POSTCARD HISTORY SERIES

McKeesport

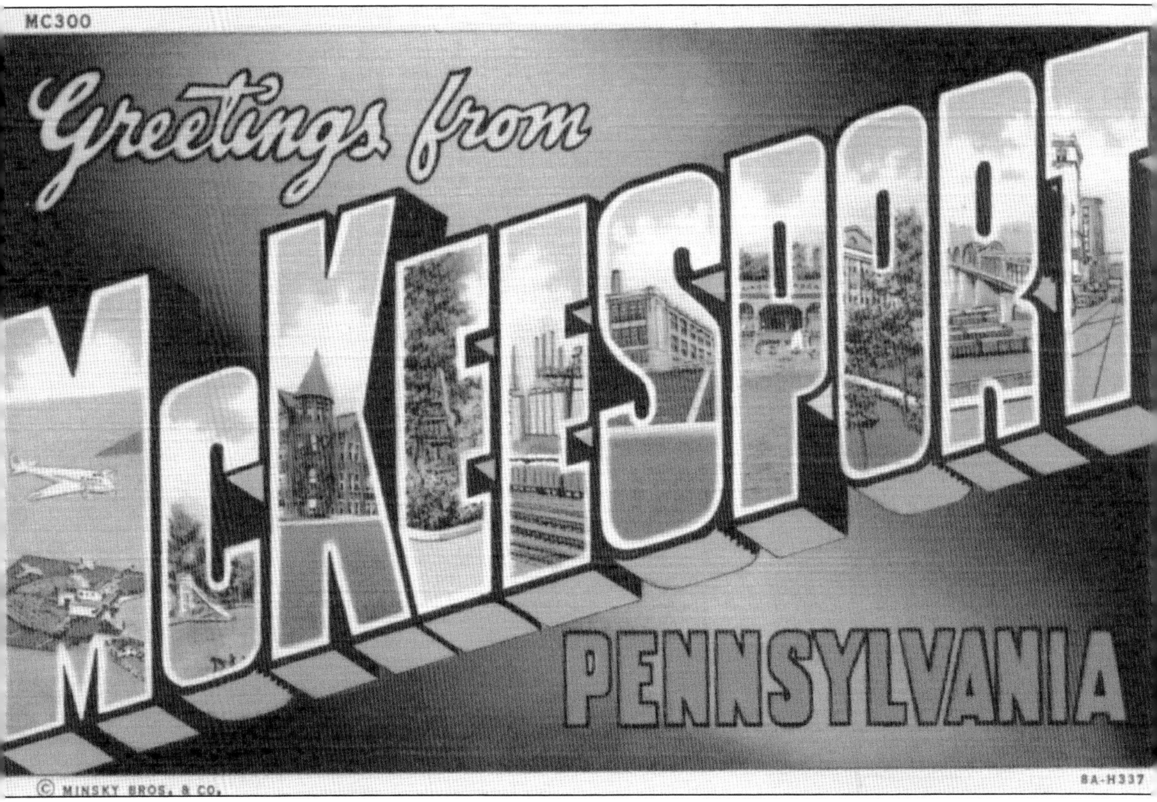

This card highlights some of McKeesport's best known sights within its letters. They are, from left to right, as follows: the Allegheny County Airport (in West Mifflin), the Municipal Pool, McKeesport Hospital, East Park, the blast furnaces of the National Tube Works, McKeesport Technical High School, Rainbow Gardens, Youghiogheny Country Club, Duquesne Bridge, and Fifth Avenue (including the People's Bank Building). (Courtesy of McKeesport Heritage Center.)

On the Front Cover: This view of Fifth Avenue, looking east from Market Street, shows the main business thoroughfare in the city of McKeesport. Built in 1929, the Memorial Theater, McKeesport's showpiece movie house, is on the right. On the left side of the street, the top two stories of the People's Bank Building, built in 1906 and still McKeesport's most recognizable building, are visible. (Courtesy of McKeesport Heritage Center.)

On the Back Cover: Seen here are the Monongahela blast furnaces of the National Tube Company, McKeesport's most famous industry. One of the world's largest manufacturers of steel pipes, the company employed thousands of local residents at its peak. The factory name gave McKeesport the nickname "Tube City." The factory complex stretched one and a half miles along the Monongahela River. (Courtesy of McKeesport Heritage Center.)

POSTCARD HISTORY SERIES

McKeesport

Michelle Tryon Wardle-Eggers and John W. Barna

ARCADIA
PUBLISHING

ISBN 978-0-7385-7564-3

Published by Arcadia Publishing
Charleston, South Carolina

Printed in the United States of America

Library of Congress Control Number: 2011920040

For all general information contact Arcadia Publishing at:
Telephone 843-853-2070
Fax 843-853-0044
E-mail sales@arcadiapublishing.com
For customer service and orders:
Toll-Free 1-888-313-2665

Visit us on the Internet at www.arcadiapublishing.com

Dedicated to the members of the McKeesport Heritage Center

Contents

Acknowledgments

To all of you who purchase and enjoy this book, thank you. You are helping support the McKeesport Heritage Center, an organization dedicated to preserving the history of McKeesport and the surrounding areas. Please take a minute to read about our organization on page 127.

We would like to start by thanking the following people who lent us their postcard collections, which we used to augment the postcards from the collections of the heritage center: Chuck Jarrell, Leonard Chemsak, Andrea (Luketic) Cartwright, Roger Reichenbach, John Barna, and Betsy Guardasoni, who lent us the Edith Graves Barrowcliff collection.

Those postcards not marked with a courtesy line came from the collection of the McKeesport Heritage Center. We would like to thank all of the people who have donated items such as postcards, photographs, archival materials, and other objects to the heritage center over the years. More than half of the postcards in this book came from the heritage center's collection, which would not exist if people like you had not donated postcards and other items to us to preserve for future generations.

Thank you to our board of directors, who supported this project: Marilyn Baldwin, John Barna, Robert Baum, J. Terrence Farrell, Robert Hauser, William Hunter, Duane Junker, Irv Latterman, Robert Messner, Daniel Piesik, JoAnne Rodgers, Francis Show, Sue Ann Striffler Galaski, Jason Togyer, and DeWayne Wivagg.

Thank you to the numerous people we cornered with questions.

A very important thank you to Gail Waite, assistant to the director at the McKeesport Heritage Center, who helped us with our research and kept the heritage center running smoothly while we were focusing our attention on this book.

And a personal thank you from Michelle: to my husband, Tom, for his support, and to my two children, Scott and Sophie, who light up my life.

INTRODUCTION

The early 20th century is considered the golden age of postcards. In 1893, postcards were printed as souvenir cards at the Columbian Exposition in Chicago. They depicted views of some of the buildings there. From that point on, postcards with views illustrating local scenes have remained popular both as souvenirs and with collectors. Numerous postcard views of McKeesport, Pennsylvania, were printed during this time, many of which are included in this book.

McKeesport is the second-largest city in Allegheny County, Pennsylvania, after Pittsburgh. It is located at the junction of the Monongahela and Youghiogheny Rivers, 12 miles southeast of Pittsburgh. David McKee purchased 306 acres at the point of the two aforementioned rivers in 1769. There, he and his sons cleared swamp and forest lands and planted an orchard and various types of grain. He also began to operate a ferry over the two rivers, giving the area the name McKee's Ferry. John McKee, one of David's sons, inherited those 306 acres in 1781, prior to his father's death in 1795. It was John who laid out the town, then called McKee's Port, in February 1795. A full 200 parcels of land were sold by lottery. In 1842, with a population of 500, McKeesport became a borough. In 1891, McKeesport was incorporated as a city, and by 1910, its population reached more than 40,000. A strong sense of civic pride was reflected by the 1910 Old Home Week festivities celebrating the dynamic progress of the city.

In the 1750s, prior to David McKee settling here, there was a small Seneca Indian population led by a matriarch known as Queen Alliquippa. Unlike other local native tribes, who supported the French, she remained a steadfast ally of the British. George Washington met her in McKeesport in 1753 on his return from a diplomatic mission. In 1755, Washington again passed through McKeesport as a member of the British army under Gen. Edward Braddock.

The town of McKeesport was laid out on the original McKee homestead in the lowlands where the two rivers meet. This area became known as the First Ward. A large tract, "the Diamond," was set aside in the town as a space for a public market house. Four lots were also set aside "for a place of worship and a seminary of learning." The first church, built jointly by the Presbyterians, Baptists, and Methodists, was erected in 1819 on one of those separate lots. The first school was built in 1832 as a private subscription school, and the first public school was built in 1841. As early as 1800, McKeesport was known for its horse racing course along the village streets, which attracted patrons county-wide.

From the 1840s through the succeeding decades, McKeesport grew from a town of log cabins and unpaved streets into a bustling city of multistory brick commercial buildings, fine residential homes, and efficient public transportation. Street paving began in 1867, and by 1894, more than 20 miles of street were covered. Both the fire and police departments began as one-man operations. In 1871, George Smith was the one paid police officer, and in 1885, William

King was the one paid fireman. The fire department grew from one company to four over the next few decades.

The city's location along the rivers provided an ideal location for development of transportation industries and coal mining. Slack water navigation was introduced with the construction of dams in 1841, making the Monongahela River navigable year-round. Beginning in the 1870s, manufacturing industries expanded rapidly. In 1872, McKeesport became the home of the National Tube Works, which was at one point the largest manufacturer of steel pipe in the world. The company ultimately became the largest employer in the city during the first half of the 20th century. Two other large manufacturers were the American Tin Plate Company and the Firth-Sterling Steel Company. Some of the smaller industries included brick making, tanneries, gristmills, sawmills, a soap factory, a glass factory, a shovel factory, distilleries, breweries, and even a windmill factory.

The Baltimore & Ohio Railroad and the Pittsburgh & Lake Erie Railroad, along with 15 miles of street railways, connected McKeesport to the world. Connecting the city to its neighbors were eight bridges. At one point, 40 churches, 14 school buildings, seven banks, two opera houses, six newspapers, more secret societies than any town of its size, and numerous small businesses served the city.

As the factories developed along the rivers, the business section of the city grew along Fifth Avenue, and the residential areas spread in a southeast direction. The city grew from one ward to nine. In 1898, the borough of Reynoldton joined the city as the 10th Ward, in 1899, the borough of Christy Park became the 11th Ward, and in 1952, the borough of Eden Park became the 12th Ward.

McKeesport served as the business and commercial hub for the surrounding boroughs and towns of the Mon-Yough area. These included Port Vue Borough and Dravosburg Borough to the west and Versailles Borough and Versailles township to the south and east.

The vibrancy of that growing city is reflected on the following pages. From the thriving downtown businesses to the expanding manufacturers, from the trolley parks and swimming pools to the churches and schools, McKeesport in the early 20th century was an exciting place to be.

One

Early McKeesport

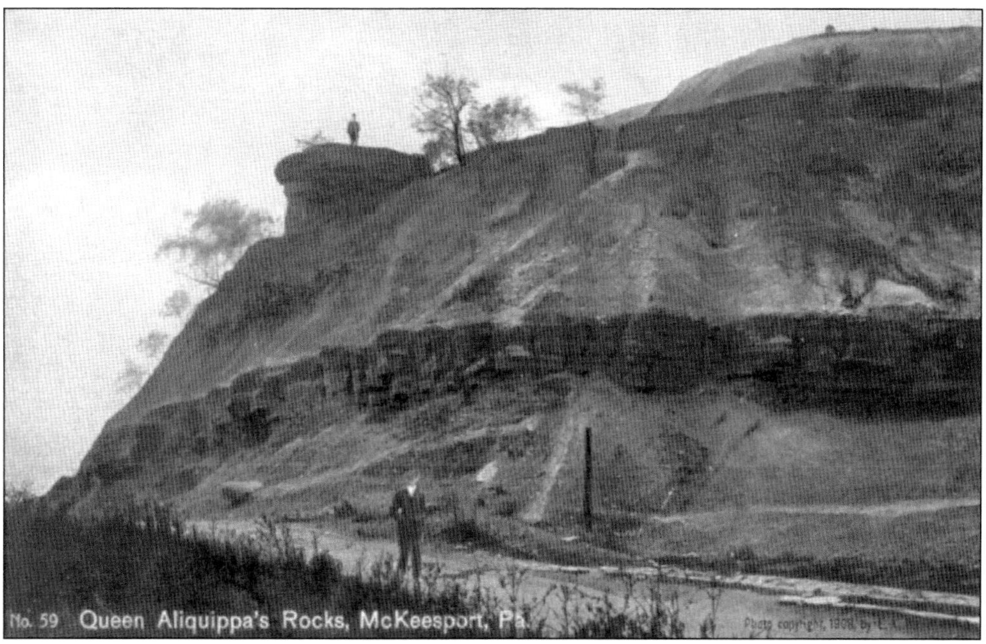

Before the first settlers came to McKeesport, there was a Seneca Indian tribe that seasonally lived in this area. Queen Aliquippa's Rock was named for the tribe's female leader. George Washington met with her in 1753 on his return trip from a diplomatic mission to Fort LeBoeuf in Waterford, Pennsylvania. This rock, which overlooked Cliff Street near the Duquesne Bridge, no longer exists.

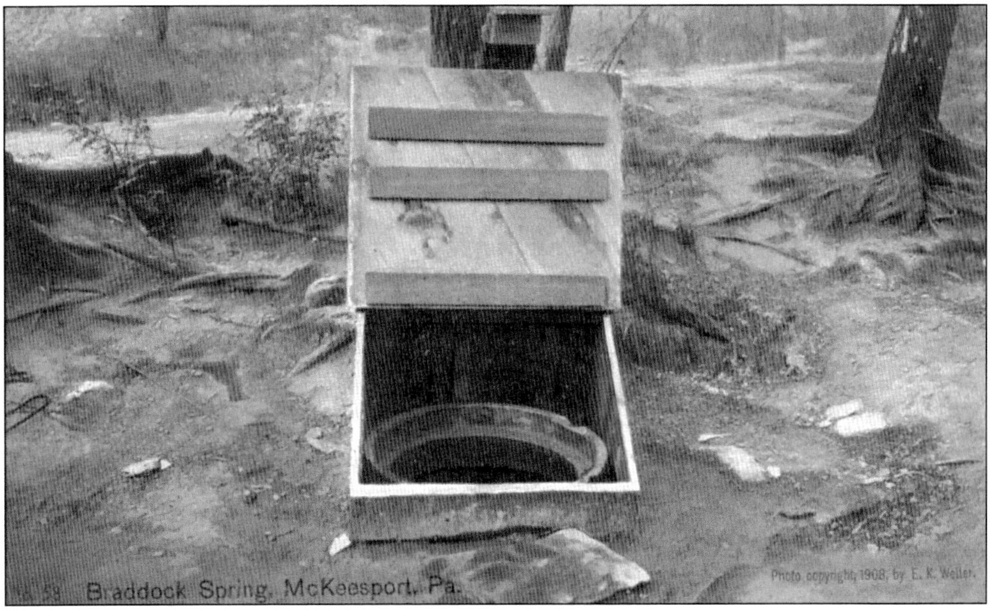

On July 8, 1755, Gen. Edward Braddock, with two regiments of the British army, camped in McKeesport, around the intersection of O'Neil Boulevard and Summit Street. They were on their way to capture Fort Duquesne from the French. The next afternoon, they suffered a disastrous defeat and retreated through McKeesport that evening. This natural spring at their campsite was destroyed by commercial construction in the late 20th century.

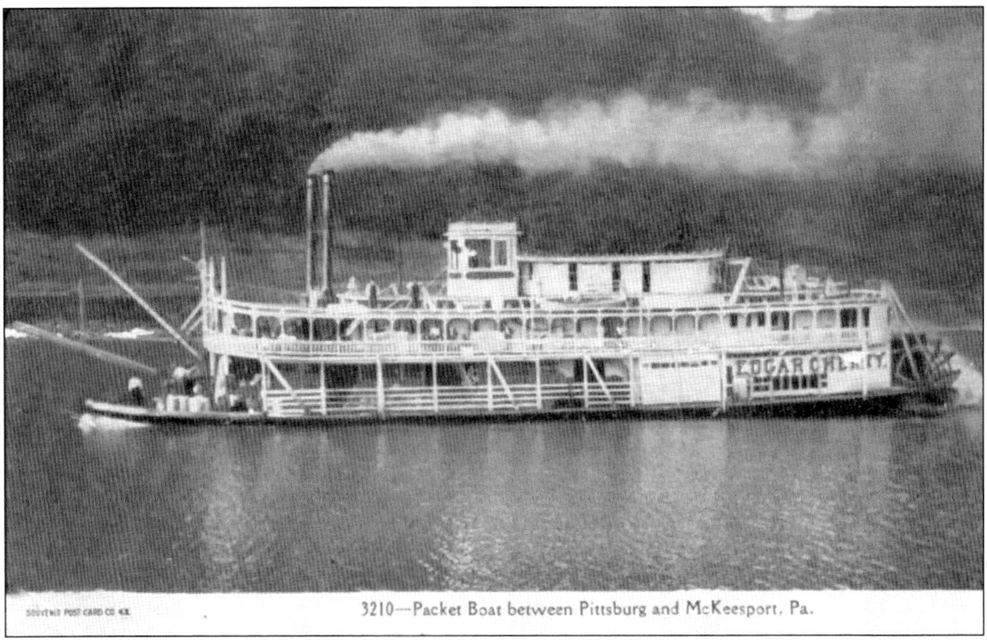

McKeesport's early industries included boat building and coal mining. Coal flats and coal barges were built to support the mining industry. The packet boat *Edgar Cherry*, built in Ohio in 1894, traveled the Monongahela River between Pittsburgh and Morgantown and sank in 1904. Packet boats carrying mail, passengers, and freight were typical of the boats seen on local rivers. (Courtesy of Chuck Jarrell.)

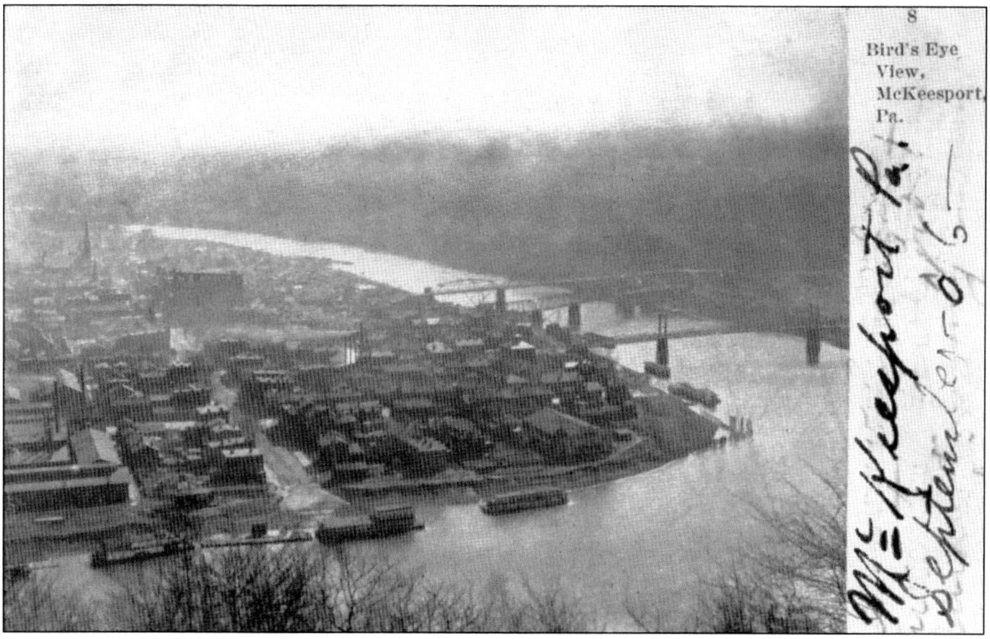

This bird's-eye view of McKeesport shows the First Ward section, where the Monongahela and Youghiogheny Rivers meet. This was the area where David McKee's homestead was located and where his son John McKee laid out the original town in 1795.

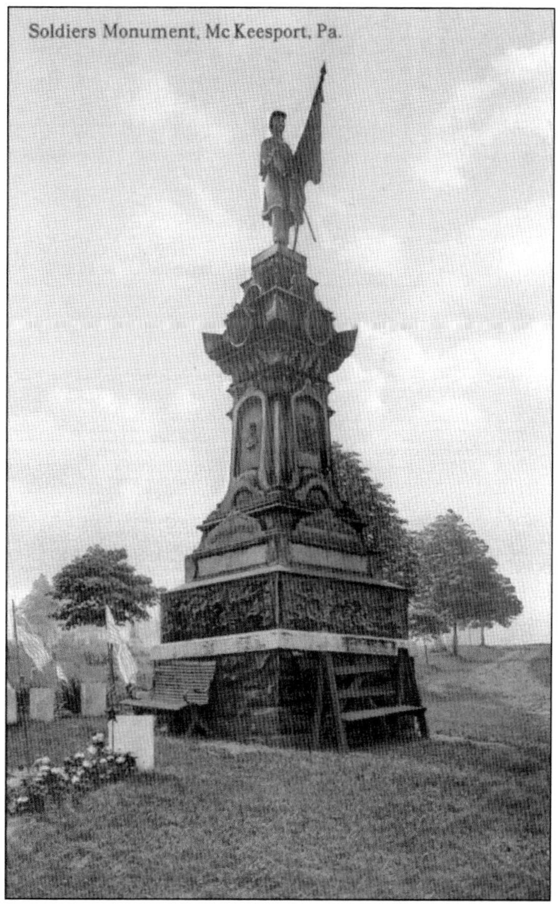

The Soldiers Monument, located in the McKeesport and Versailles Cemetery, was dedicated on July 4, 1892, to commemorate all of the soldiers and sailors from McKeesport who died in the Civil War. Three companies of soldiers were recruited from McKeesport for that conflict, and some men from McKeesport fought with companies recruited elsewhere.

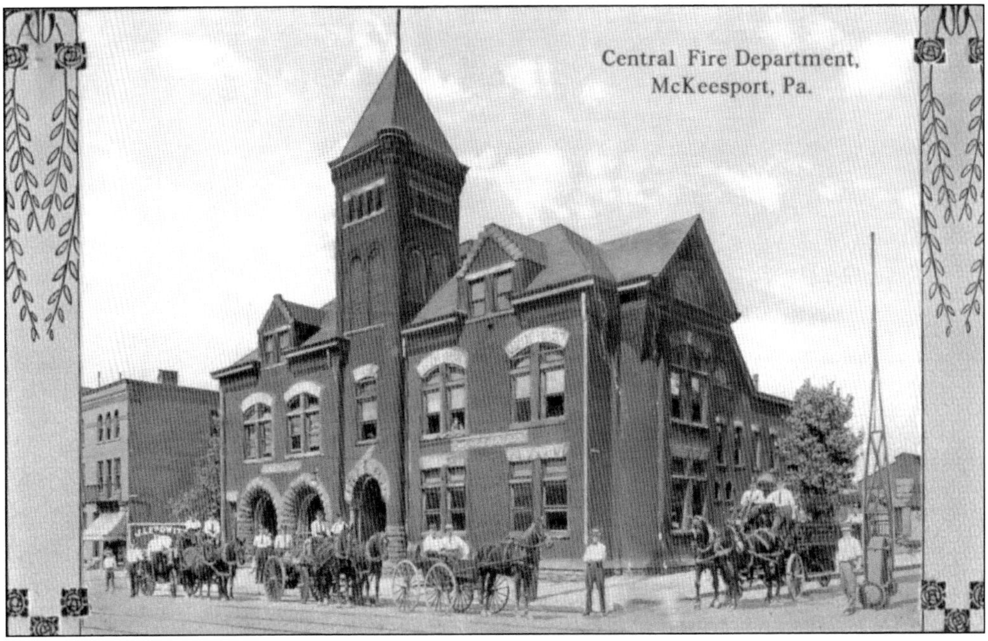

The Central Fire and Police Station was perhaps the most recognizable building in the First Ward. Built in 1894, it was located at the northeast corner of the Diamond, at Fourth Avenue and Market Street. The building was designed by Henry J. Lohman, a McKeesport architect. The tower was 50 feet high.

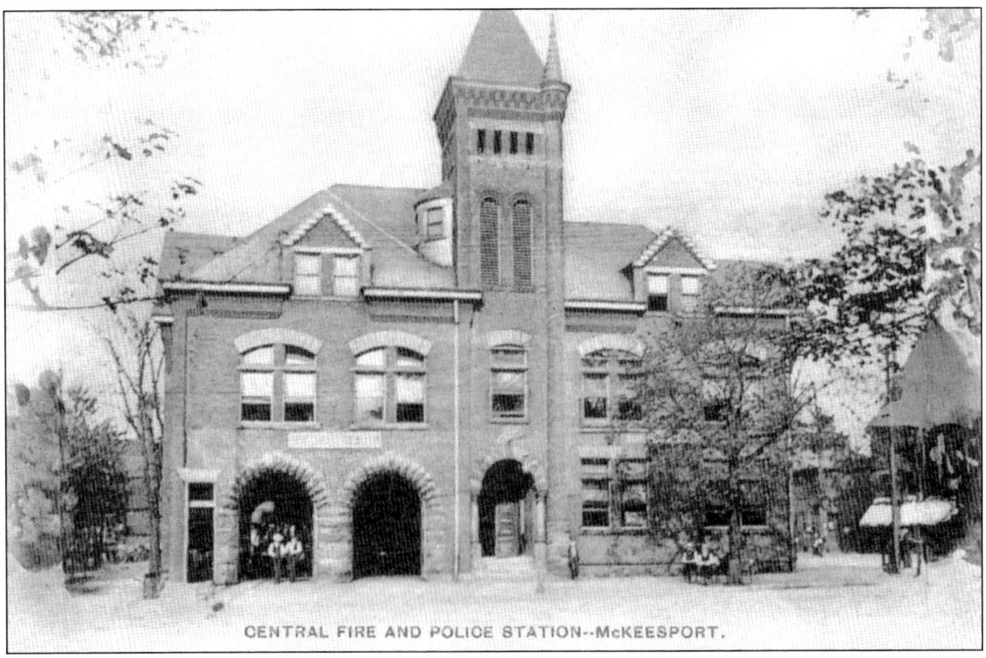

The fire department was established in 1885. At first, it consisted of one paid man and volunteers. This building continued to be used as a fire station until 1958, when the new municipal building on Lysle Boulevard was constructed. In March 1960, Central Station was demolished as part of McKeesport's First Ward Redevelopment Program. (Courtesy of Leonard Chemsak.)

Two

INDUSTRY

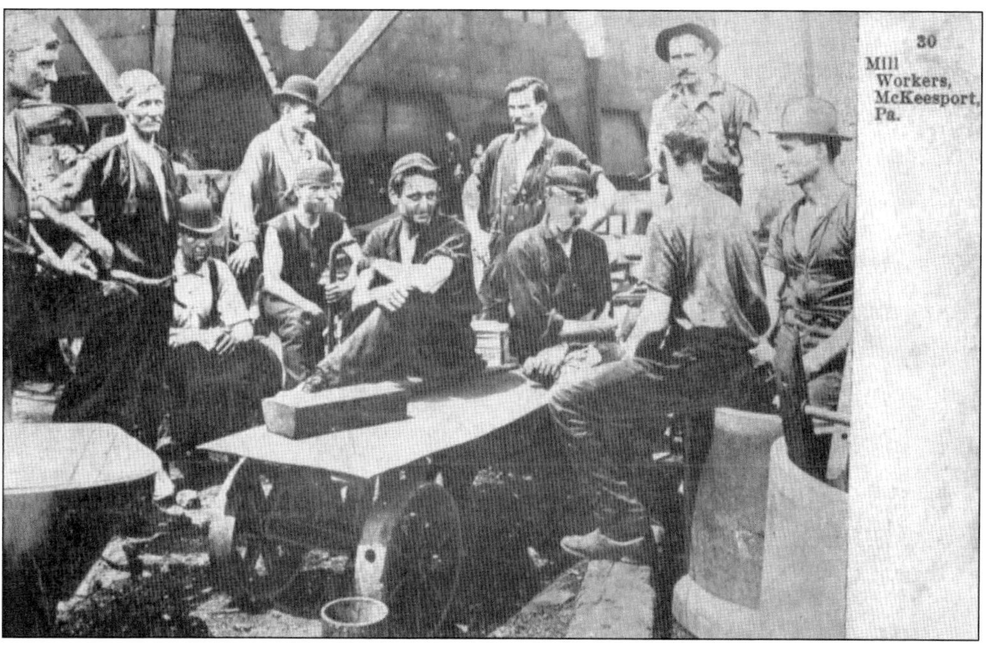

These mill workers typify the workforce that drove the city. With numerous manufacturers in McKeesport, many people were attracted to the job opportunities here. Factory agents recruited workers for the mills from among immigrants as they arrived at Ellis Island and other ports of entry. These people made McKeesport into the ethnically diverse city it is today. (Courtesy of the Edith Greaves Barrowcliff collection.)

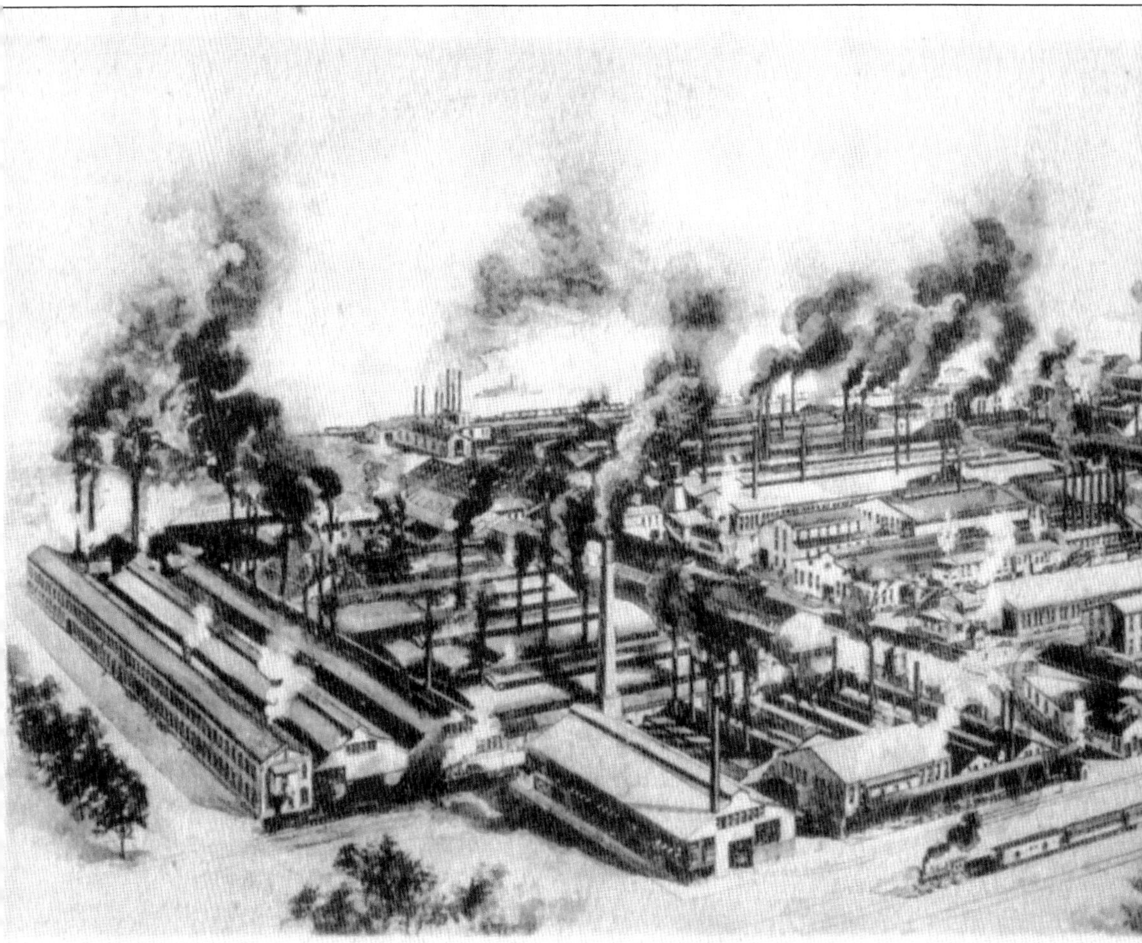

National Tube Company, National Dept., McKeesport, Pa.

In 1872, John H. Flagler and John C. Converse, from Boston, Massachusetts, were looking for a new site for their tube mill. They found that site in McKeesport. The former Fulton, Bollman and Company Rope factory was purchased. It was located between Walnut Street, Huey Street, Fourth Avenue, and the Monongahela River. That factory burned down in 1873 and was immediately rebuilt the same year. A number of expansions followed, including the

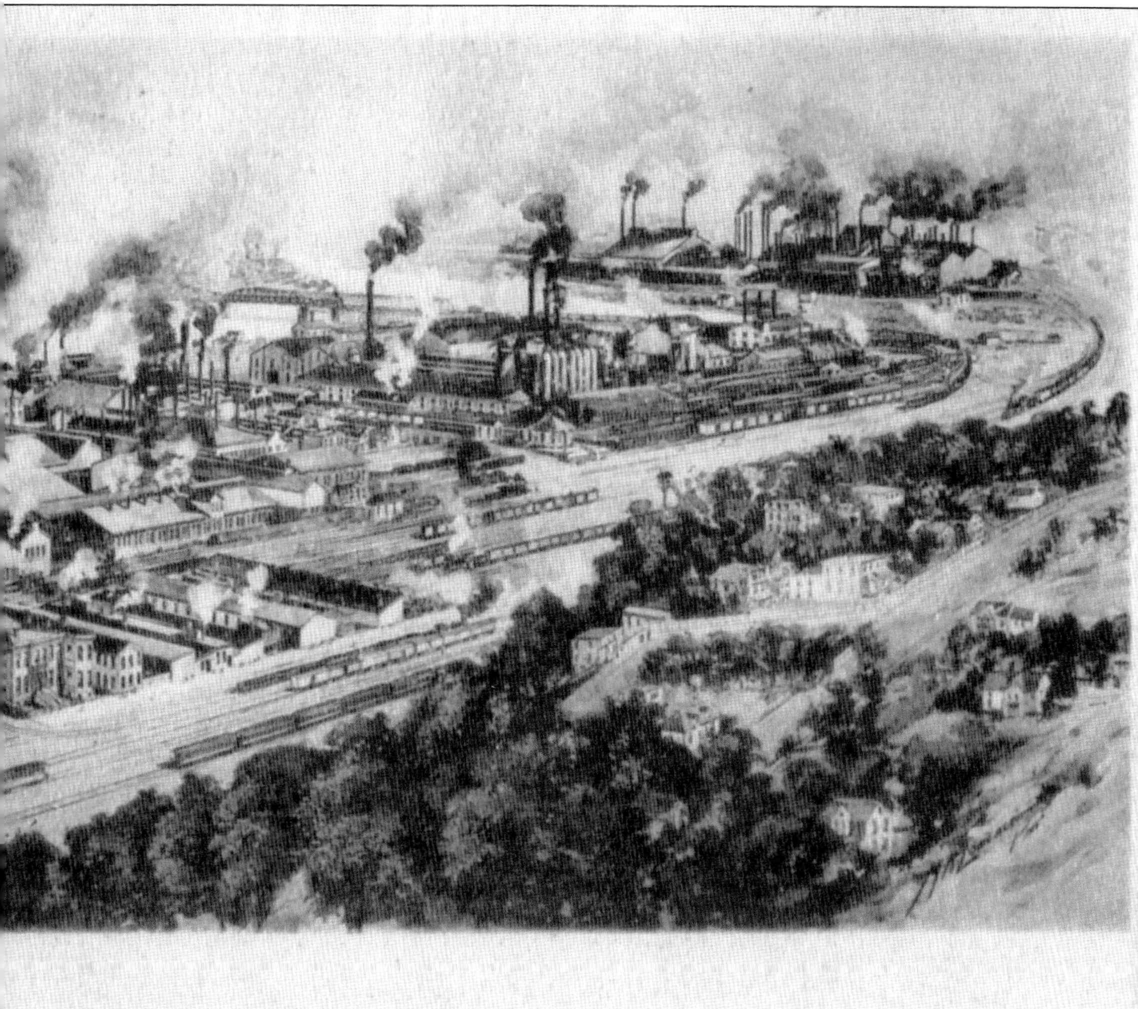

Butt Weld Mill in 1874, the rolling mill in 1879, the Monongahela Furnaces in 1890, and the Monongahela Steel Works between 1892 and 1893. By 1894, the National Tube Works was considered the largest mill of its type in the world, covering 66 acres, 50 of which were under roof. (Courtesy of John Barna.)

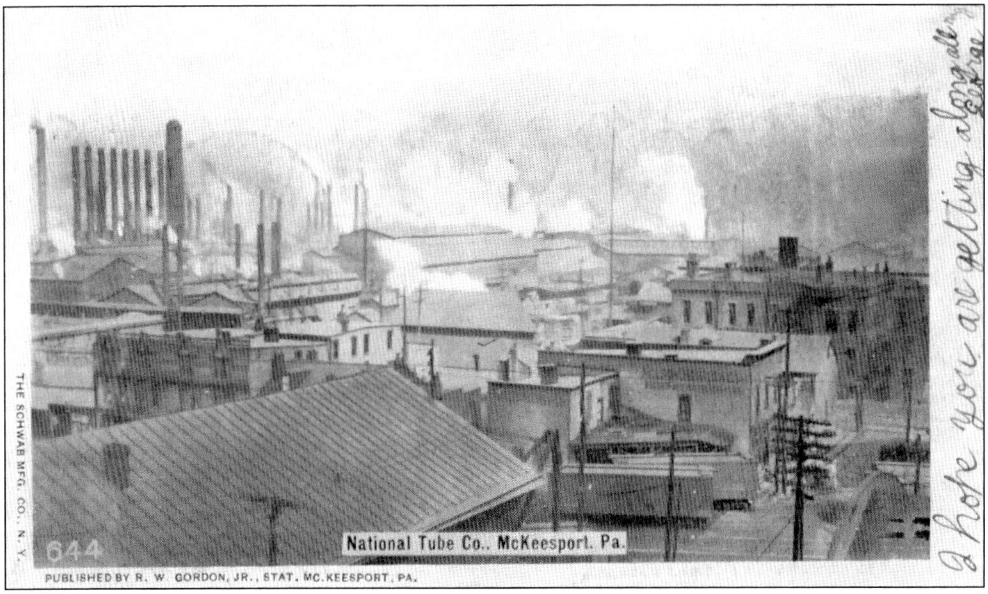

This view of the tube works was shot looking north from Sinclair Street toward the river. In the upper left corner, a portion of the W. Dewees Wood Works, McKeesport's earliest factory (established in 1851), is visible. In 1900, the Wood Works was acquired by US Steel and became its American Sheet and Tin Plate division. US Steel acquired National Tube Works at this same time. (Courtesy of Leonard Chemsak.)

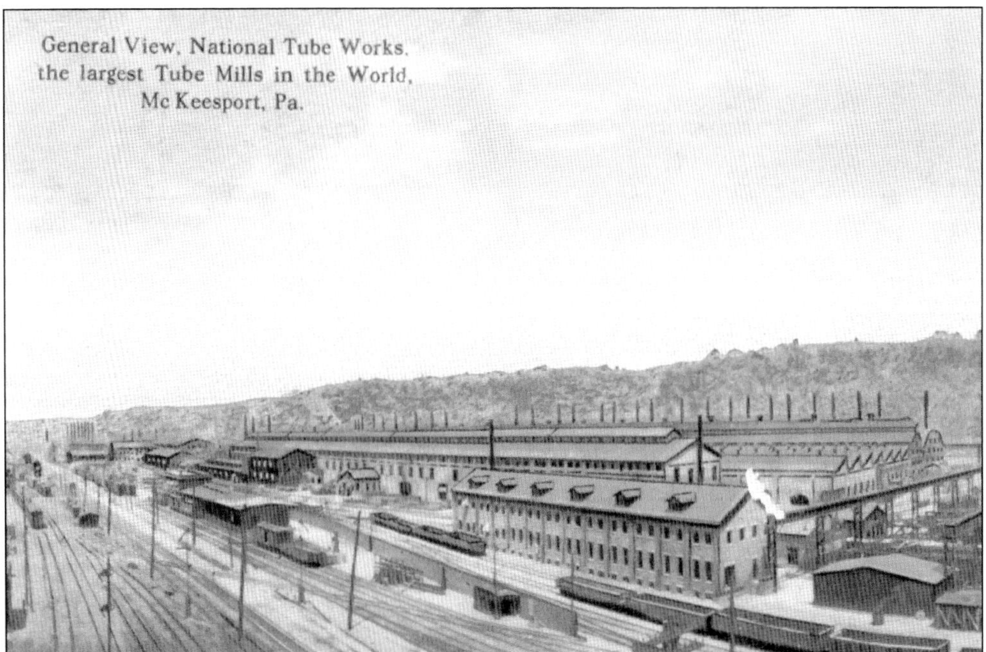

This photograph was taken from the roof of the old McKeesport Brewing Company at Jerome Street and Ryan Alley. The building in the foreground was the stores building, with the pipe mill in the background, storage yards to the right, and the Pennsylvania Railroad freight station to the left.

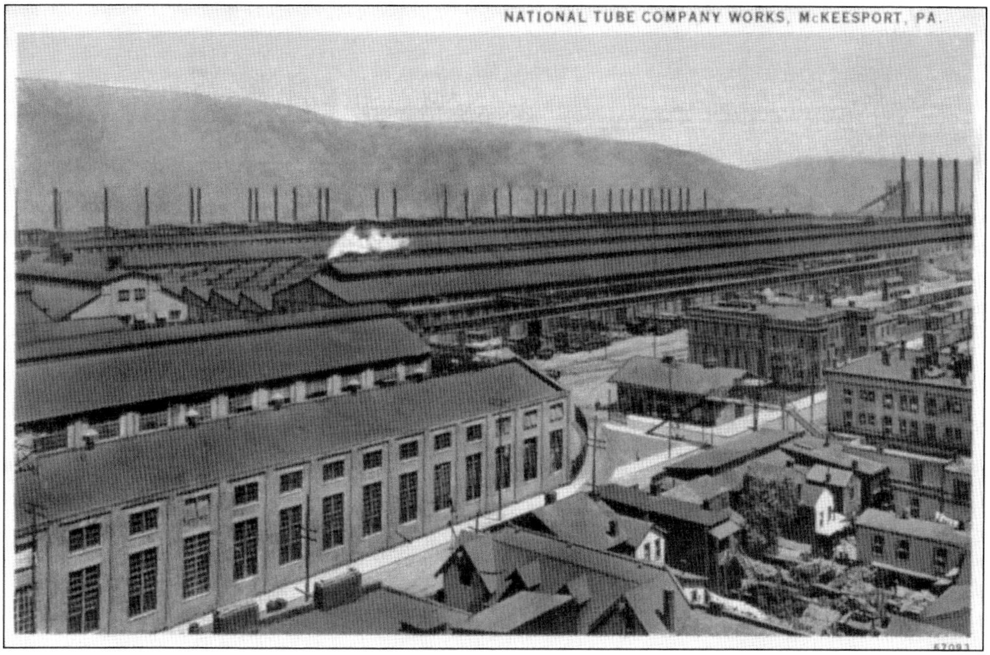

This photograph includes the Locust Street Gate to the tube works. To the left is the machine shop, to the right is the main office, and in the back is the huge expanse of the pipe mill. Between 1904 and 1905, the tube works bought the old Bowery district, a residential section in the old Third Ward, for a $10 million expansion.

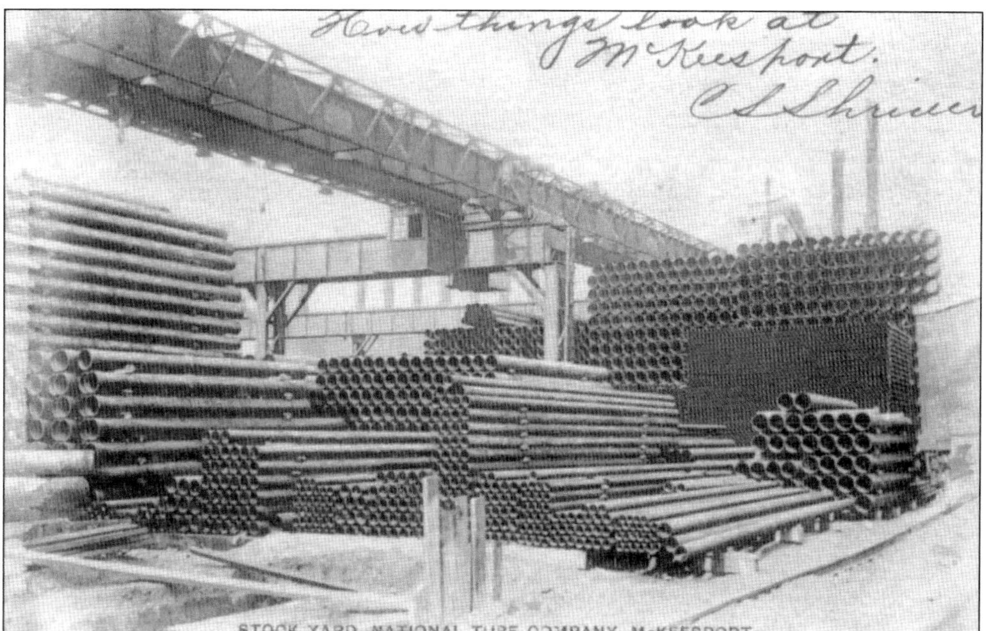

This shows the steel pipe that was manufactured by the National Tube Works. In 1910, annual output was 450,000 tons of pipe, which was used by the gas and oil industries, among others. (Courtesy of Leonard Chemsak.)

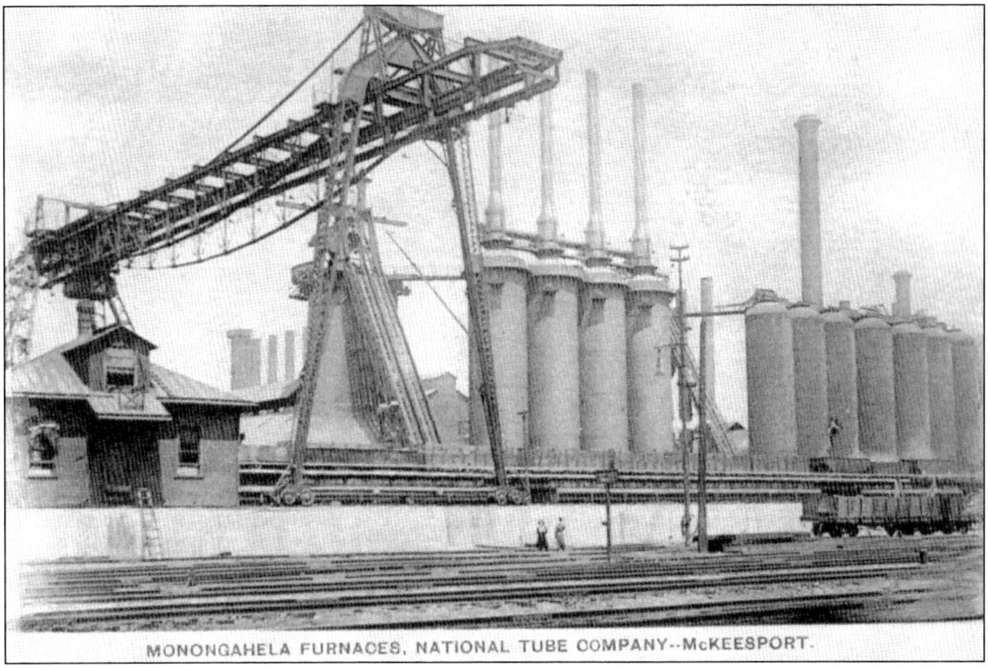

The Monongahela Furnaces were located east of Center Street. This is where iron was made. Molten iron from these blast furnaces was then taken to the Bessemer converter to produce steel. From there, steel ingots went to the rolling mills where they were rolled into round billets. Those billets were then taken to the seamless pipe mill for processing into pipe. (Courtesy of Chuck Jarrell.)

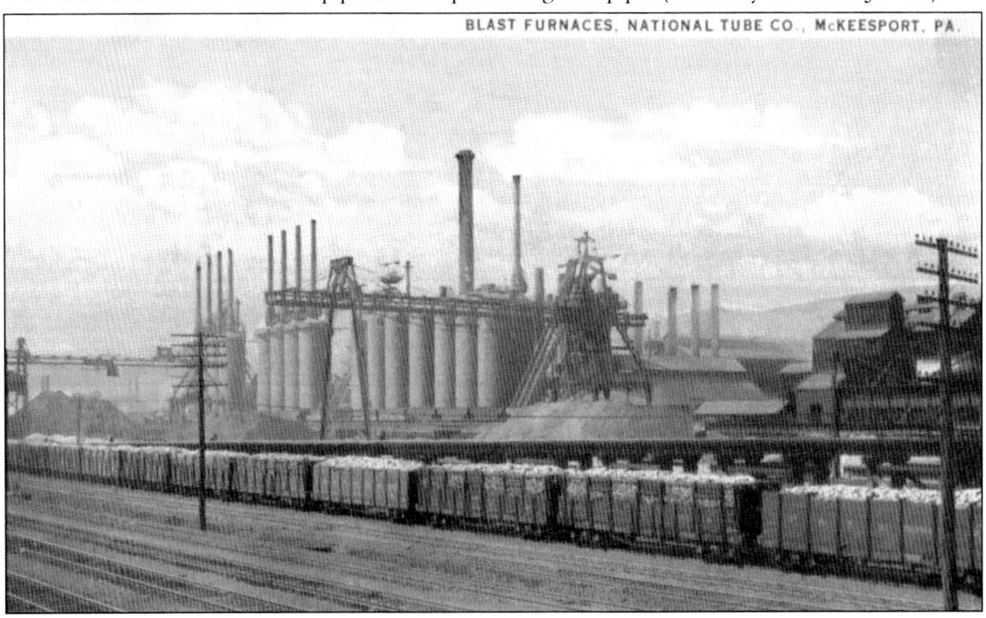

This more recent view of the blast furnaces shows the railroad lines serving the mill. Beginning in 1889, the McKeesport Connecting Railroad, an industrial line, operated several miles of track within the mill. The main lines of the Pittsburgh & Lake Erie Railroad, Baltimore & Ohio Railroad, Union Railroad, and a branch line of the Pennsylvania Railroad also served the mill. (Courtesy of Chuck Jarrell.)

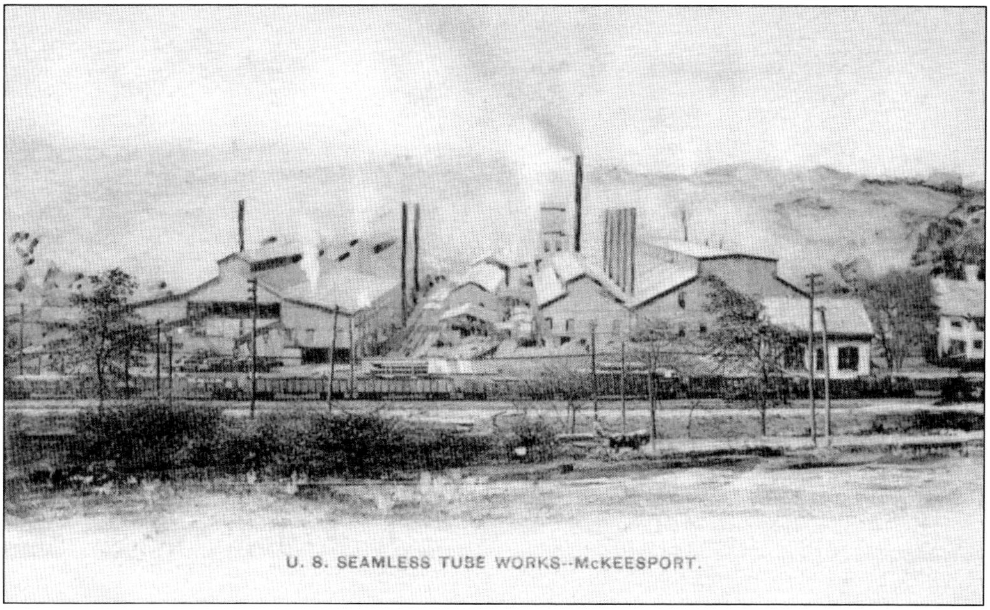

In 1893, National Tube Works built the seamless mill in the then borough of Christy Park. In 1899, Christy Park was annexed by McKeesport and became the 11th Ward. The National Tube Company's Christy Park Works covered 34 acres along Stockdale Avenue, now Walnut Street, at what is now Iowa Street. (Courtesy of Leonard Chemsak.)

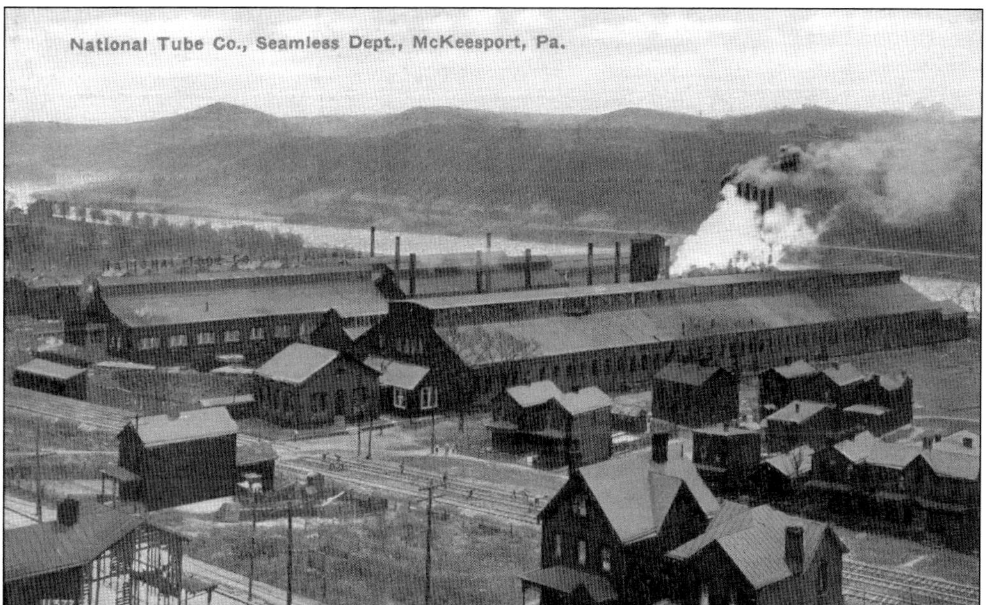

In this second view of the mill, Walnut Street is to the left in the foreground, and the Baltimore & Ohio Railroad tracks are behind the houses. The empty hills of what is now Liberty Borough are across the Youghiogheny River. During World War II and the Vietnam War, ordnance materials, such as bomb casings, were manufactured here. (Courtesy of Leonard Chemsak.)

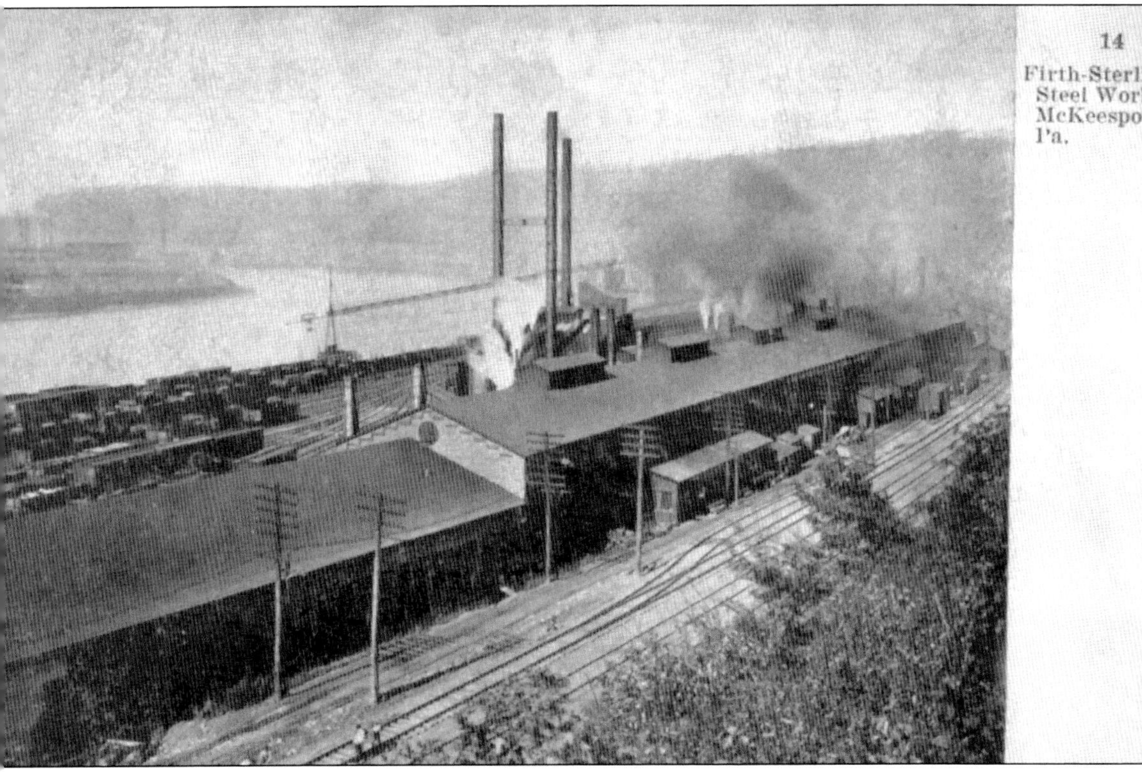

The Firth-Sterling Company was created when Thomas Firth & Sons, from England, were looking for an American outlet and bought Sterling Steel Company of Pittsburgh. Sterling Steel's plant was located in Demmler, in the old Third Ward of McKeesport along the Monongahela River. Firth-Sterling was founded in 1897. It manufactured specialty steels, including tool steels. The armor piercing shells used in the Battle of Manilla Bay during the Spanish-American War in 1898 were manufactured here. During World War I, Firth-Sterling became the first American producer of stainless steel and continued to produce munitions for the United States and the Allies. Later, the company branched out into the fields of wire and powder metallurgy. Firth-Sterling also owned its own tungsten mines in Colorado. (Courtesy of Chuck Jarrell.)

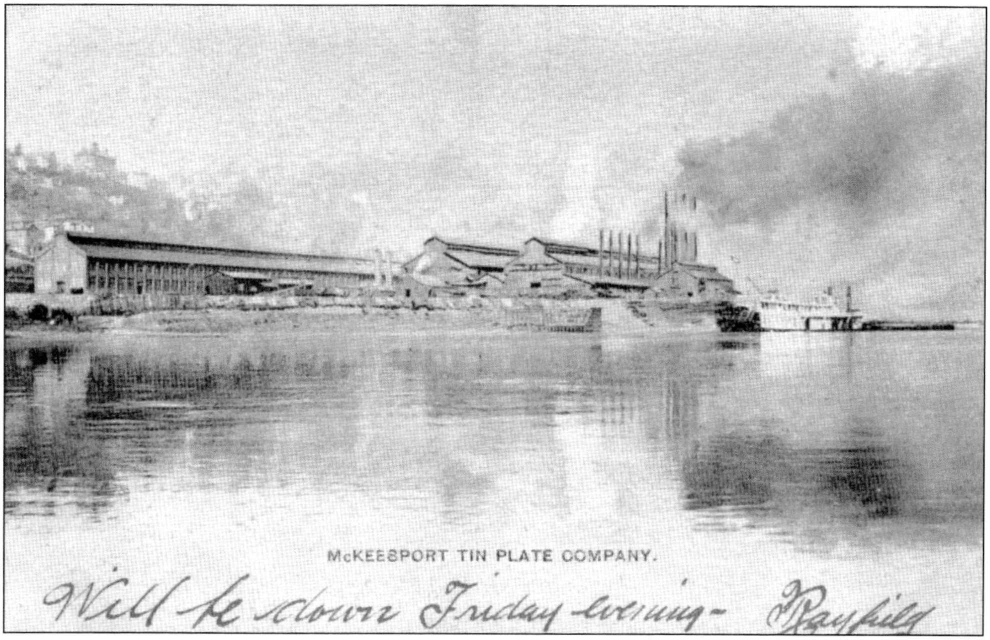

The McKeesport Tin Plate Company, founded in 1902, was located on 13 acres of the old Dale Farm in Port Vue, along the Youghiogheny River. Edwin R. Crawford was one of the original 11 subscribers to the company stock and became its first president.

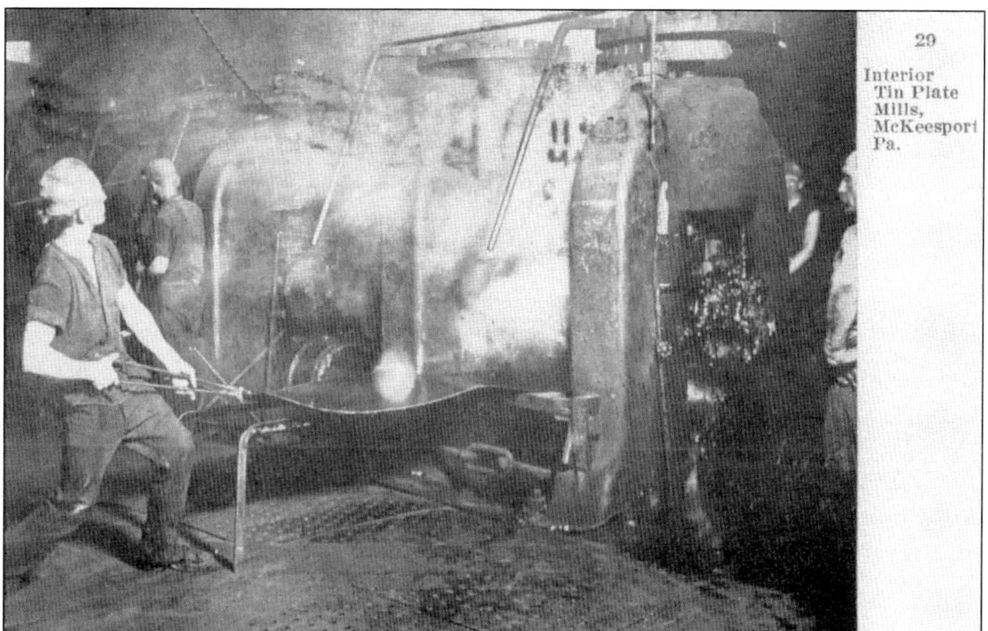

The original plant consisted of 10 hot mills, 10 cold mills, and 19 tin pots with annealing furnaces. The plant employed 1,400 workers who would roll bars of steel into sheets, which were then treated with acid and plated with molten tin. Production remained steady through the Depression.

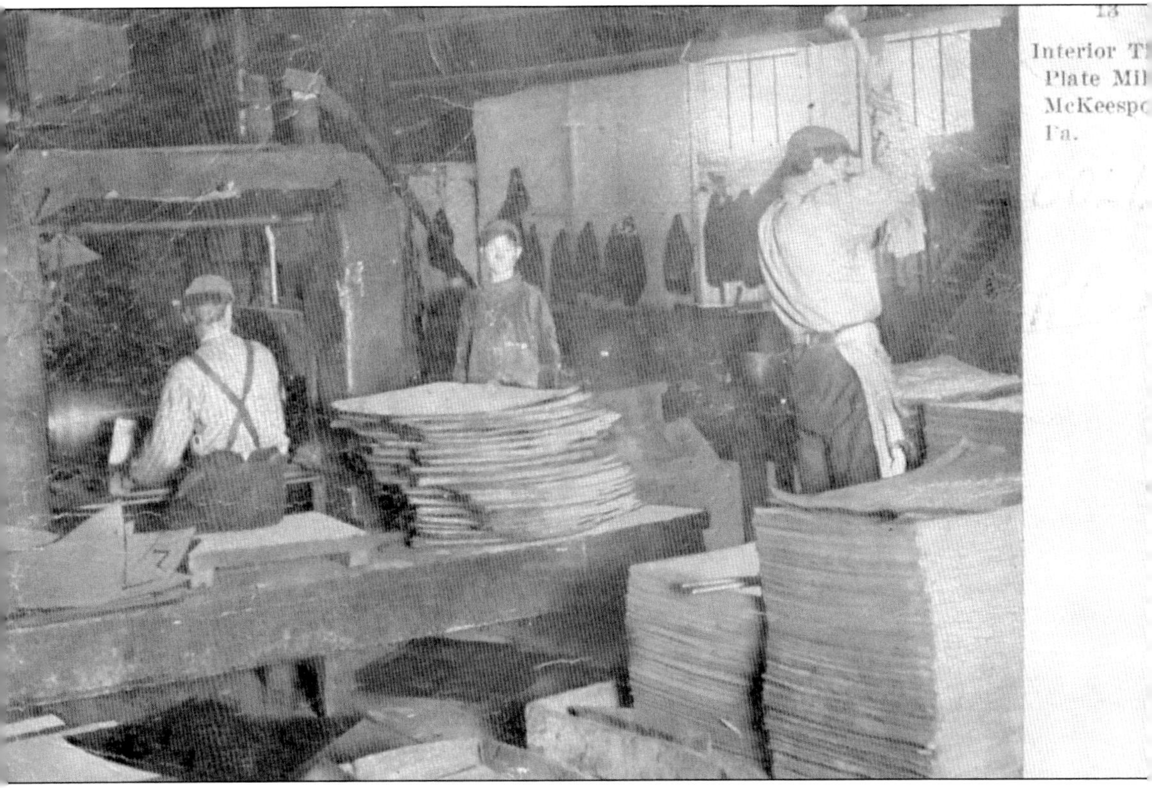

The factory closed in 1939 because of increasing competition. Other companies developed new processes for making tin plate, and it was decided that the millions of dollars needed to upgrade the factory made doing so unfeasible.

Three

Bridges and Bird's-eye Views

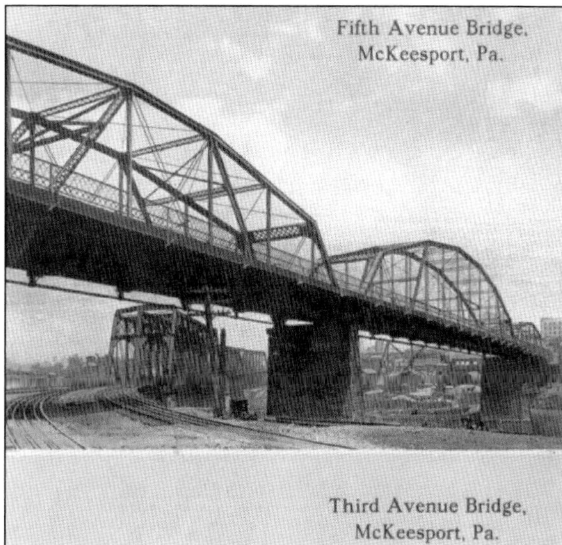

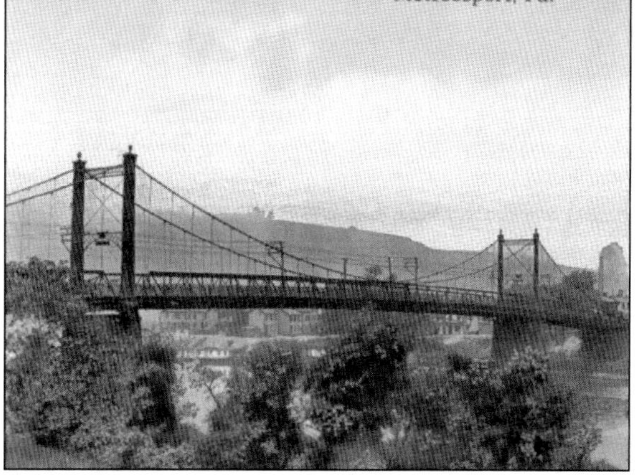

The Fifth Avenue Bridge (above) and the Third Avenue Bridge (below) were the two main bridges into McKeesport across the Youghiogheny River. The Third Avenue Bridge, built in 1884, was the first bridge to span either of McKeesport's rivers. This suspension bridge connected the First Ward to the borough of Reynoldton, now the 10th Ward. It was dismantled in 1961 as part of the First Ward Redevelopment Program.

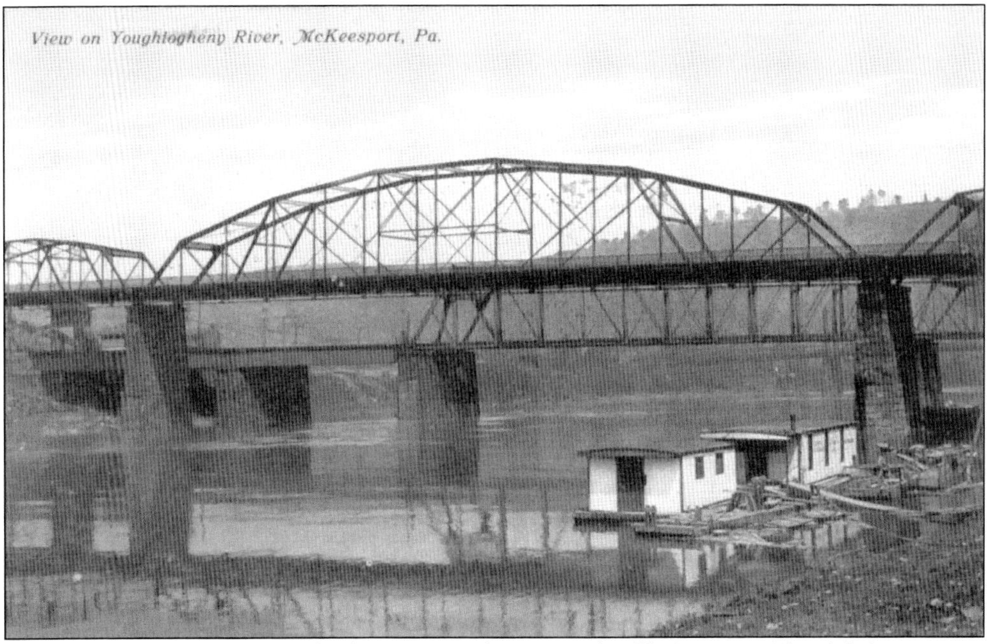

The Fifth Avenue Bridge was built in 1895 and connected Fifth Avenue with High Street, now West Fifth Avenue, in the former borough of Reynoldton. It was replaced by the present Jerome Street Bridge in 1937. There was an entrance off the sidewalk of this bridge into the second floor of the Palisades dance hall. (Courtesy of Chuck Jarrell.)

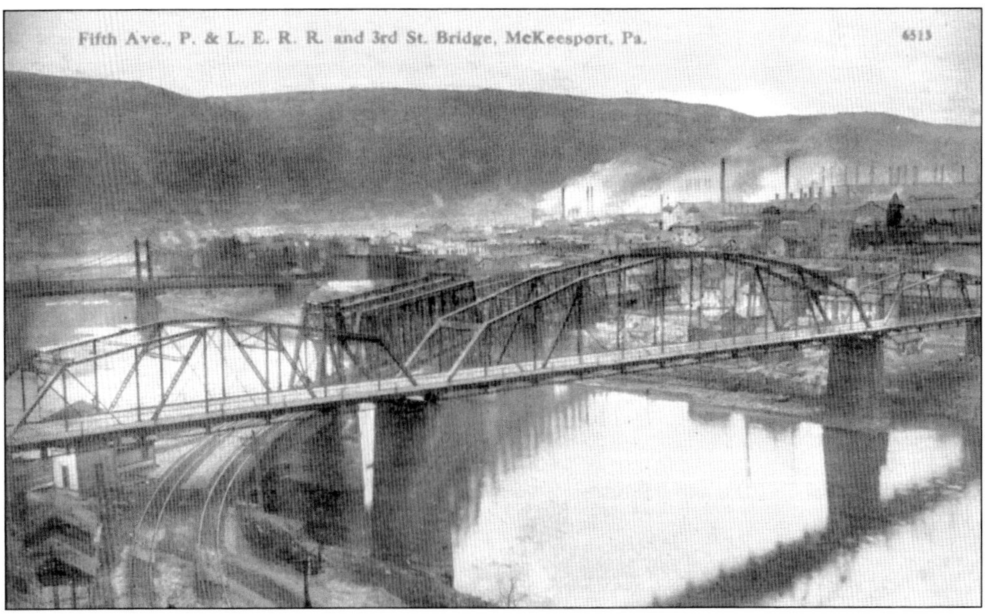

Pictured are three of McKeesport's bridges: the Fifth Avenue Bridge is in the foreground; the Pittsburgh, McKeesport & Youghiogheny Railroad Bridge is in the center; and the Third Avenue Bridge is in the distance. The railroad bridge crossed the river at Fourth Avenue. It was built in 1883, widened in 1898, and demolished in 1970. (Courtesy of Leonard Chemsak.)

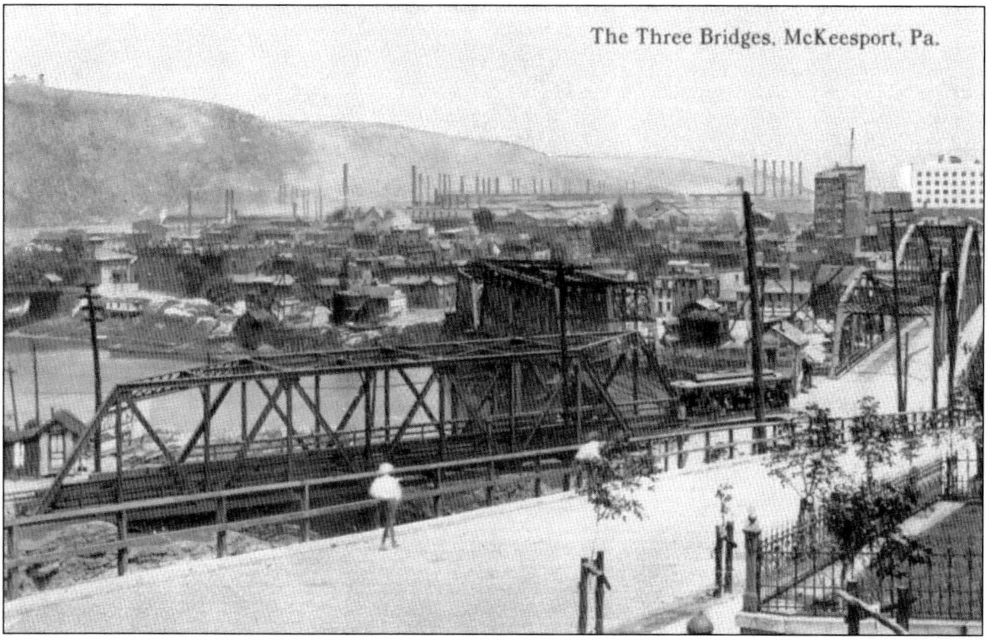

The three bridges pictured are the Fifth Avenue Bridge (right), the railroad bridge (center), and the trolley viaduct (left). The trolley viaduct was built in 1898 by the United Traction Company, later Pittsburgh Railways, to eliminate a railroad grade crossing in the Tenth Ward. Trolley Route 56 to Pittsburgh used this bridge until it was demolished in 1953.

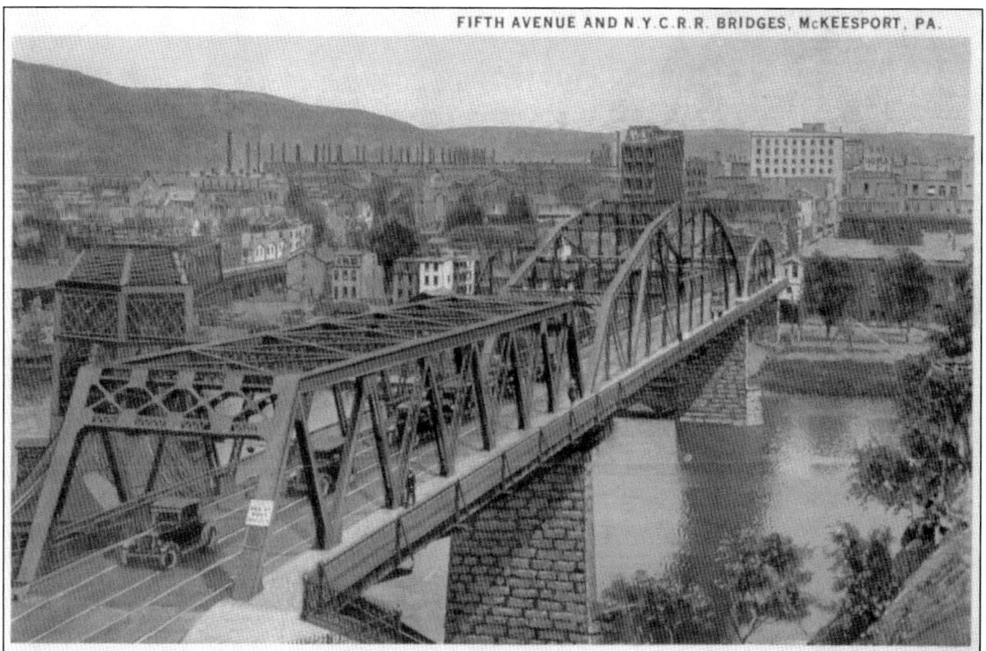

The Fifth Avenue Bridge and the railroad bridge are pictured with a view of the city in the background. The Palisades is across the river at the right, the People's Bank building is in the background, and Stone's Furniture building is to its left. Early vehicular bridges charged tolls until the "free bridge" movement of around 1910.

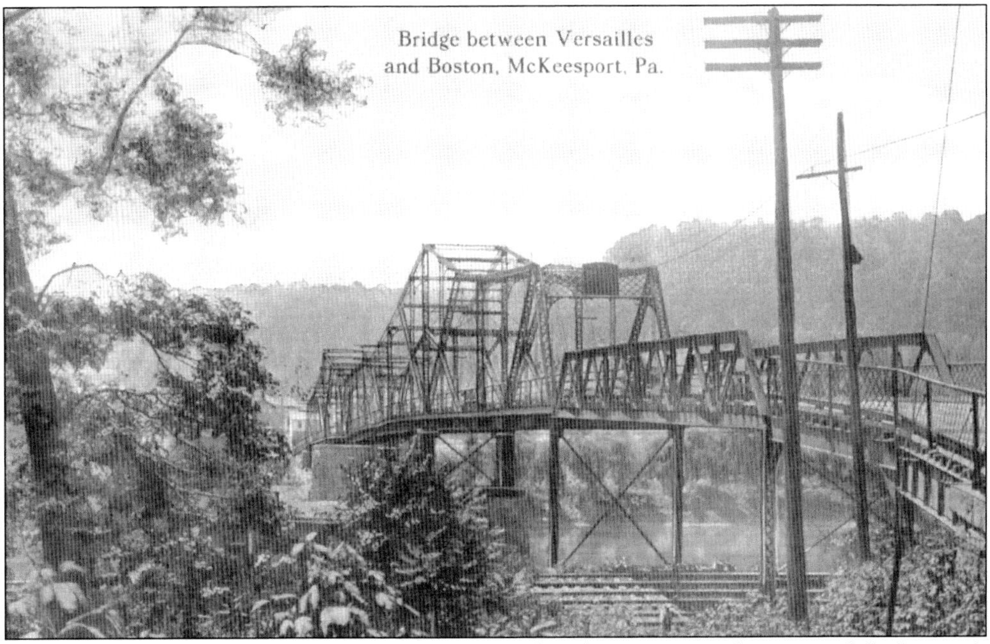

The Boston Bridge, built in 1892, crossed the Youghiogheny River and connected the borough of Versailles, just south of McKeesport, to the Village of Boston in Elizabeth Township. In 1900, the Versailles end was raised 23 feet to eliminate the trolley line grade crossing of the Baltimore & Ohio railroad tracks. It was replaced by the current Boston Bridge in 1932.

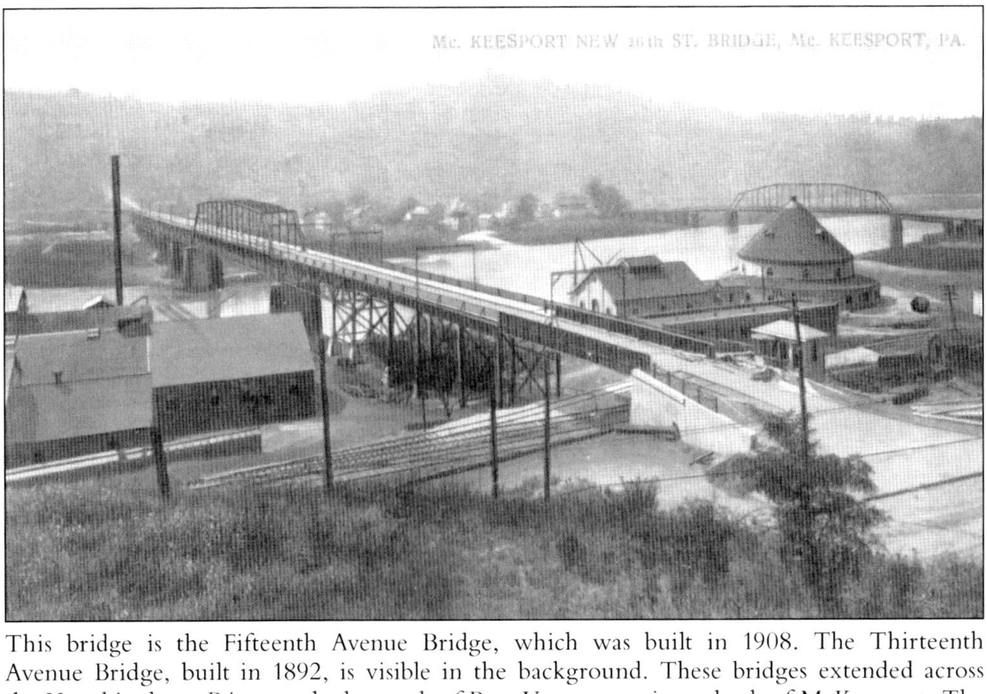

This bridge is the Fifteenth Avenue Bridge, which was built in 1908. The Thirteenth Avenue Bridge, built in 1892, is visible in the background. These bridges extended across the Youghiogheny River to the borough of Port Vue, a growing suburb of McKeesport. The McKeesport and Port Vue Bridge Company built the Fifteenth Avenue Bridge to carry trolley cars. (Courtesy of John Barna.)

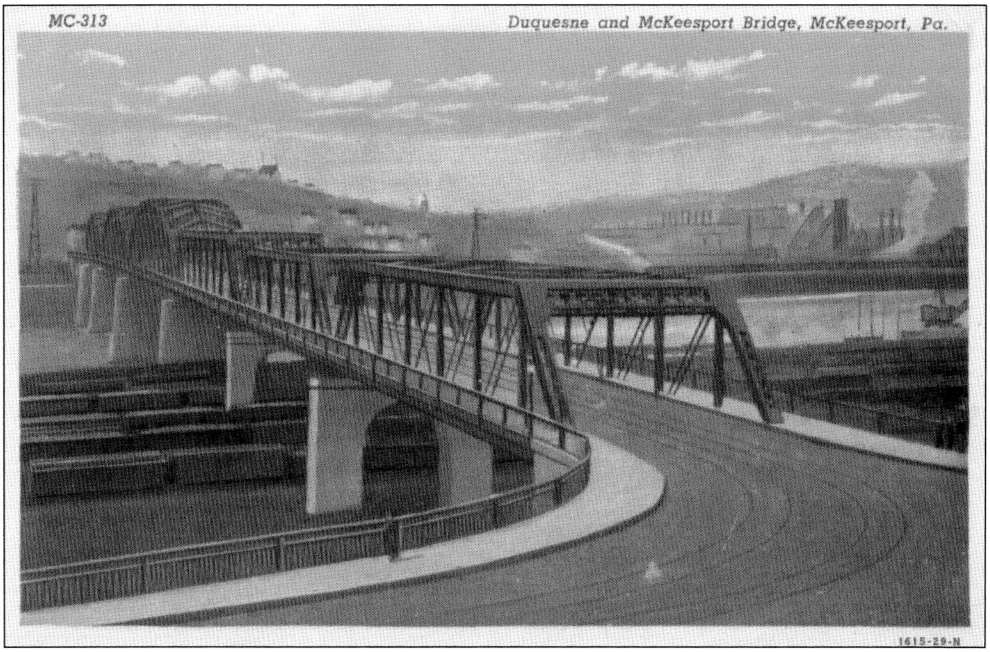

The McKeesport and Duquesne Bridge, also referred to as the Cliff Street Bridge, was built in 1927. It replaced the old Riverton Bridge and eliminated an extremely dangerous railroad crossing. Spanning the Monongahela River at the mouth of Crooked Run, it marks the location where General Braddock and his army forded the river in 1755.

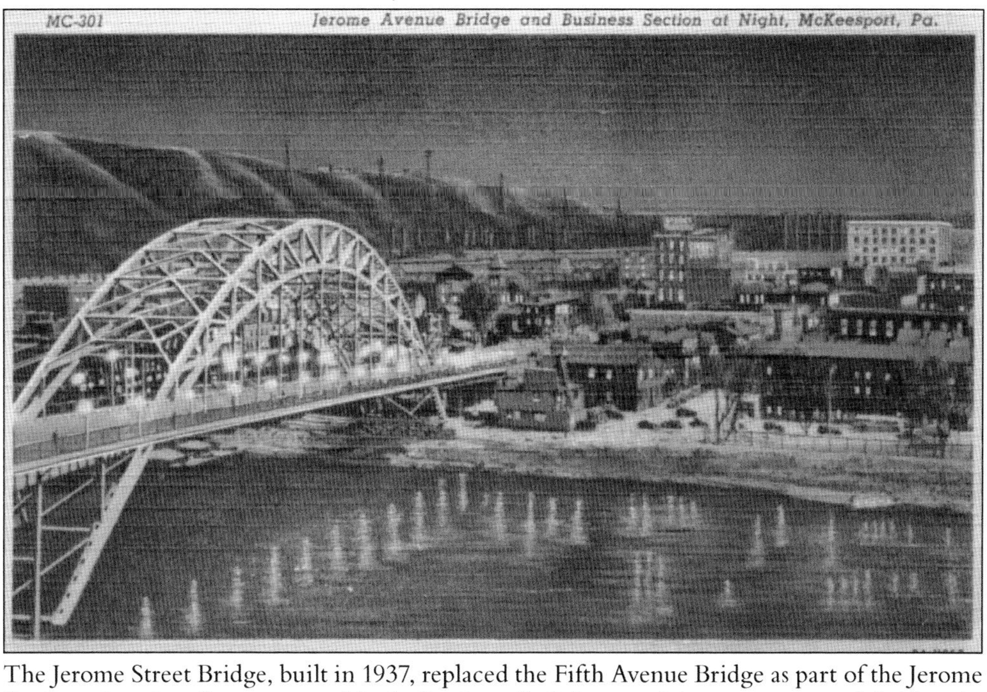

The Jerome Street Bridge, built in 1937, replaced the Fifth Avenue Bridge as part of the Jerome Boulevard project (later renamed Lysle Boulevard). It is one of three crescent arch bridges in Allegheny County, and its main span across the Youghiogheny River is 455 feet. The Water Street abutment of the bridge records the high-water mark from the 1936 flood.

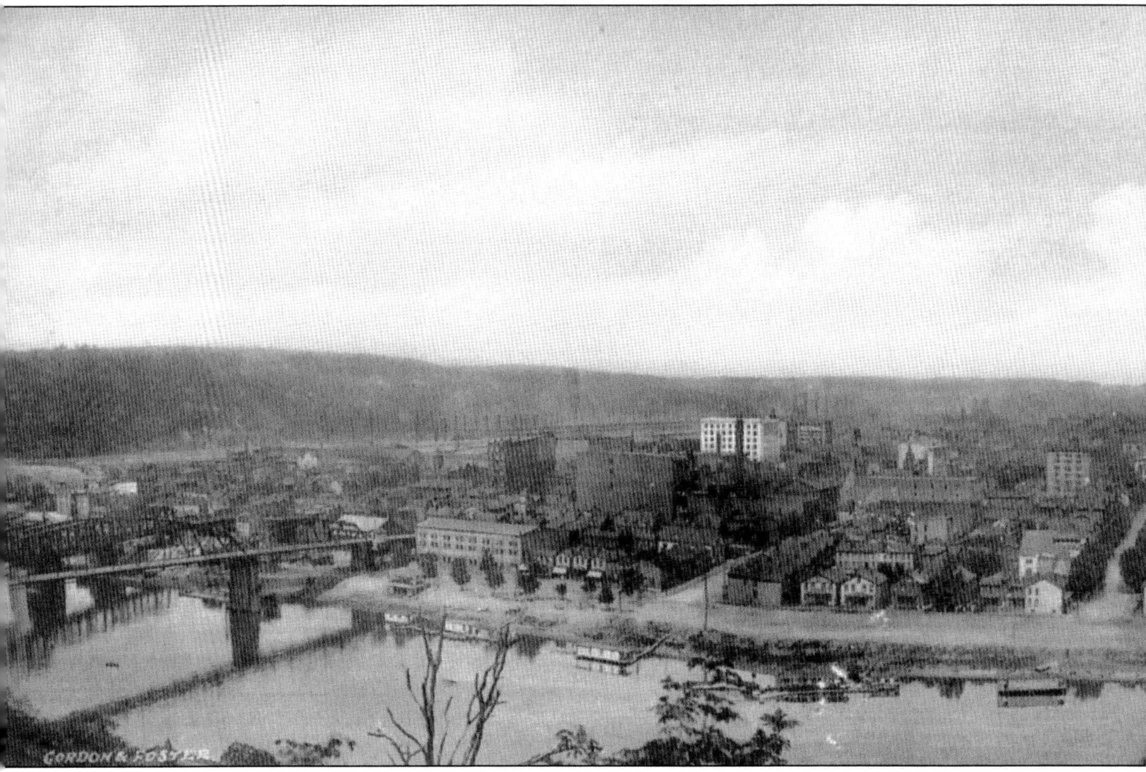

This c. 1910 panoramic view was taken from Arlington Avenue in Port Vue, across the Youghiogheny River. It includes Third Avenue to Fifteenth Avenue. The heavily residential area pictured along Water Street has largely disappeared, being replaced by the McKee's Point Marina, Gergely Riverfront Park, Riverside Nursing Home, and Kane Hospital. This initially

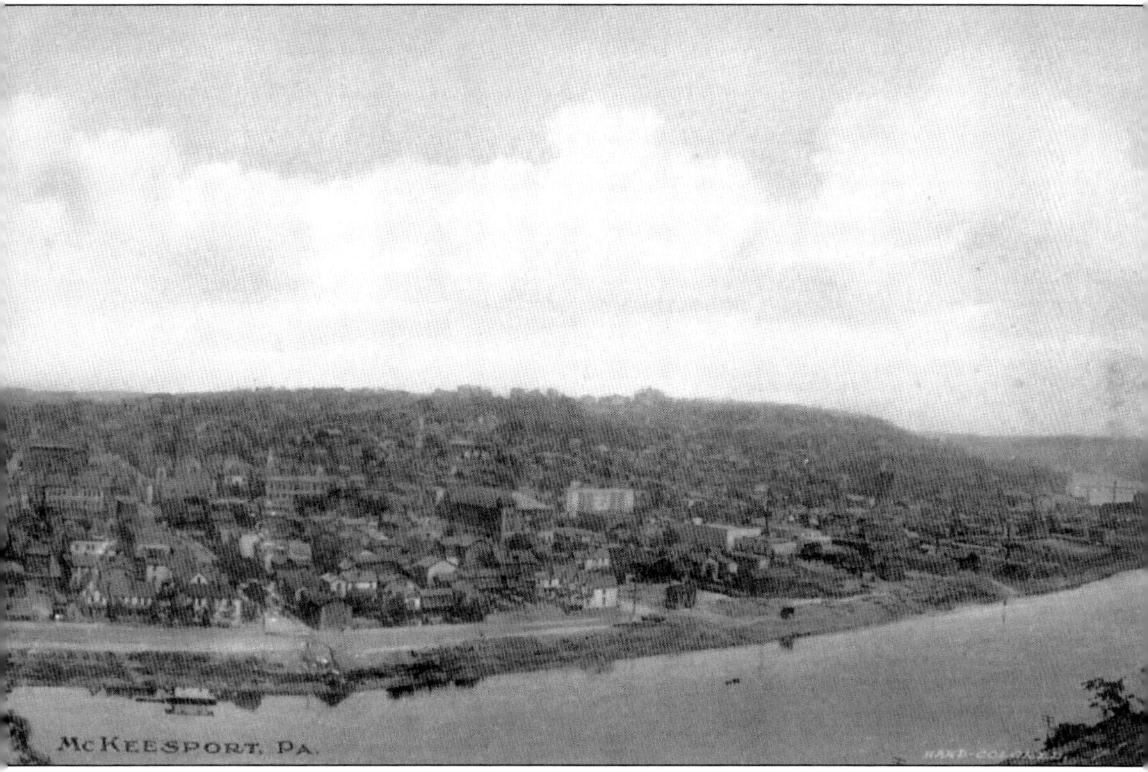

residential area was developed in the mid-19th century and includes both the Second and Third Ward sections of McKeesport. The People's Bank building is visible above the other downtown buildings, and the smokestacks from the mills can be seen in the background. (Courtesy of Leonard Chemsak.)

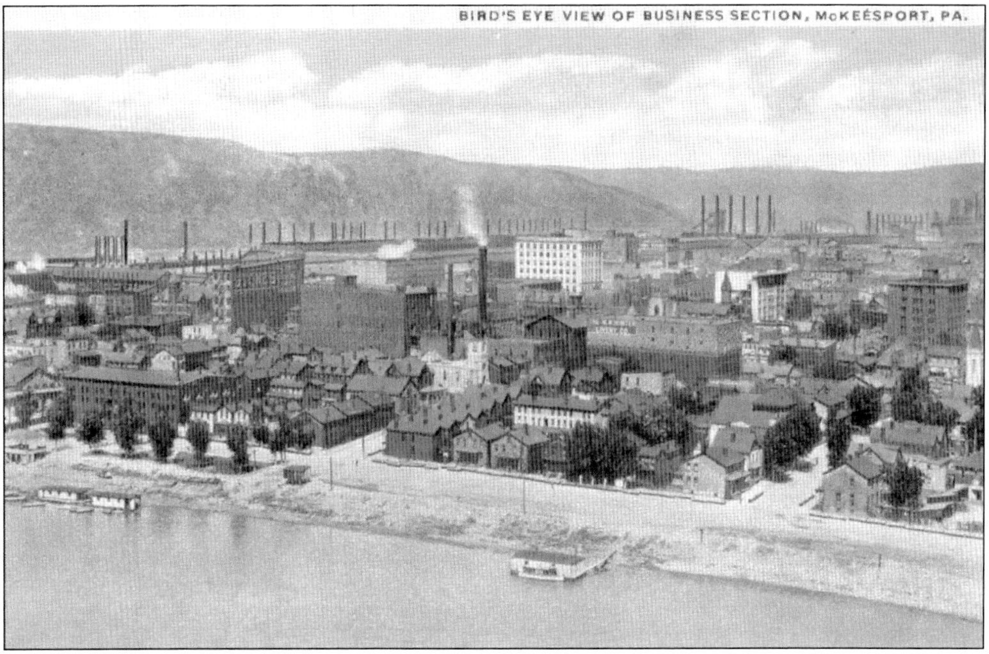

The next three photographs were also taken from Arlington Avenue. The Palisades (bottom left), built in 1901, still serves the community as an event center. The Market Street School (middle) was built in 1863. The W.W. Hunter Livery Company, to the right of the school, was built in 1893. It later became a garage and service station, and finally a storage facility.

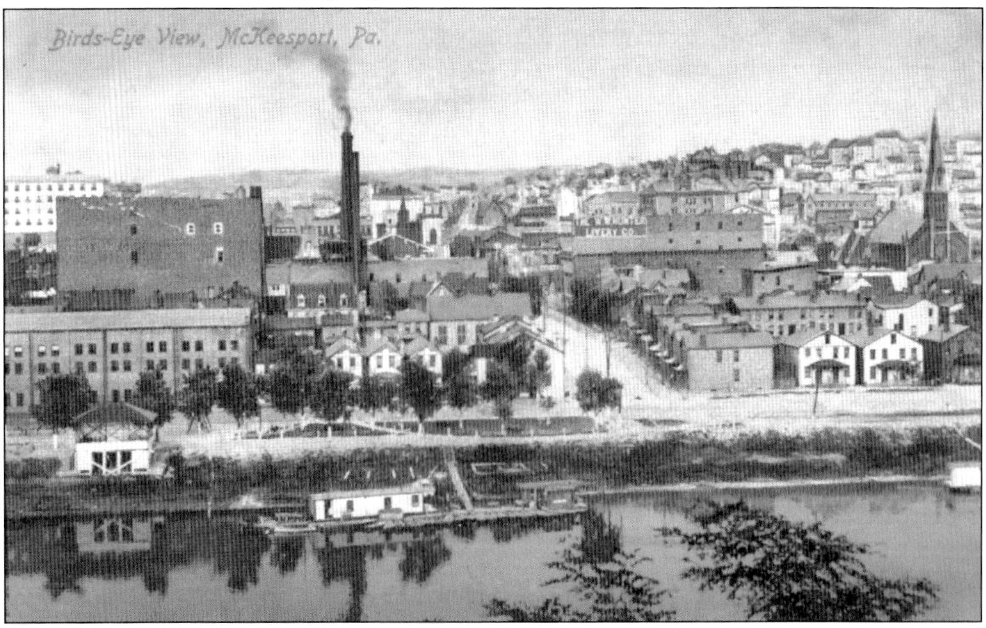

This closer view includes the Palisades (left), and behind the Palisades is the old Altmeyer Theater, built in 1892. After an 1896 fire, it became the People's Light and Storage Company and later the Crown Chocolate Company. On February 8, 1920, twenty-four years later to the day, the building was destroyed by another fire. The Penn McKee Hotel was later built on this site. (Courtesy of Leonard Chemsak.)

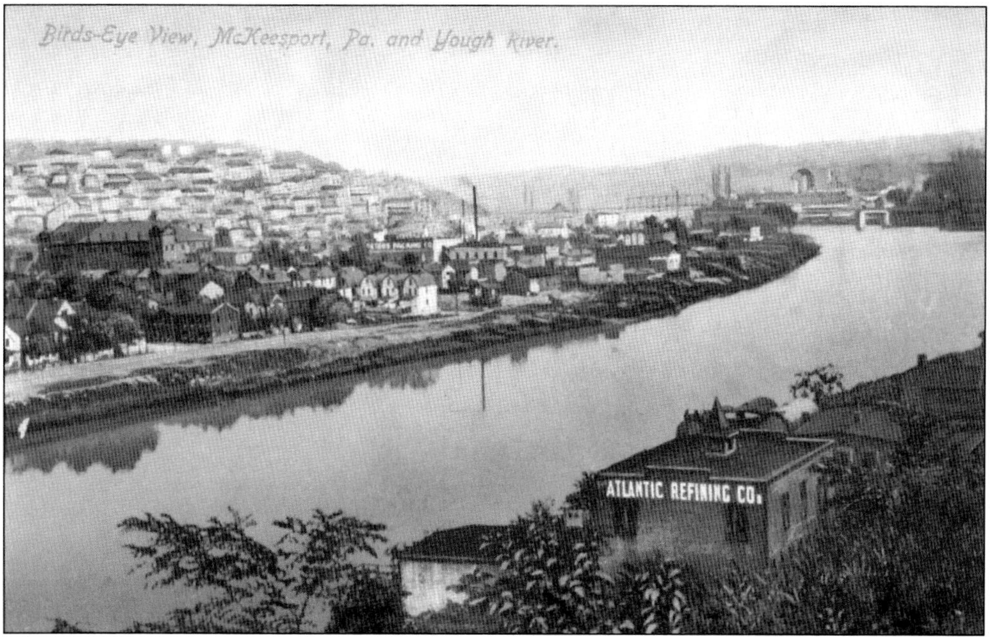

Looking up the Youghiogheny, this card includes the Atlantic Refining Company on River Road in Port Vue. To the left, the large building is Noble's Livery Stable. Barely visible at the center is Peter's Packing Company, and at the upper right the Fifteenth Avenue Bridge can be seen. Across the river to the right is the McKeesport Tin Plate Company in Port Vue. (Courtesy of Leonard Chemsak.)

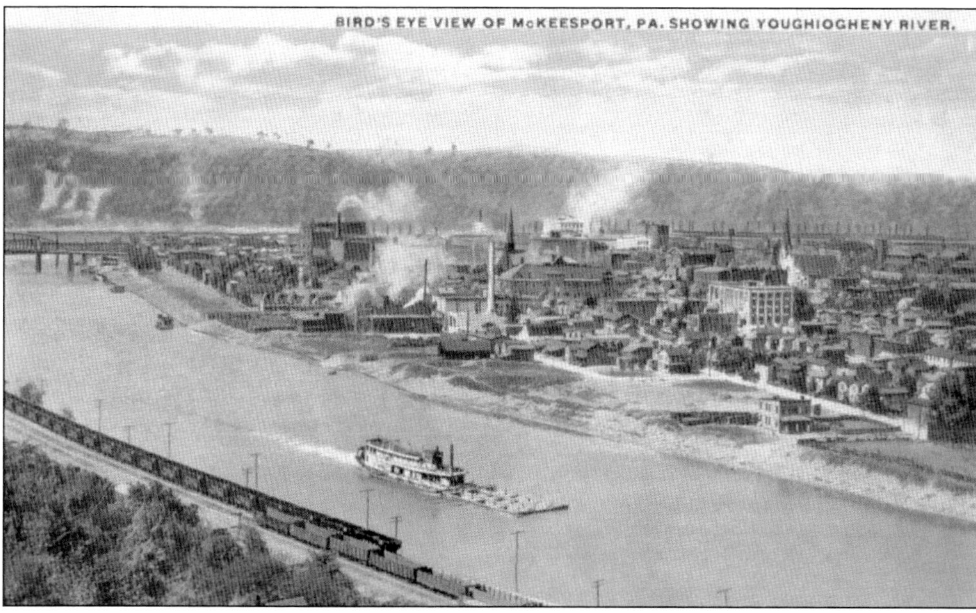

Taken from Laredo Street in Port Vue, the Pittsburgh & Lake Erie railroad tracks are in the foreground along River Road. The view takes in downtown McKeesport from the Fifth Avenue Bridge to Eleventh Avenue. The original Potter-McCune warehouse is the four-story building to the right. This was a triangular-shaped building located between the Baltimore & Ohio railroad tracks and Peebles Lane. (Courtesy of Roger Reichenbach.)

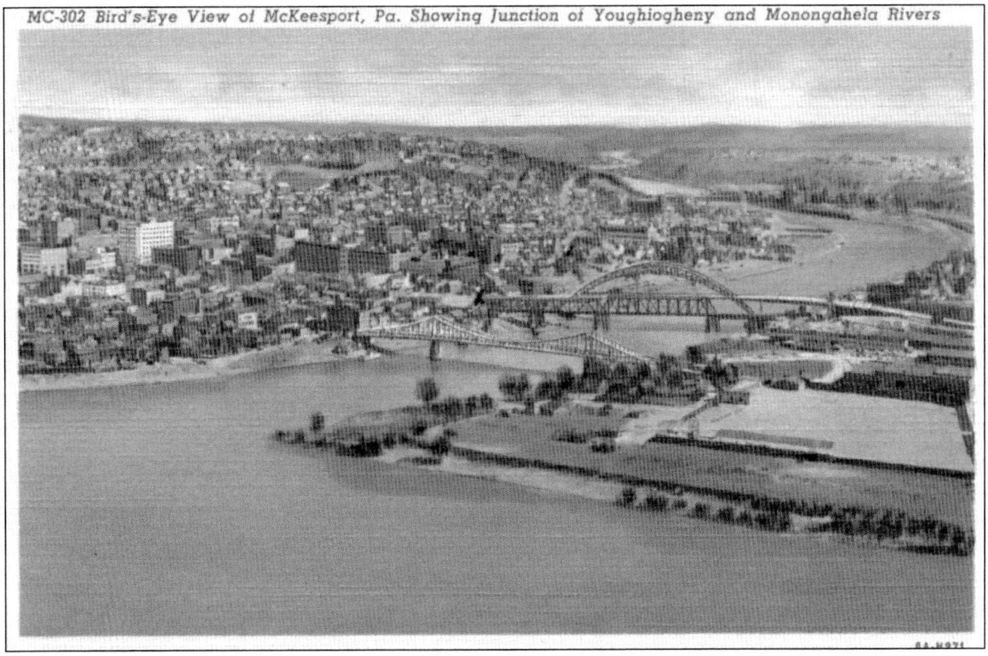

The junction of the rivers and the Third Avenue Bridge, Jerome Street Bridge, and the railroad bridge are captured on this card. Downtown McKeesport is to the left, and Cycler Park—Tenth Ward's popular ball field—is to the right. The old ballpark, which at times also hosted traveling circuses and carnivals, is now the site of the McKeesport Sewage Authority treatment plant. (Courtesy of Leonard Chemsak.)

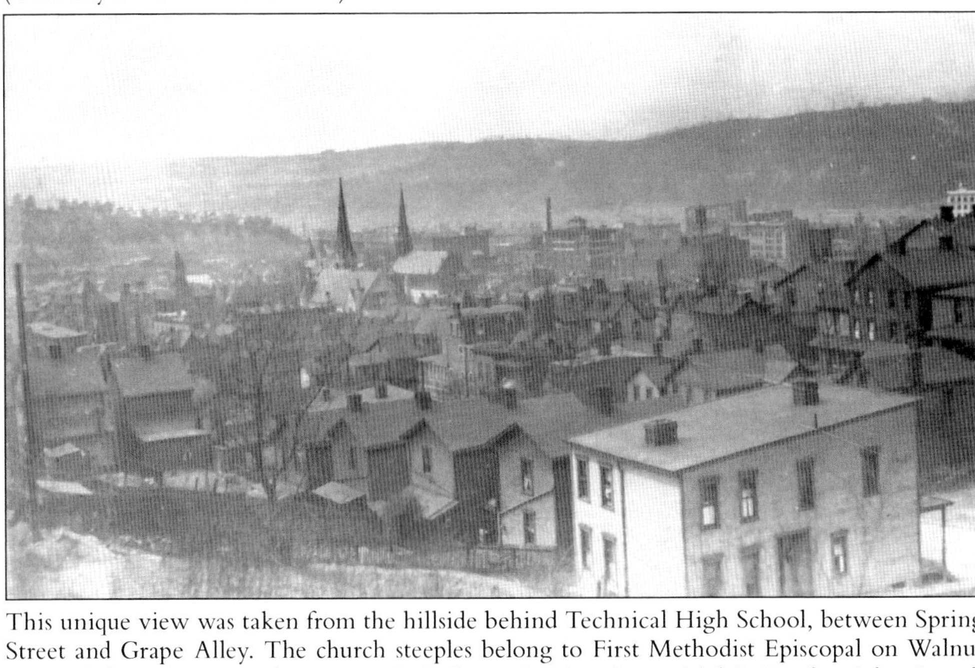

This unique view was taken from the hillside behind Technical High School, between Spring Street and Grape Alley. The church steeples belong to First Methodist Episcopal on Walnut Street (left) and St. Peter's Roman Catholic on Market Street (right). To the right, Stone's Furniture, the Masonic Temple, and a corner of the People's Bank Building can be seen. (Courtesy of the Edith Greaves Barrowcliff collection.)

Four

Downtown Scenes

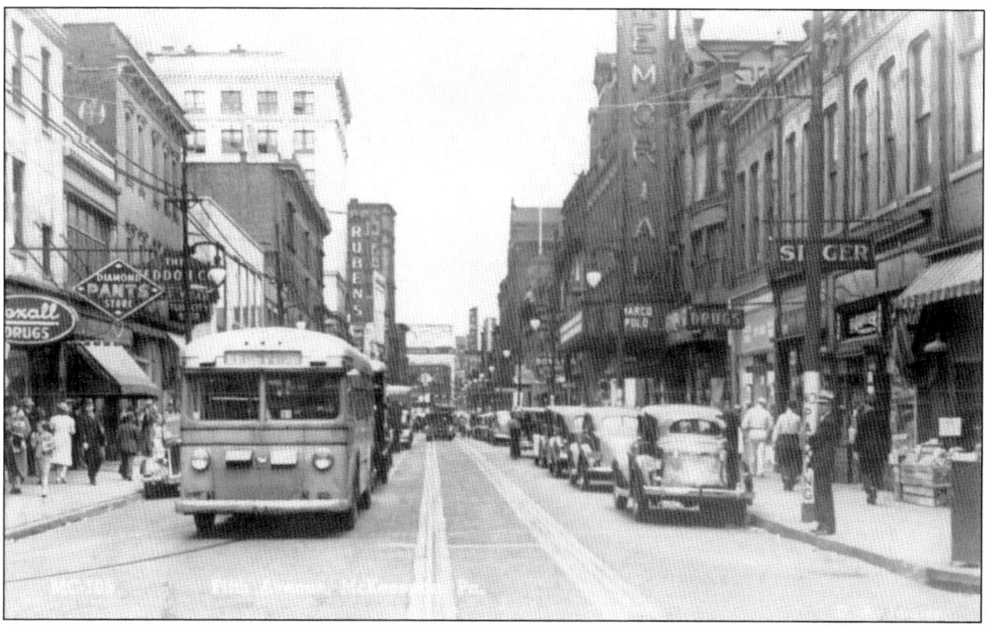

This east-facing view of Fifth Avenue, taken around 1938, shows a bustling downtown. Numerous stores lined the street, along with the Memorial Theater and the People's Bank. Busses, trolleys, and cars crowded McKeesport's main thoroughfare.

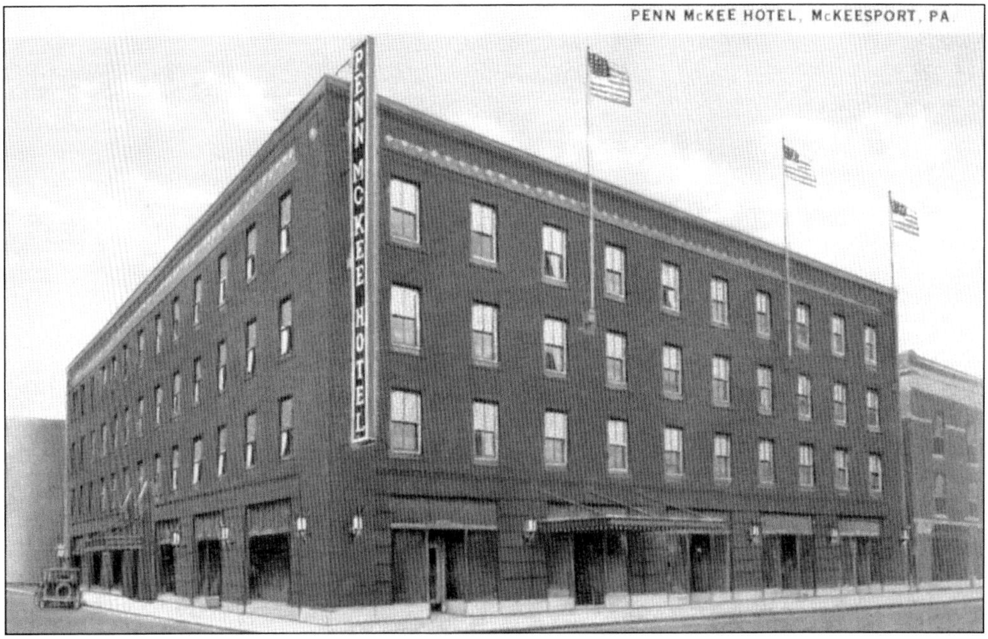

The Penn McKee Hotel still stands at the corner of Fifth Avenue and Strawberry Alley, built by the Community Hotel Company of McKeesport in 1926. Designed by Benno Janssen, a prominent Pittsburgh-area architect, it was the site of the first Kennedy-Nixon debate on April 22, 1947.

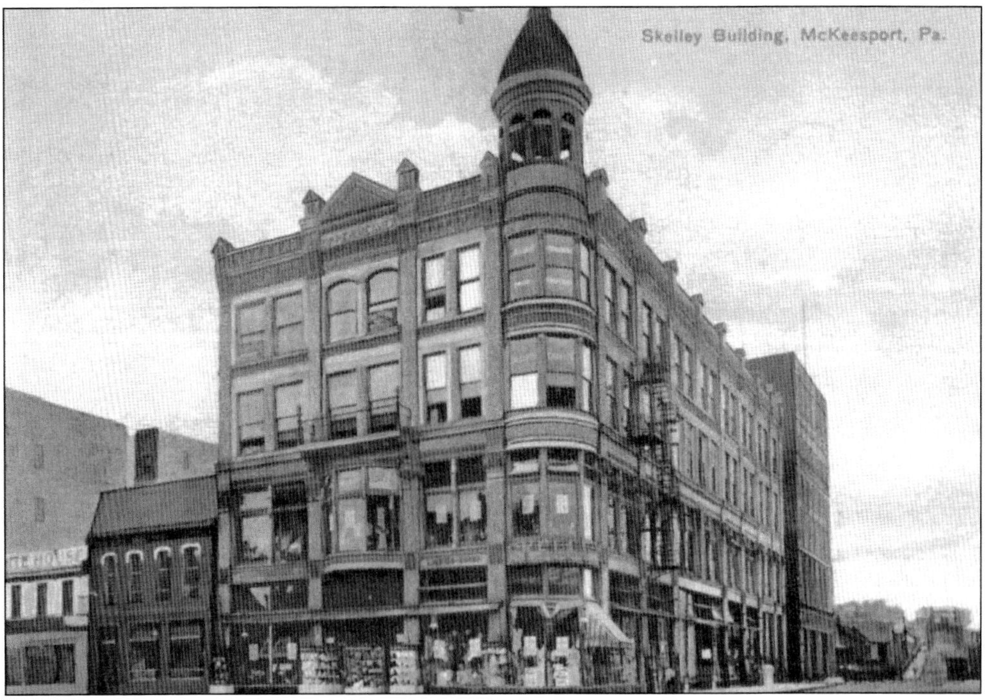

At Fifth Avenue and Market Street, was the Oppenheimer Building, erected in 1893. It was the location first of Skelley's and later the Famous Department Store. The turret was removed during World War I, and in the 1950s, the building was covered with a metallic skin. It was destroyed in 1976 during the "Famous Fire."

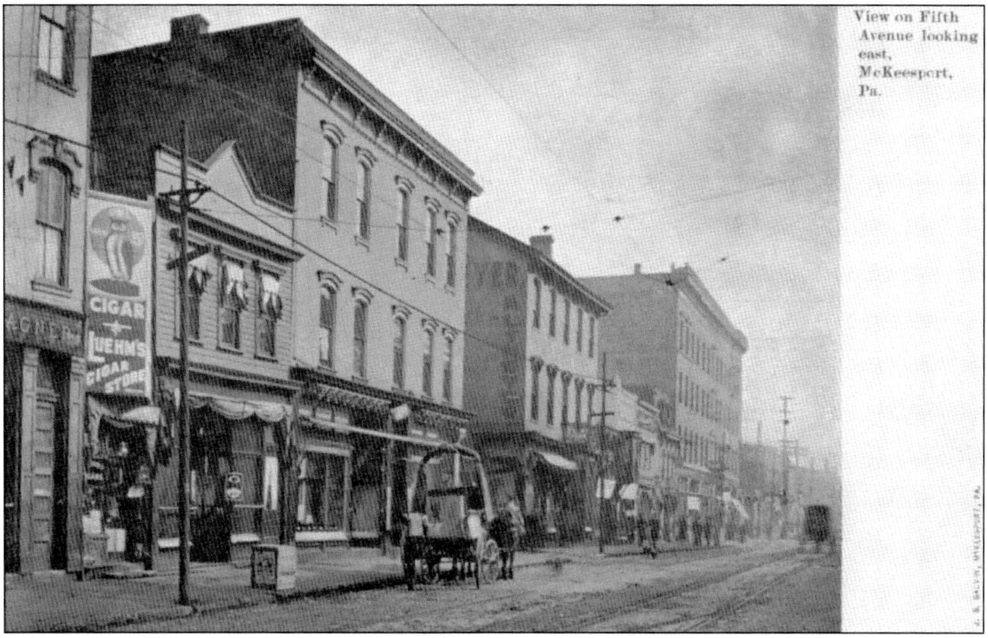

This image shows the north side of Fifth Avenue, between Market and Walnut Streets, around 1904. Between the Ruben Building (right) and the Lysle and Van Kirk building (left of center) was Altmeyer's. Over its lifetime, Altmeyer's was a saloon, restaurant, and theater. It was converted to the Harris State Theater and later became Jaison's Department Store. (Courtesy of Leonard Chemsak.)

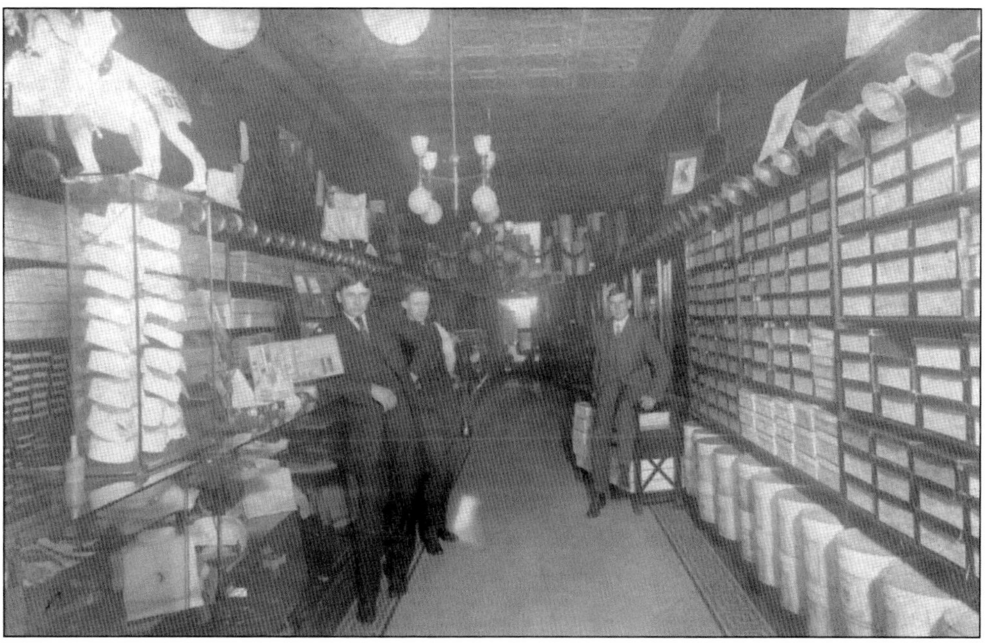

The interior of W.H. Myers's store, listed in the 1910 city directory as a "Hatter and Furnisher," was located at 213 Fifth Avenue. His store sold hats, collars, ties, and other accessories for men. Myers was one of 14 stores on Fifth Avenue that sold men's furnishings. Fred Emerson has been identified as the man on the right.

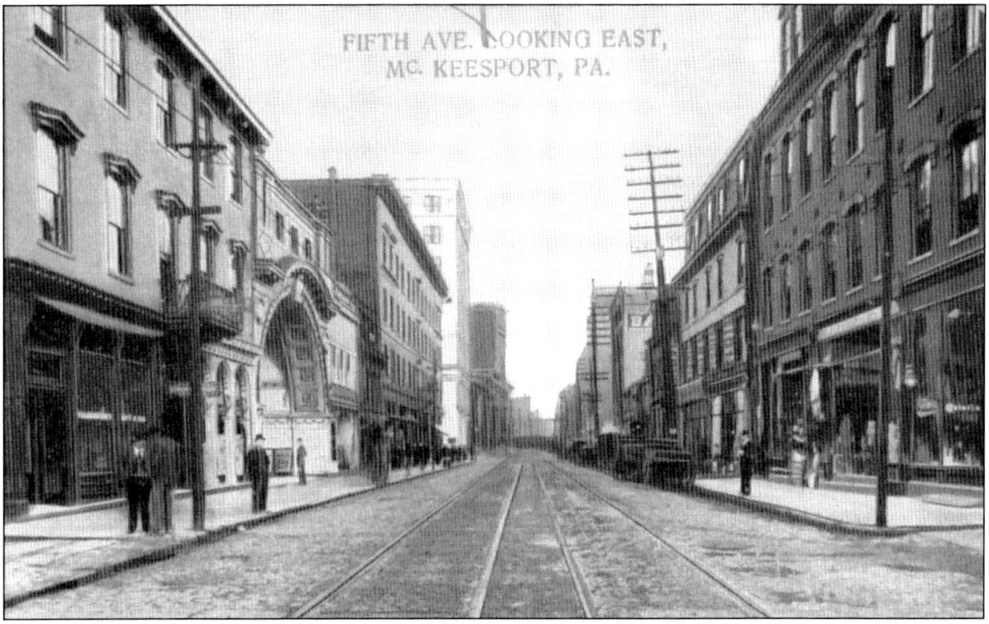

By 1908, Altmeyer's, the building on the left with the arched entrance, had become part of the Harris Amusement Company. On the right is the Wyant Building. The upper floor was the headquarters of the Masonic lodges before the Masonic Temple was built in 1906. Just beyond the Wyant Building is the National Hotel, which later became the site of Cox's Men's Store.

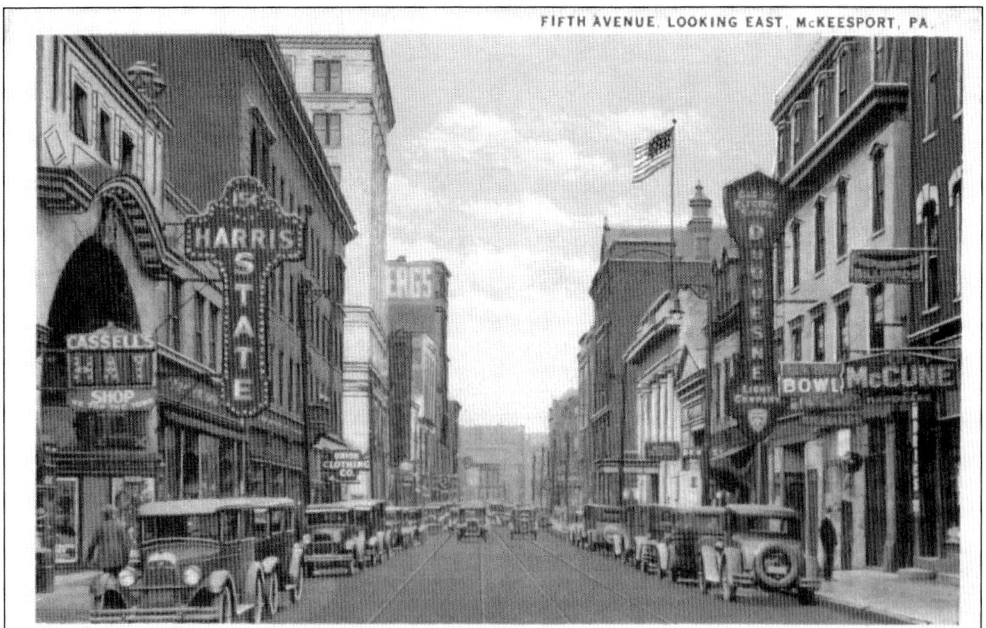

This view is of the same section of street, shown in the 1920s. The National Hotel had become an office for the Duquesne Light Company, and there was bowling upstairs. Continuing up the street is the First National Bank and the old White's Opera House. On the left, Altmeyer's is now the Harris State Theater. Beyond that is the Ruben Building and the People's Bank. Hirshberg's is in the distance.

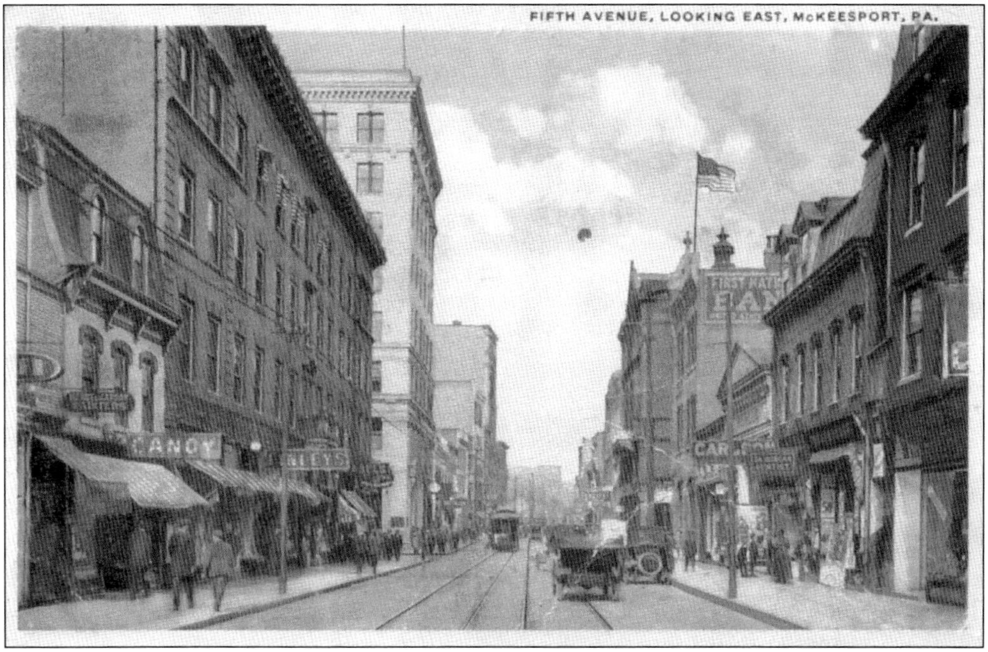

Moving half a block up Fifth Avenue, Carroll's Candy Kitchen is the first small building on the left. Next is the Ruben Building, with store signs for Finley's dry goods and Abel's jewelry store. On the right is the corner of the old National Hotel. In the next building there are store signs for Doctor Duncan, a dentist, and Carlson's shoe store. (Courtesy of John Barna.)

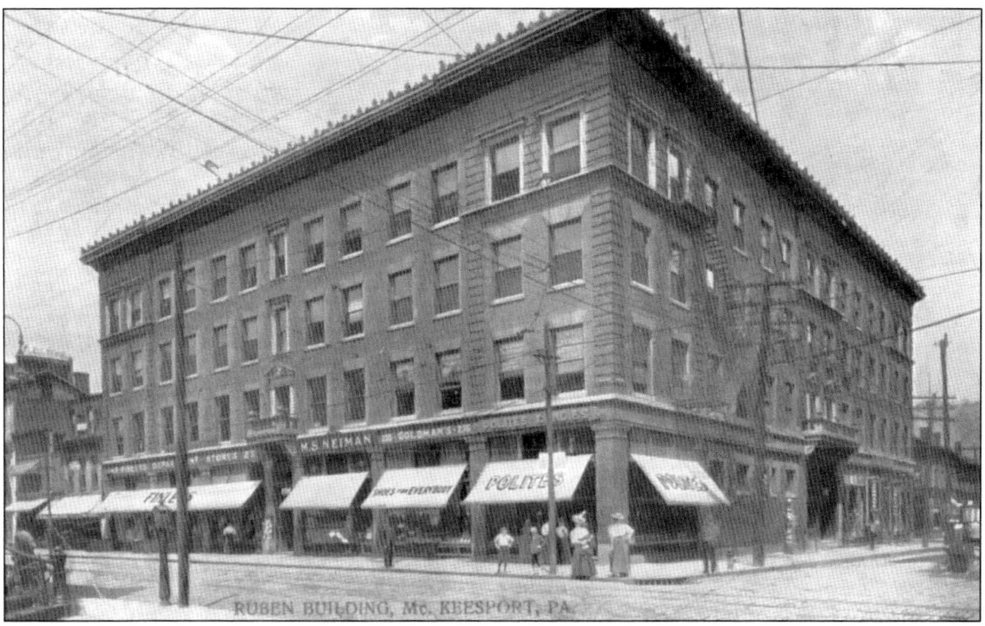

The Ruben Building was constructed in 1902 at the northwest corner of Fifth Avenue and Walnut Street. This image was shot in 1905, and the storefronts at the time were Finley's Department Store, M.S. Neiman's jewelry store, Goldman's shoe store, and, at the corner, Polites Brothers confectioners. The upper floors were offices and apartments. This building burned in February 1945. (Courtesy of John Barna.)

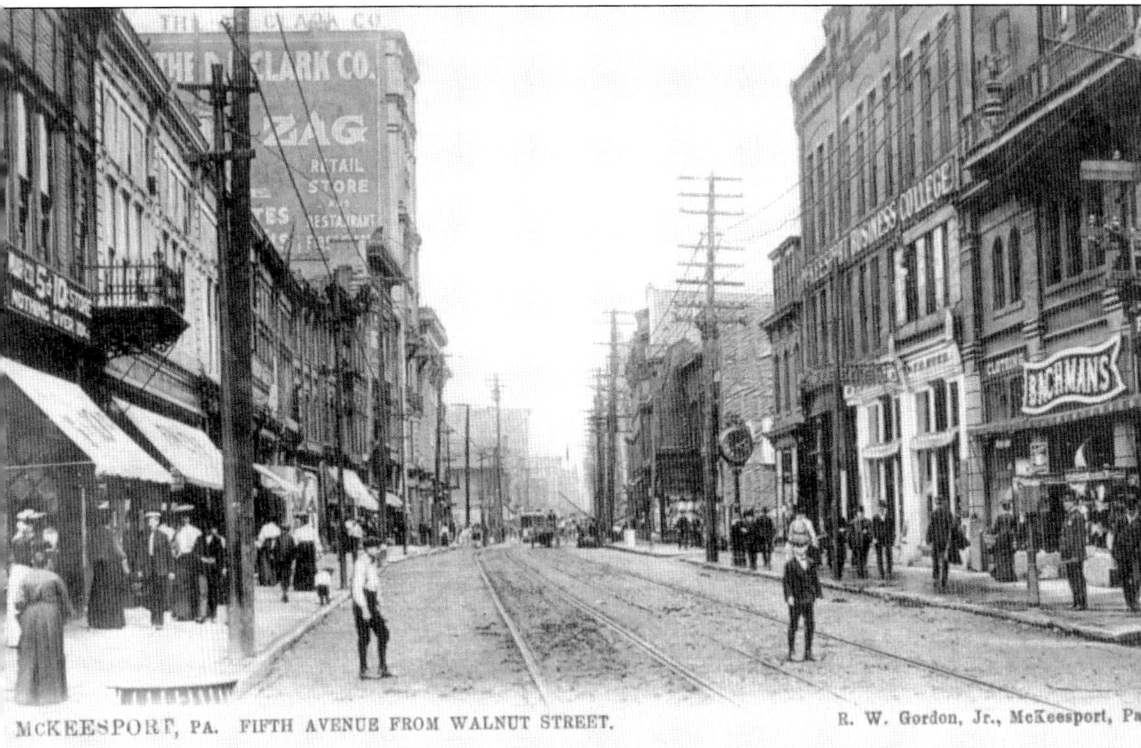

On the left is the Hartman Block, built in 1878. The corner storefront, at 301 Fifth Avenue, was the first location of the G.C. Murphy 5 & 10 store, which opened around 1899. In 1904, George Clinton Murphy sold his company, and this store closed. He later opened a new store at 545 Fifth Avenue. In the background is the D.L. Clark Candy Company. On the right side of the street is Bachmans men's clothing store in the White's Opera House building. The next building is the Lyceum Building, home to the McKeesport Business College on the upper floors, with F.O. Reed Shoes in the first-floor storefront. This building at one time also contained a roller rink. The small structure with the clock in front next to the Lyceum Building, at the corner of Tube Works Alley, was Henry Reineman's jewelry store. (Courtesy of Leonard Chemsak.)

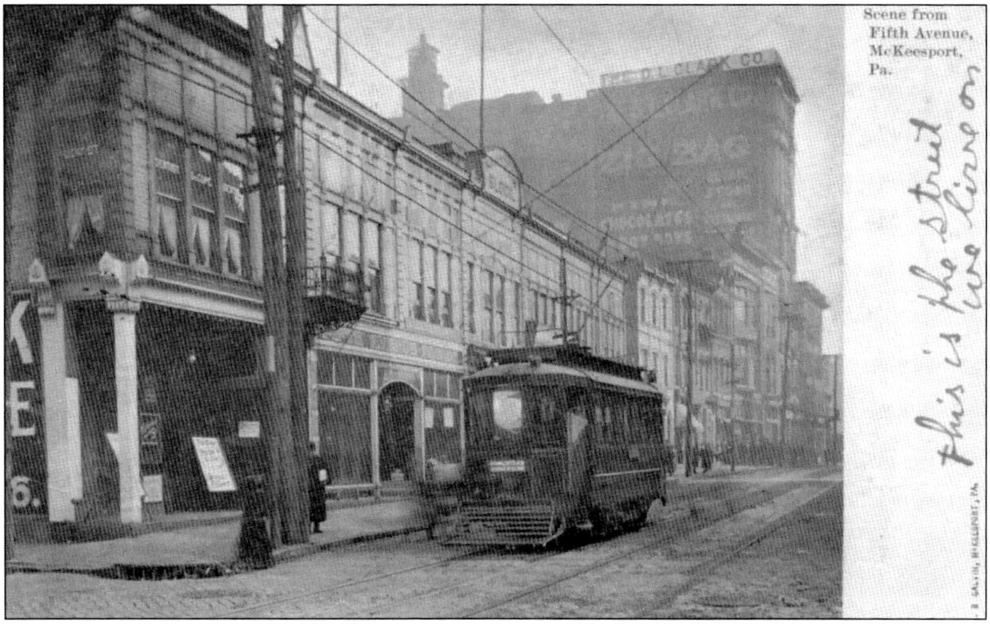

This image of the Hartman Block is from 1905. It includes the first nickelodeon in McKeesport, where the first G.C. Murphy store had been. This was one of the earliest nickelodeons in the world, opened shortly after the first one in Pittsburgh. Most of the Hartman Block was replaced by the People's Bank in 1906. (Courtesy of Andrea [Luketic] Cartwright.)

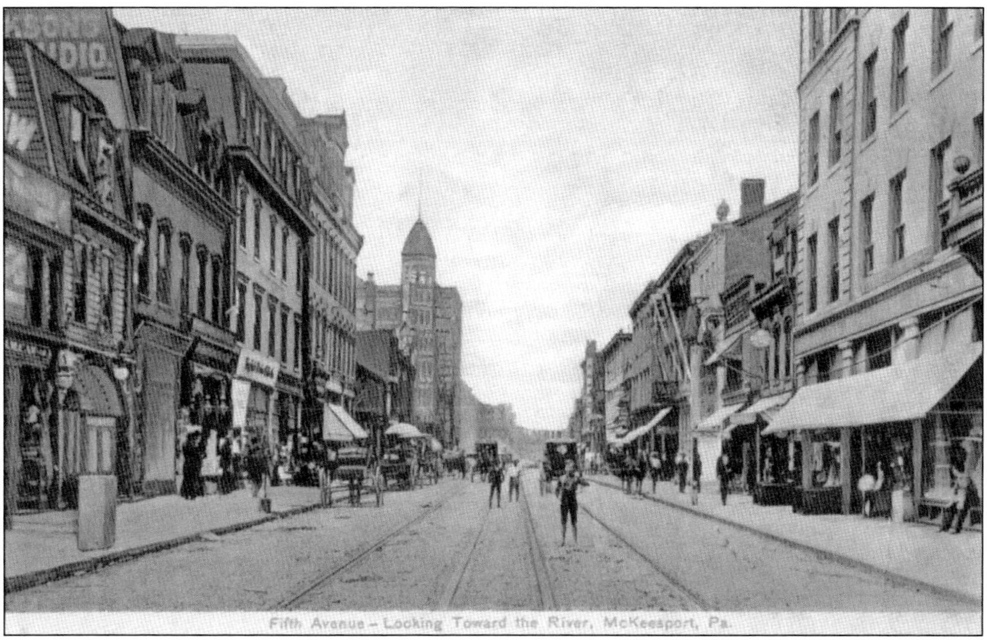

This westward-facing view of Fifth Avenue includes the Ruben Building (right). The first building on the left, with the arched entrance, is Dreamland Theater, another early nickelodeon. In the distance is the Oppenheimer Building with its turret.

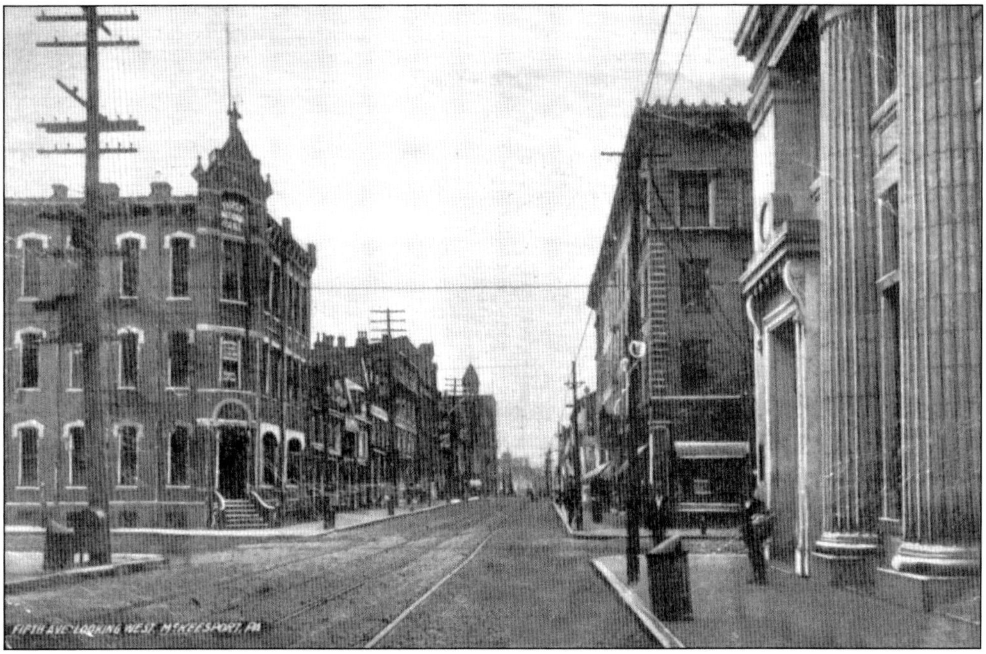

Slightly up the road is the corner of People's Bank Building (right), and the Ruben Building is just behind it. First National Bank (left) was built in 1881. There were offices upstairs and a barbershop in the basement. (Courtesy of Andrea [Luketic] Cartwright.)

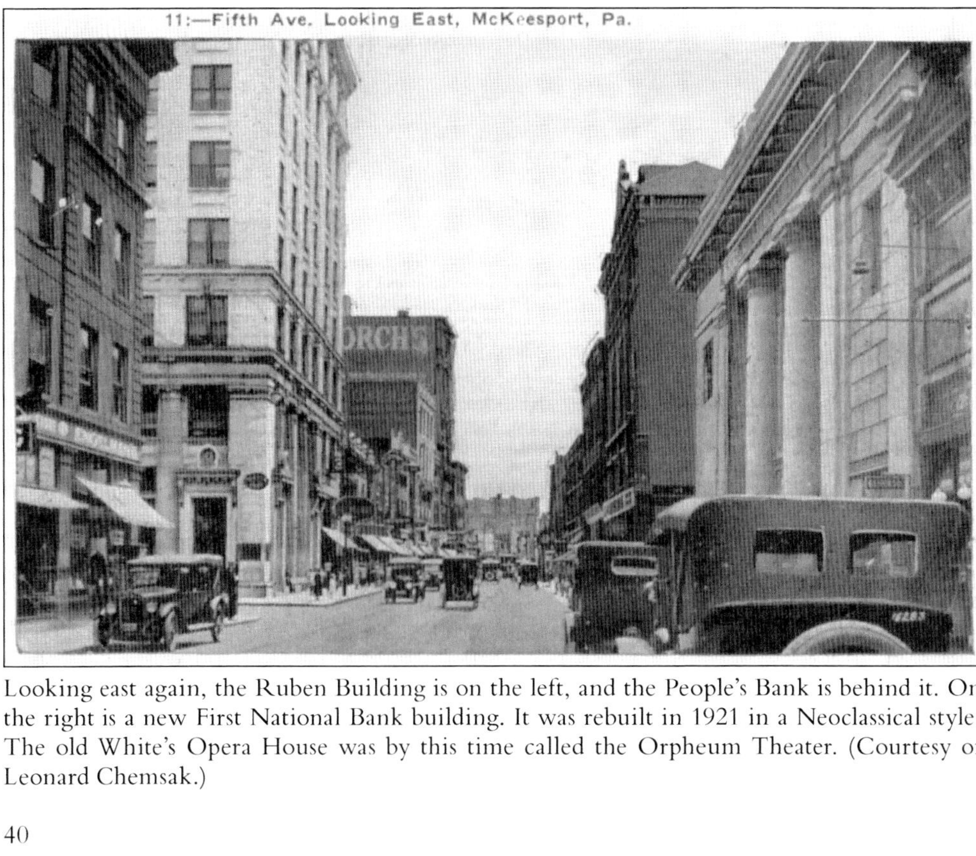

Looking east again, the Ruben Building is on the left, and the People's Bank is behind it. On the right is a new First National Bank building. It was rebuilt in 1921 in a Neoclassical style. The old White's Opera House was by this time called the Orpheum Theater. (Courtesy of Leonard Chemsak.)

The People's Bank Building was located at the northeast corner of Fifth Avenue and Walnut Street. Built in 1906, it was designed by Mowbrey and Uffinger, architects from New York. This replaced the old Hartman Block and was the second location of the People's Bank, following its original location at Fifth Avenue and Market Street.

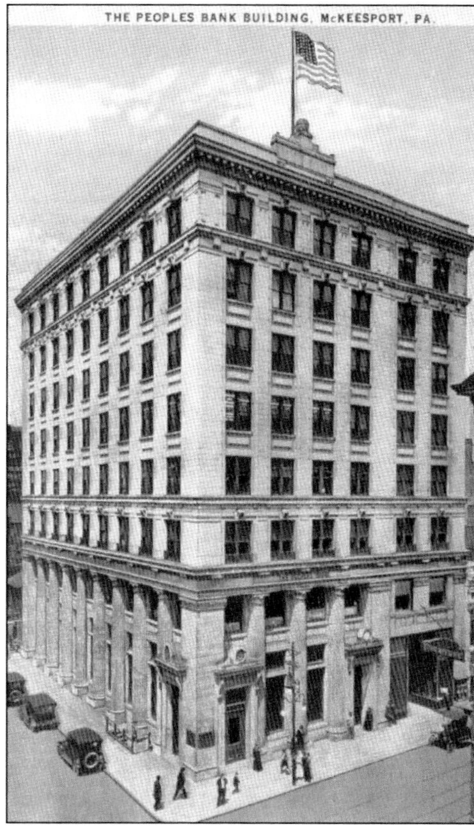

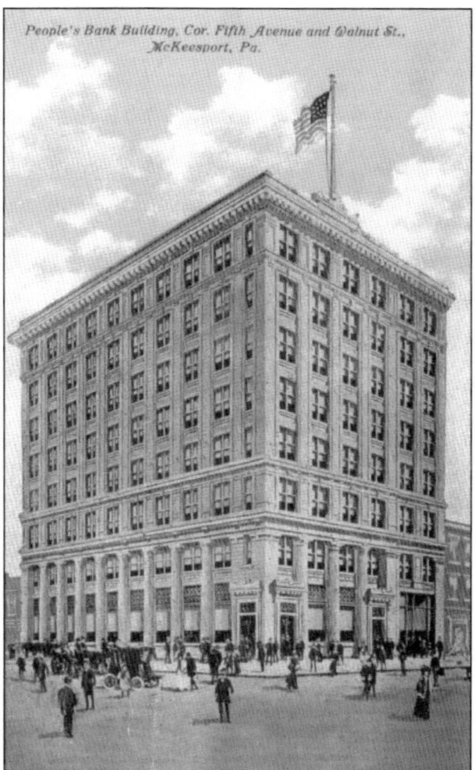

At almost 100 feet high, this building contained 200 to 300 tons of structural steel. It was faced with glazed white terra-cotta and had 11 four-foot-diameter columns of Bethel granite. The bank was at street level, and 100 offices were located on the upper floors. There was an earlier plan from 1897, before the bank bought the property, to build a large hotel on this site.

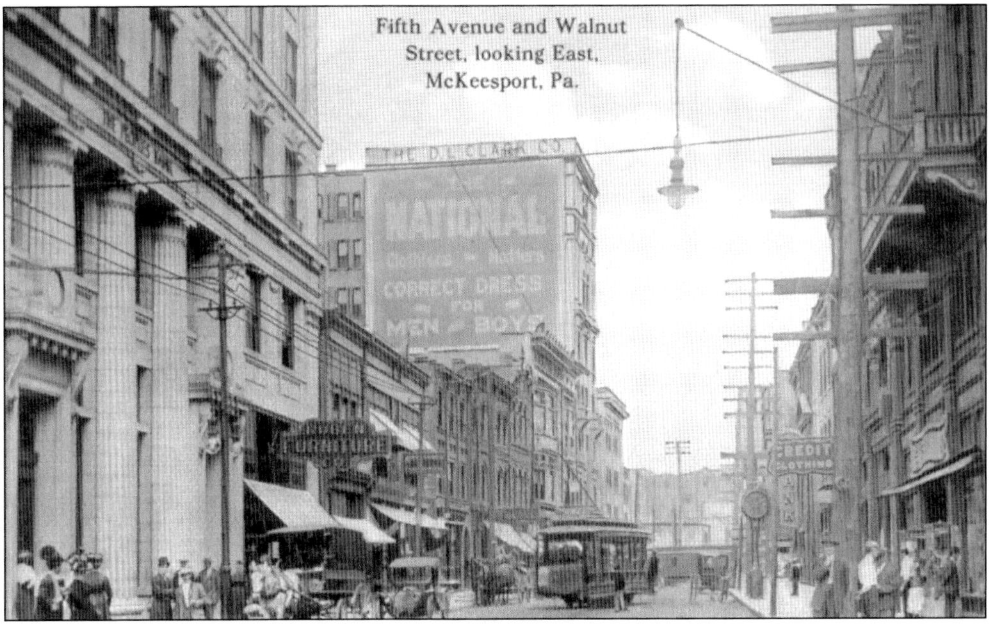

Beyond the People's Bank, at 331 Fifth Avenue, was the D.L. Clark Candy Company. Built between 1903 and 1904, the building was approximately 110 feet high. The candy kettles were on the fourth, fifth, seventh, and eighth floors. The Zig-Zag department was on the sixth floor, where the popular molasses-covered popcorn confection was made. The structure was demolished in 1970. (Courtesy of Chuck Jarrell.)

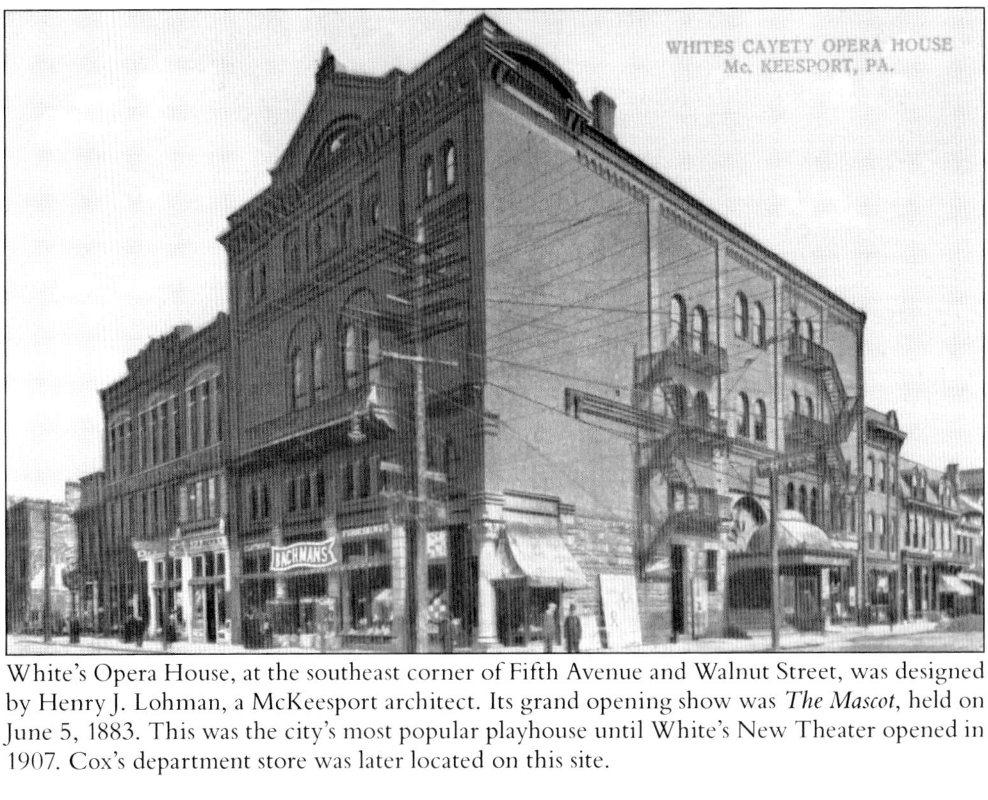

White's Opera House, at the southeast corner of Fifth Avenue and Walnut Street, was designed by Henry J. Lohman, a McKeesport architect. Its grand opening show was *The Mascot*, held on June 5, 1883. This was the city's most popular playhouse until White's New Theater opened in 1907. Cox's department store was later located on this site.

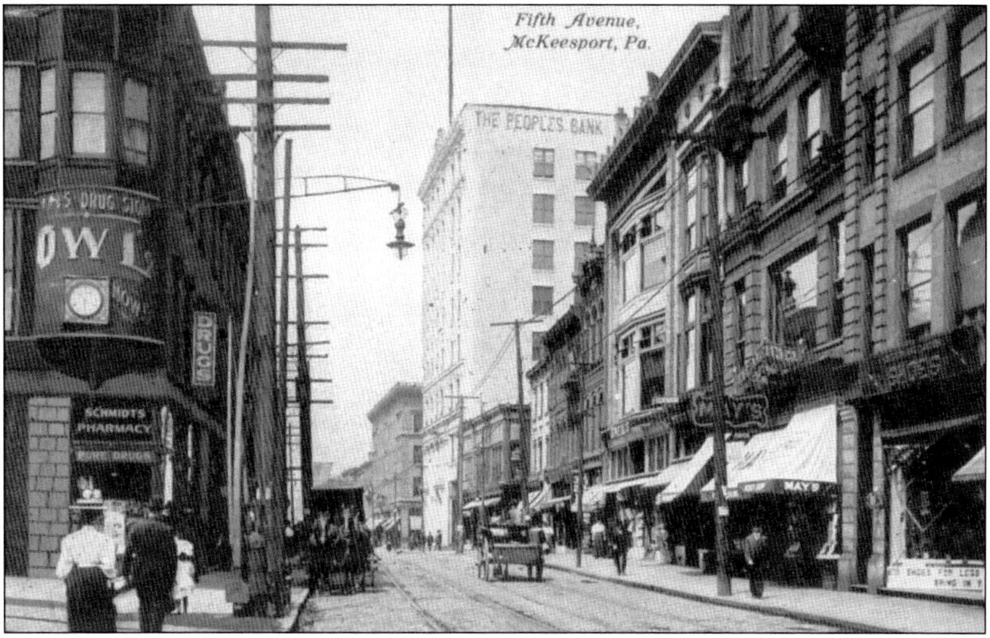

Looking west along Fifth Avenue from the railroad crossing, this 1910 image shows the corner of the Fifth Avenue Hotel at the right. The May Drug Company is next door in the storefront of the Clark Building with O'Neil's department store beyond. On the left is Schmidt's Pharmacy, later the site of Harold Blid's Pharmacy.

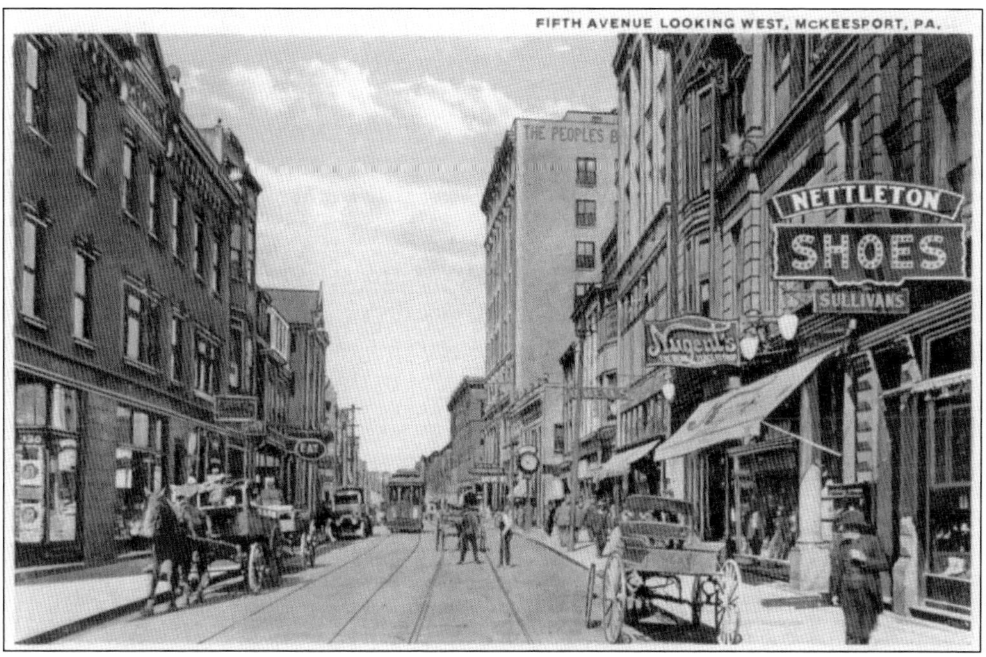

Looking west around 1912, Nugent's department store now occupies the Clark Building. To the right, Sullivan's Shoes occupies the storefront of the Fifth Avenue Hotel. The clock on the sidewalk stands in front of the Sheehan Building. The Schmidt Building is on the left.

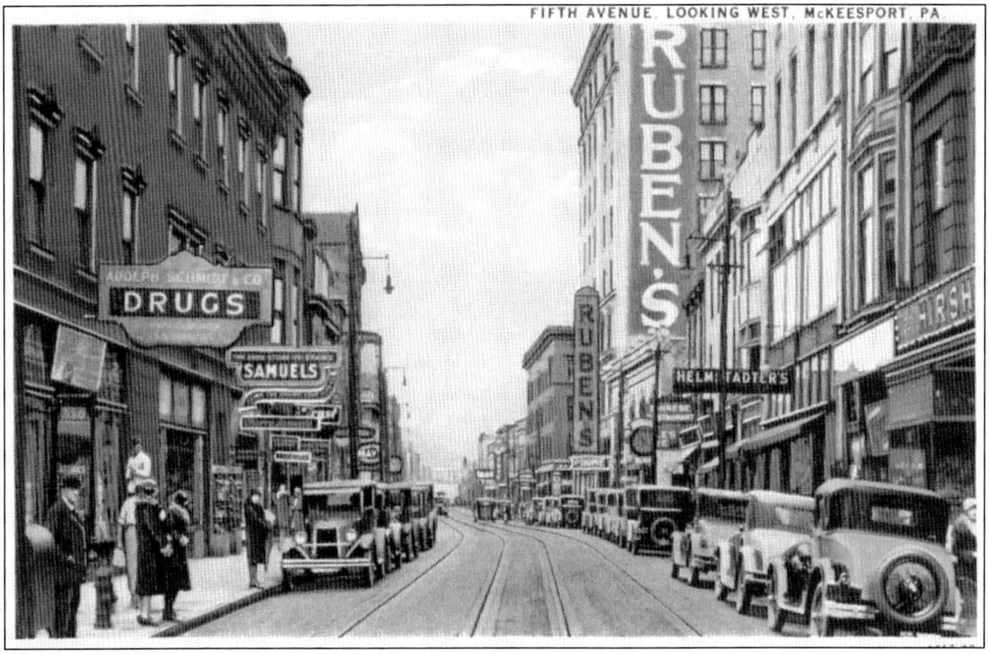

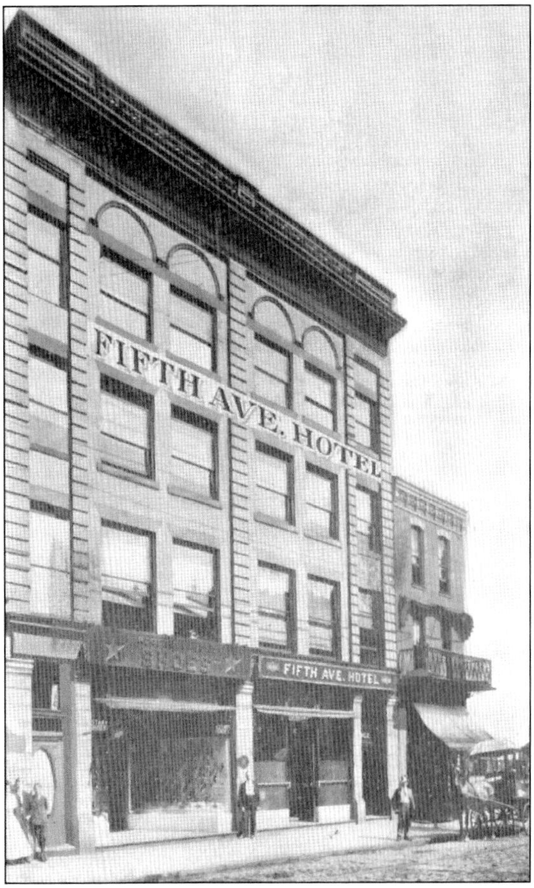

Showing practically the same view as the previous page, this postcard is from around 1925. Hirshberg's Furniture is now in the Clark Building, and O'Neil's is now Helmstadter's department store. Ruben's Furniture now occupies part of the People's Bank Building. Ruben's remained in that location until it closed in the early 1970s. (Courtesy of Chuck Jarrell.)

The Fifth Avenue Hotel was built around 1885 and remodeled around 1900. It had 37 guest rooms, a bar, and dining room. This later became the Hotel Pershing in 1921, an A&P store in the 1930s and 1940s, and then the R.E. Kaplan Furniture Company. The Patterson Block is the building to the right, along the Baltimore & Ohio railroad tracks. (Courtesy of Roger Reichenbach.)

Regensburger's Shoes was located in the Fifth Avenue Hotel storefront, at 335 Fifth Avenue. Its advertisements were found on the back of a number of McKeesport postcards. Sullivan's Shoes later occupied this same site. (Courtesy of Leonard Chemsak.)

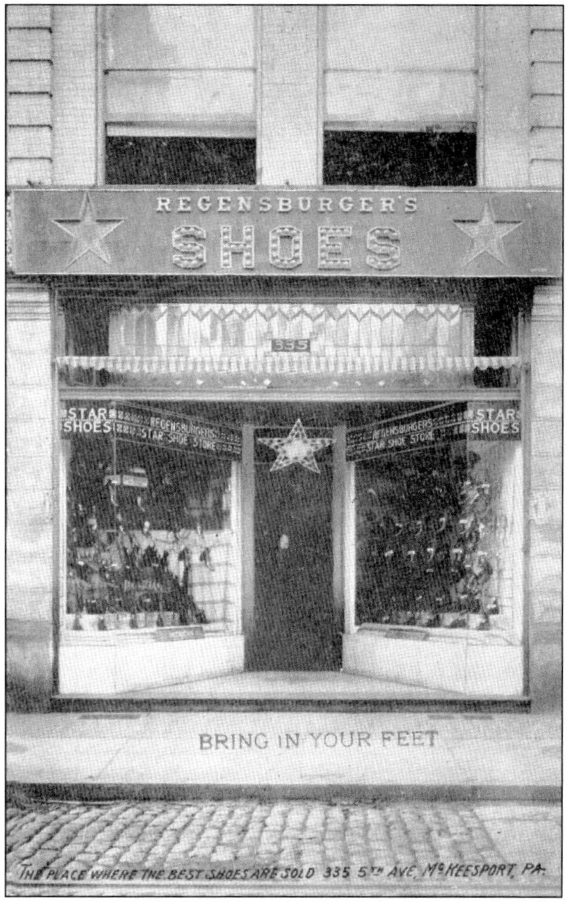

Looking west, on the right is the front of the Patterson Block, along the Baltimore & Ohio railroad tracks. The roof of the Fifth Avenue Hotel peeks over the top. The tower on the left is the Schmidt Building. The second building on the left is the Volk Hotel, at Fifth Avenue and Locust Street. (Courtesy of Leonard Chemsak.)

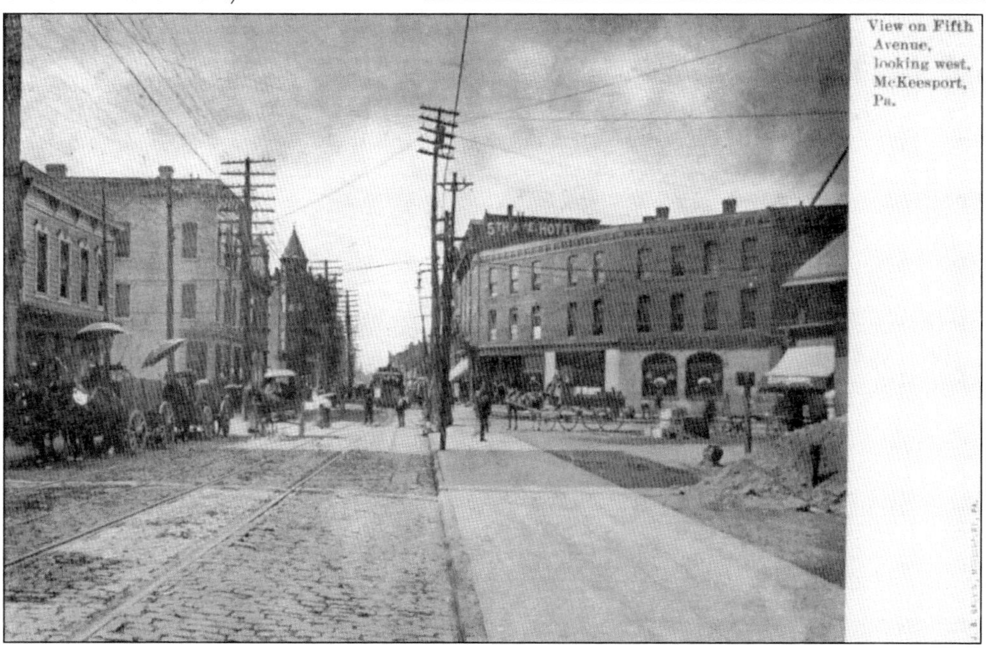

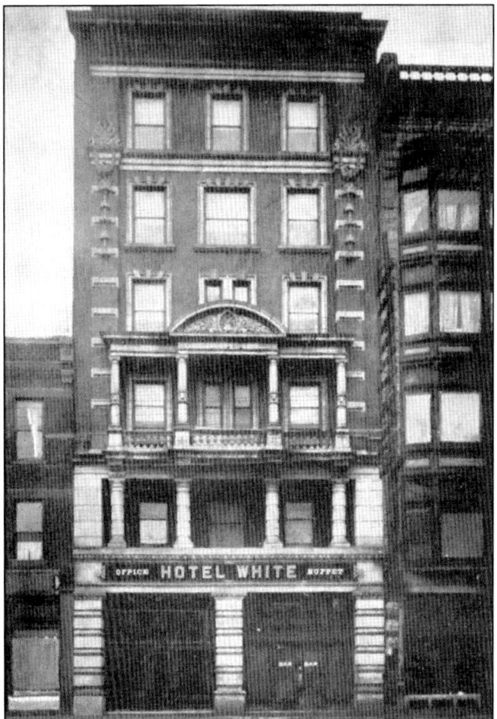

32. New Hotel White, McKeesport, Pa.

The New Hotel White was located at 408 Fifth Avenue. Built around 1905, it replaced the earlier hotel on the same site. Mabel Connelly, mother of Marc Connelly—McKeesport's Pulitzer Prize–winning playwright—was the proprietress in the early 20th century. Later, it was called the Hotel Waldo, the Clinton, and finally, the McKeesporter.

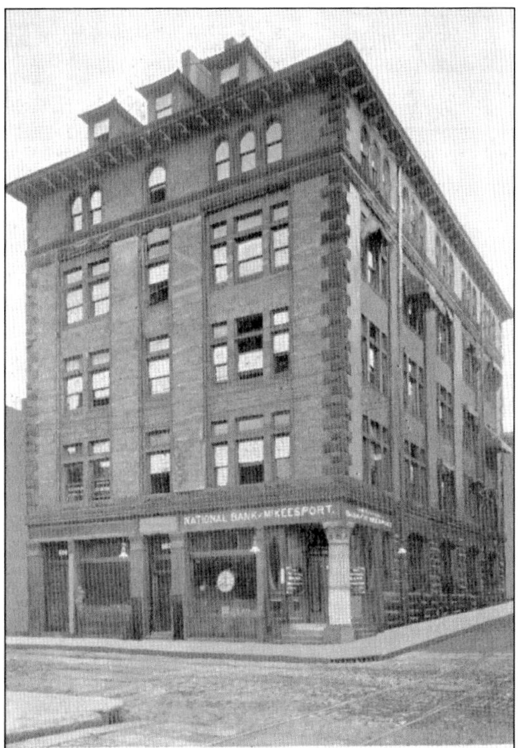

7 National Bank of McKeesport, McKeesport, Pa.

The National Bank Building was located at 500 Fifth Avenue, on the site of Dunshee's apple orchard. Built in 1889 at a cost of $35,000, it was designed by Pittsburgh architects Alden, Harlow, and Longfellow. It is now the city hall of McKeesport. (Courtesy of Leonard Chemsak.)

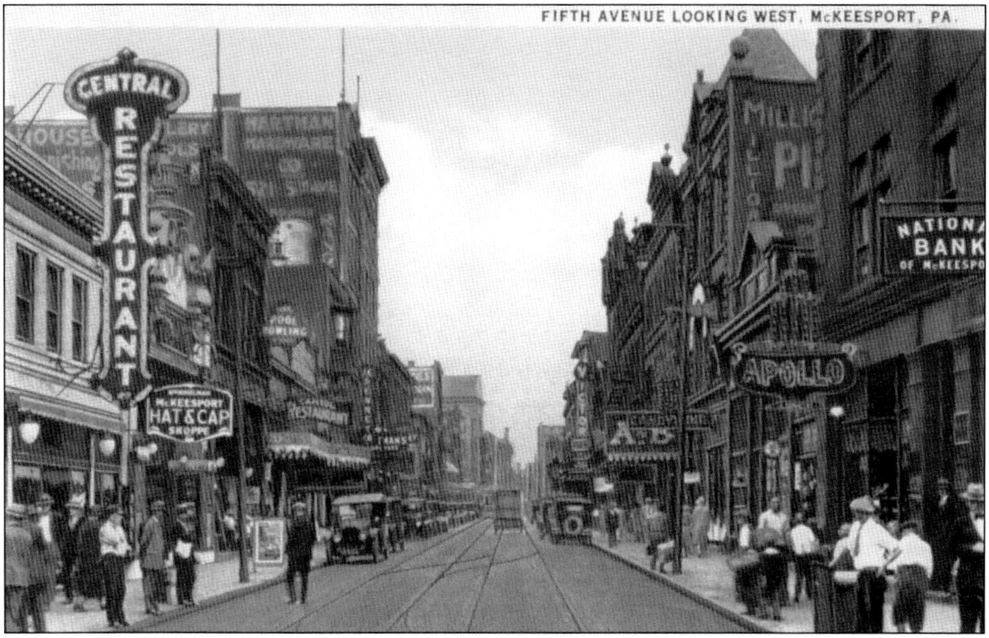

Looking east, the National Bank Building is at the right. The sign for the Victor, one of the four theaters along this block of Fifth Avenue in the 1920s, is on the right farther down the street. There is a sign for J.C. Penny Co. on the building next to Hartman Hardware. The Hartman Building later became part of the G.C. Murphy Company General Offices.

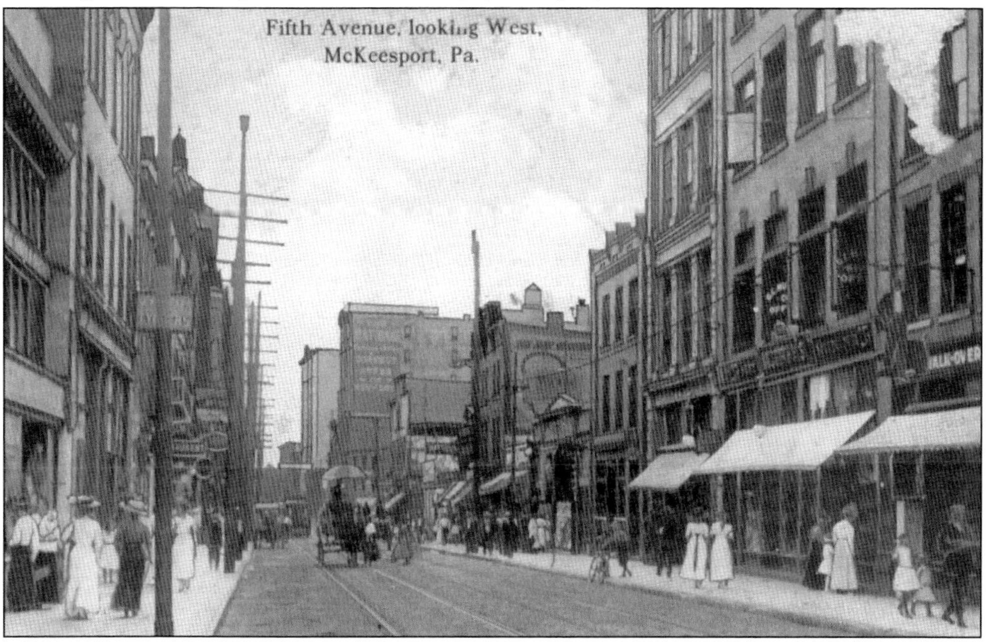

Looking west, this slightly earlier view includes the G.C. Murphy 5 & 10 and its company offices on the right. Hartman Hardware is next to that. On the opposite side of the street was the McKeesport Natatorium, at 512–514 Fifth Avenue, featuring Russian, Turkish, and Roman baths. This building later became the Liberty Theater. (Courtesy of the Edith Greaves Barrowcliff collection.)

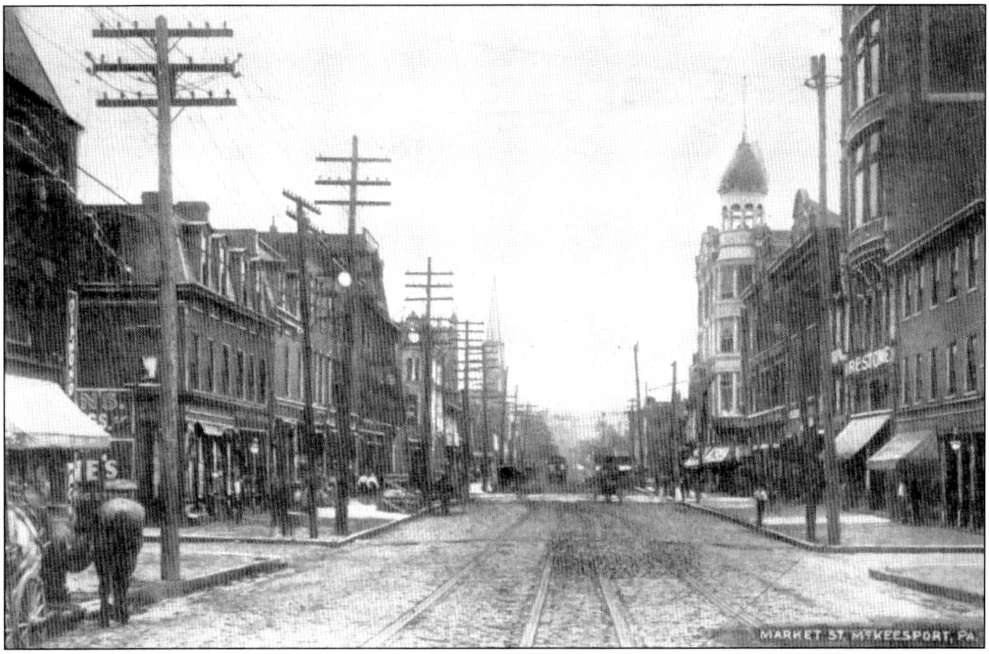

Moving to Market Street, looking south at South Diamond Street, is the corner of the old Market House on the left. In the next block were the Tube City Hotel and the Market Street Hotel. On the right, the Montezuma Hotel is next to Stone's Furniture, followed by the Haber Building. The tower of the Oppenheimer Building overlooks the corner of Fifth Avenue and Market Street.

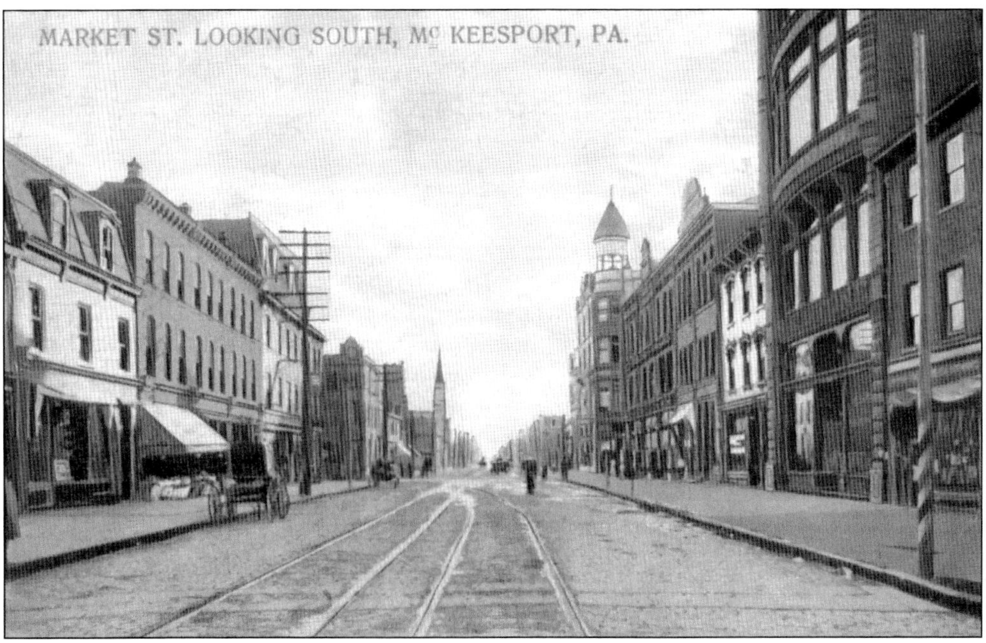

The same view, taken just a few years later, includes the Market Street Hotel on the left. Also visible is the original People's Bank Building at the corner of Market Street and Fifth Avenue, opposite the Oppenheimer Building. In the distance is the steeple of St. Peter's Church.

This building, located at 412 Market Street, was the second location of Stone's Furniture. Built in 1896 and designed by McKeesport architect Henry J. Lohman, it stood 86 feet high. Stone's had previously been located in another building on this same block. The store closed in 1931 after 45 years in business. (Courtesy of Leonard Chemsak.)

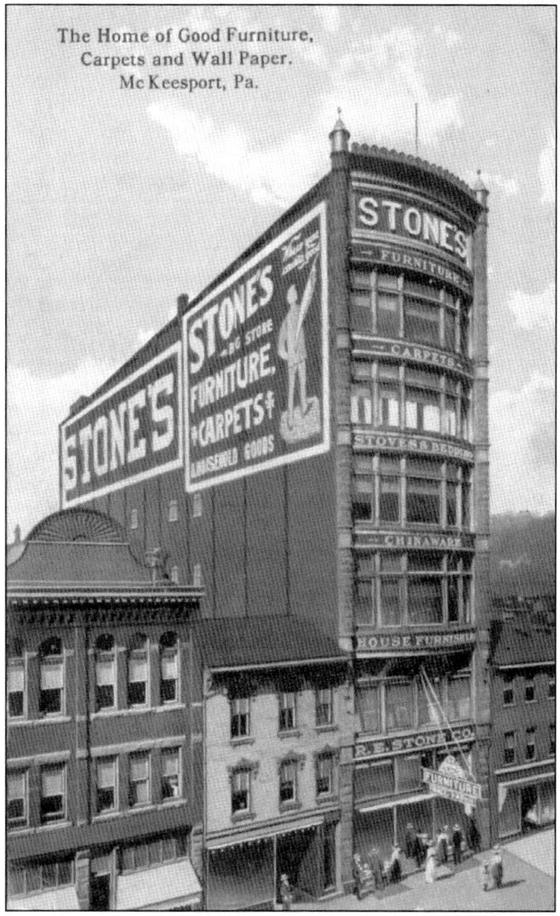

Pictured is the interior of Stone's sales floor. The store's well-known slogan was "Try Stone's for Soft Beds." In 1953, lightning struck the building, causing a fire that destroyed the top two floors. Only 10 years later, lightning struck again, causing another fire that destroyed what was left of the building. (Courtesy of Leonard Chemsak.)

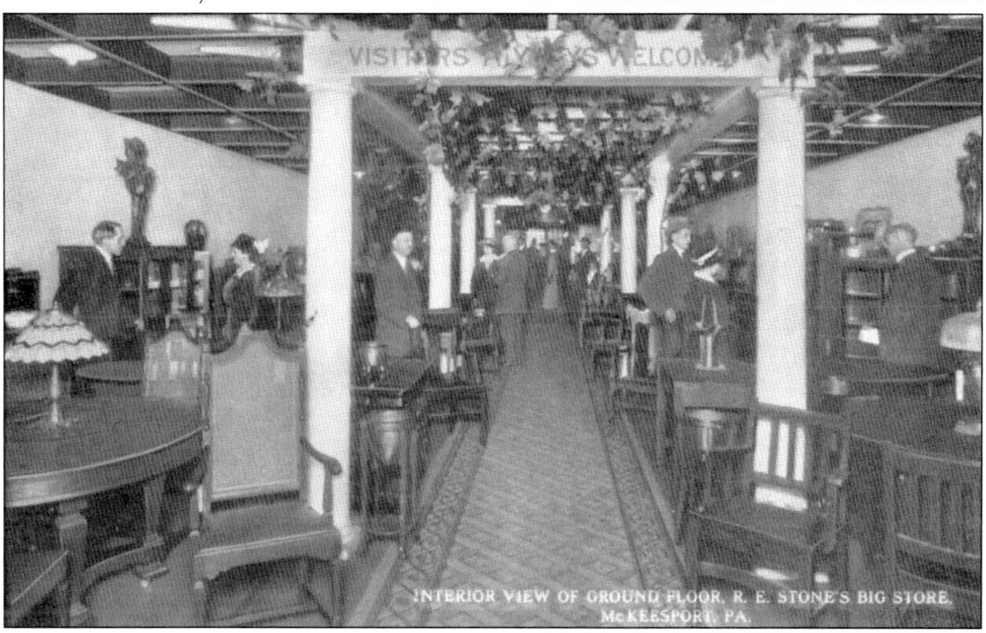

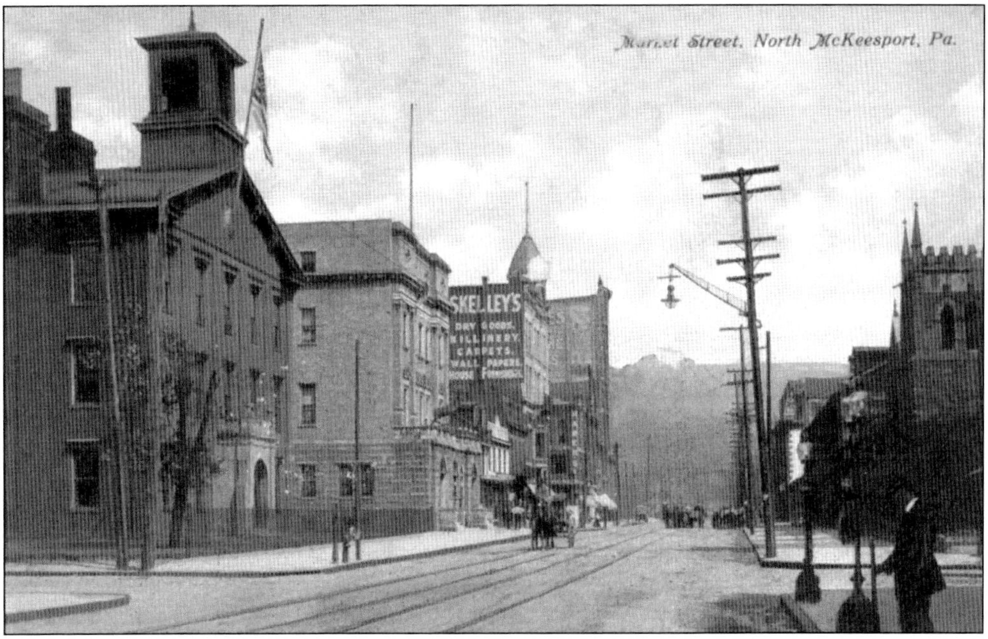

Looking north at the intersection of Market Street and Sixth Avenue, the old Market Street School is the first building on the left. Built in 1863, this was the second school on the site, replacing another brick building from 1849. The tower of First Presbyterian Church is just visible across the street. When he laid out the town in 1795, John McKee dedicated these lots for school and church use.

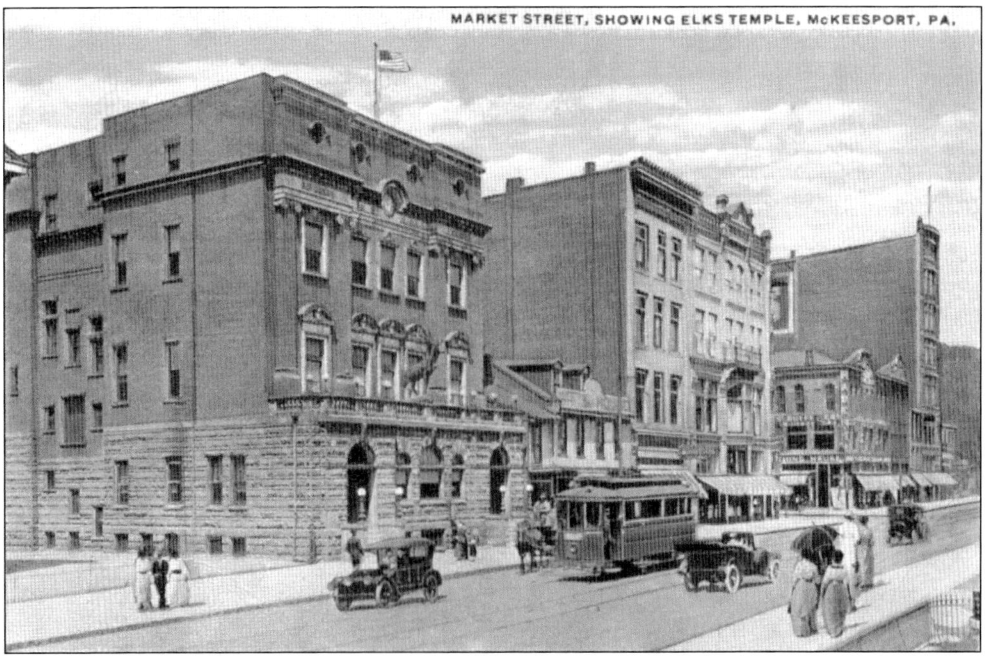

Showing the west side of Market Street, one can see the Elks Temple, the White House Hotel, Edmundson's Store, and the Oppenheimer Building without its tower. Stone's Furniture is the tall building farther down the street. The trolley car seen here ran to Ninth Street.

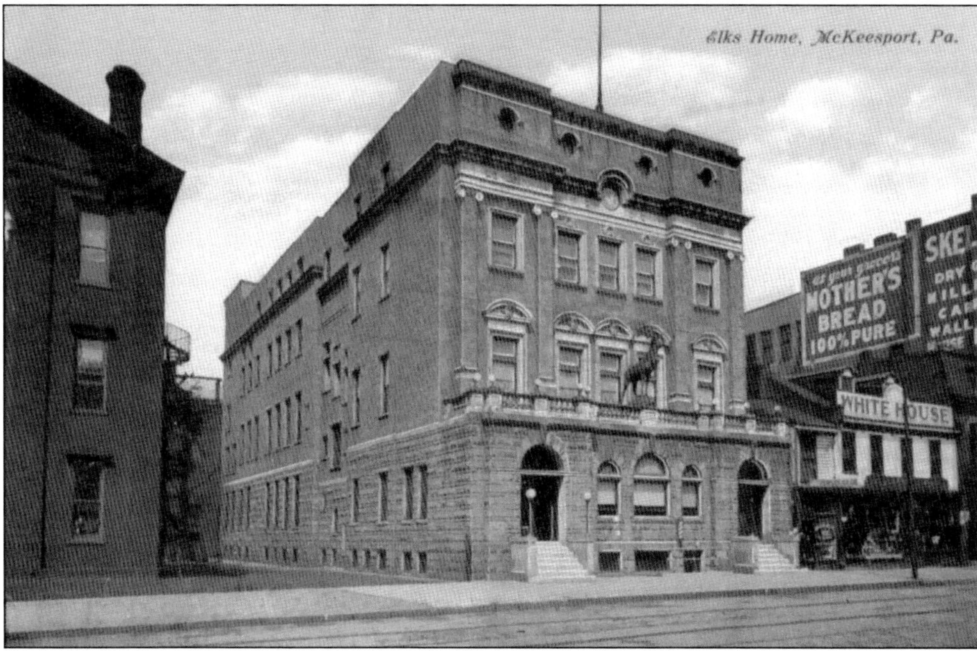

The Benevolent and Protective Order of Elks Lodge 136 was founded in 1889. This temple's cornerstone was laid in 1904, and the building opened in 1906. To the right of the Elks Temple is the White House Hotel, dating from 1853. (Courtesy of Leonard Chemsak.)

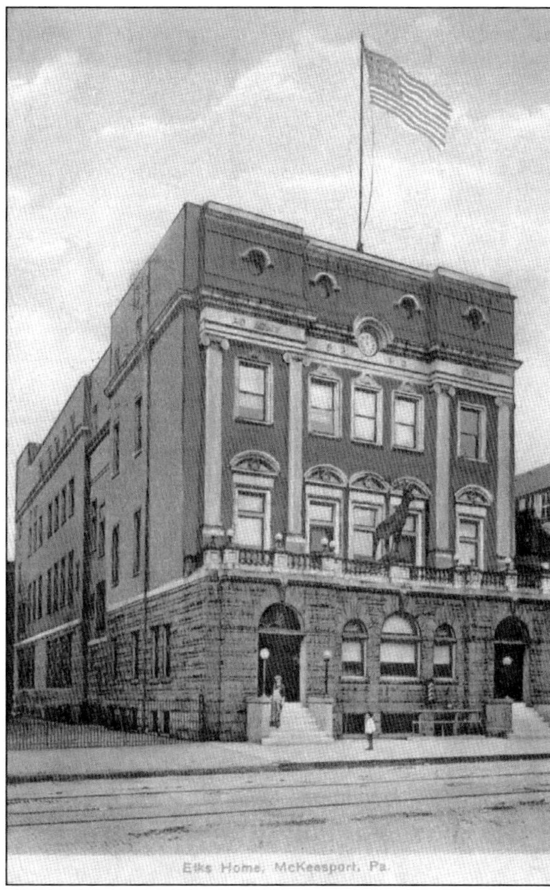

The Elks Temple contained a restaurant on the first floor, a barbershop in the basement, and a stage with a balcony on the third floor. Later, the studios of radio station WMCK were located here. The bronze elk statue was a landmark in town until the building burned during the 1976 fire, which destroyed this entire block.

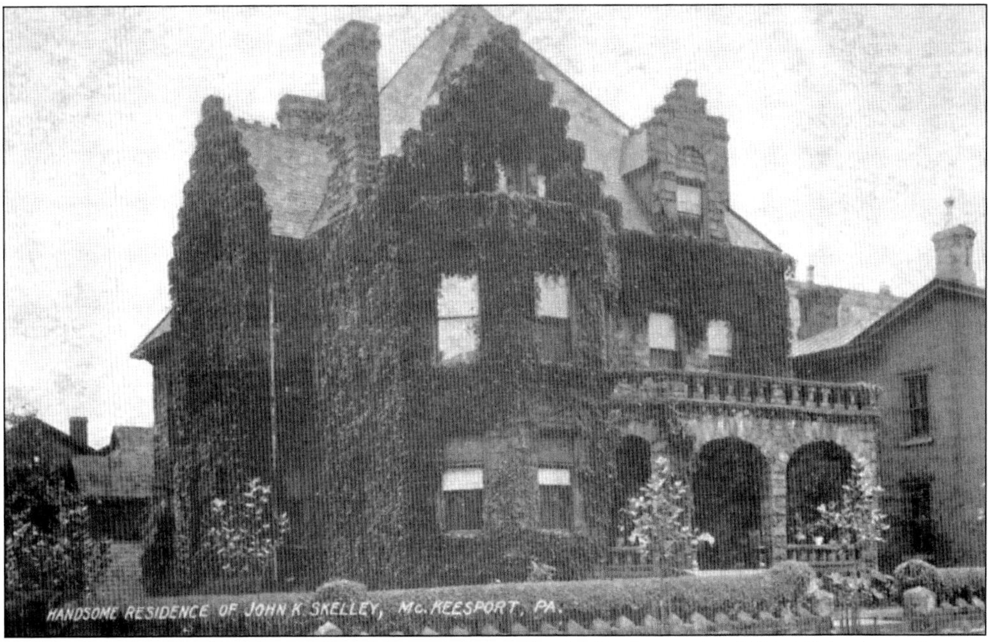

Located at 626 Market Street, Dr. Henry Hitzrot built this house in 1892. This showpiece in stone was his residence for only a few short years, until John K. Skelley bought the house in 1901. Frederich Sauer, a Pittsburgh architect, designed this opulent home, incorporating a carved staircase, leather-covered walls, Egyptian motif fireplaces, a third-floor ballroom, and a billiard room.

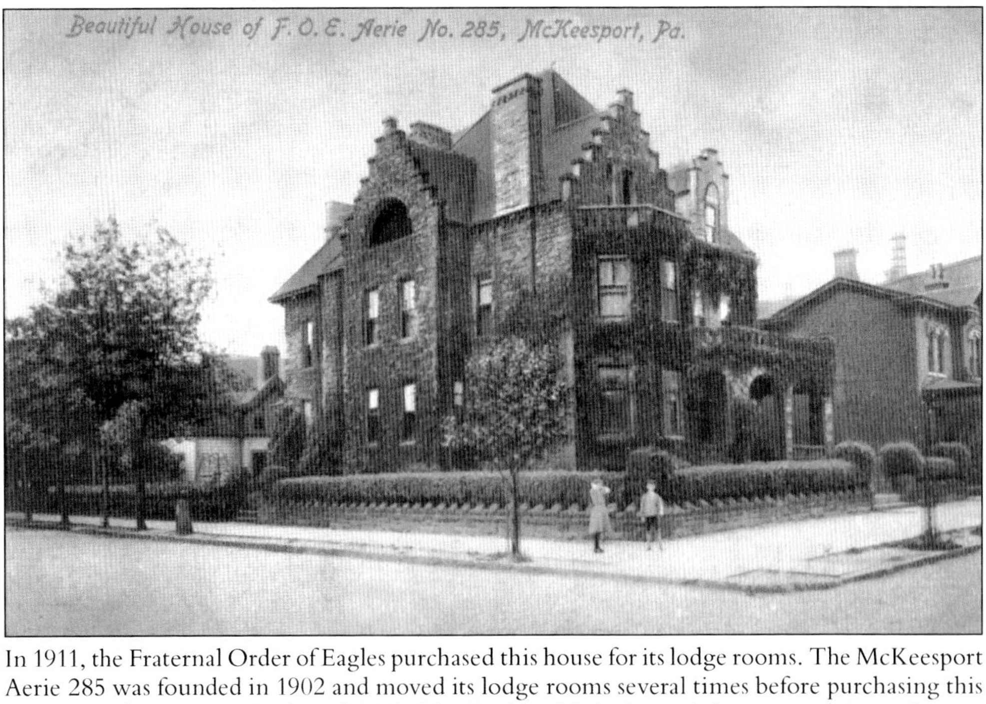

In 1911, the Fraternal Order of Eagles purchased this house for its lodge rooms. The McKeesport Aerie 285 was founded in 1902 and moved its lodge rooms several times before purchasing this property, where it remained until 1991. The Eagles added a large club room and dance floor to the rear of the building in 1924. To the right was the Stuckslager home, dating from the 1880s. (Courtesy of the Edith Greaves Barrowcliff collection.)

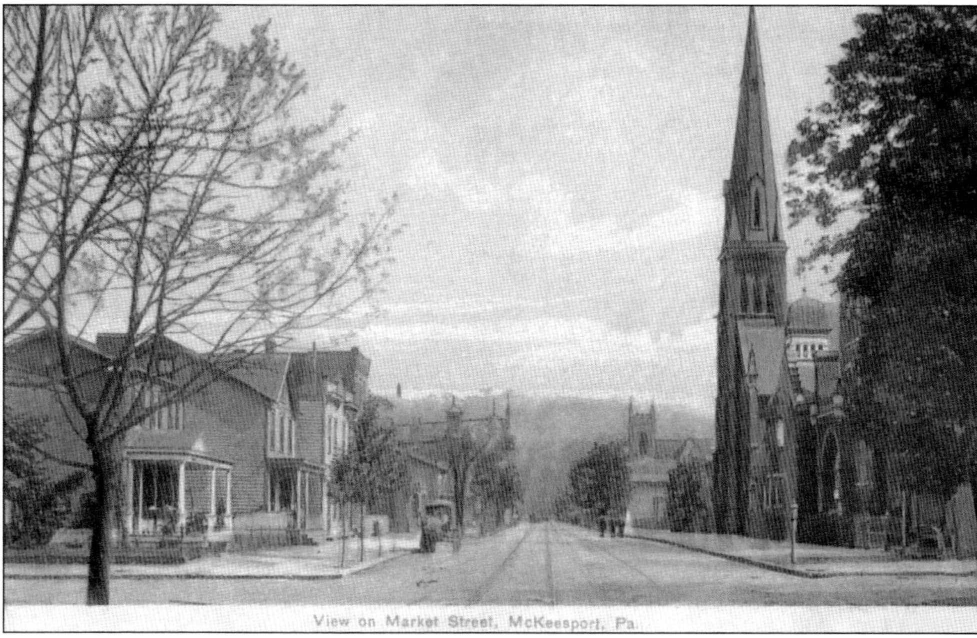

Looking north from Eighth Avenue down Market Street, St. Peter's school, convent, and church are on the right. In the distance is the tower of First Presbyterian Church, located at Sixth Street. As seen on the left side of the photograph, this section of Market Street was more residential than the area closer to Fifth Avenue. (Courtesy of Andrea [Luketic] Cartwright.)

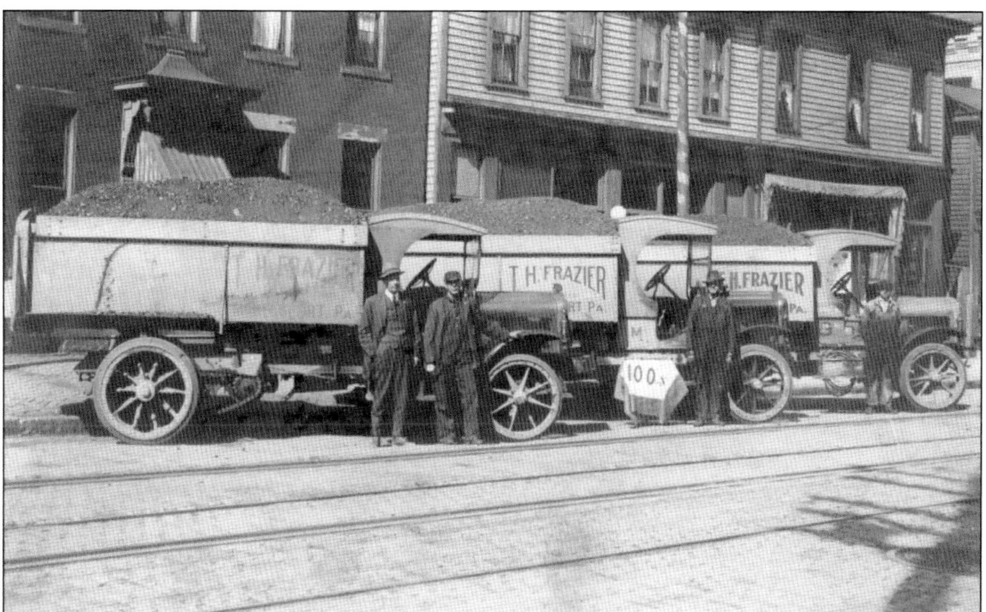

This photograph of the T.H. Frazier trucks was taken in front of Abe Walfish's meat market, at 432 Shaw Avenue, on the right. Charles F. Walker, undertaker, was in the building on the left in 1927. The trolley tracks ran along Shaw Avenue and turned onto Jenny Lind Street. (Courtesy of Leonard Chemsak.)

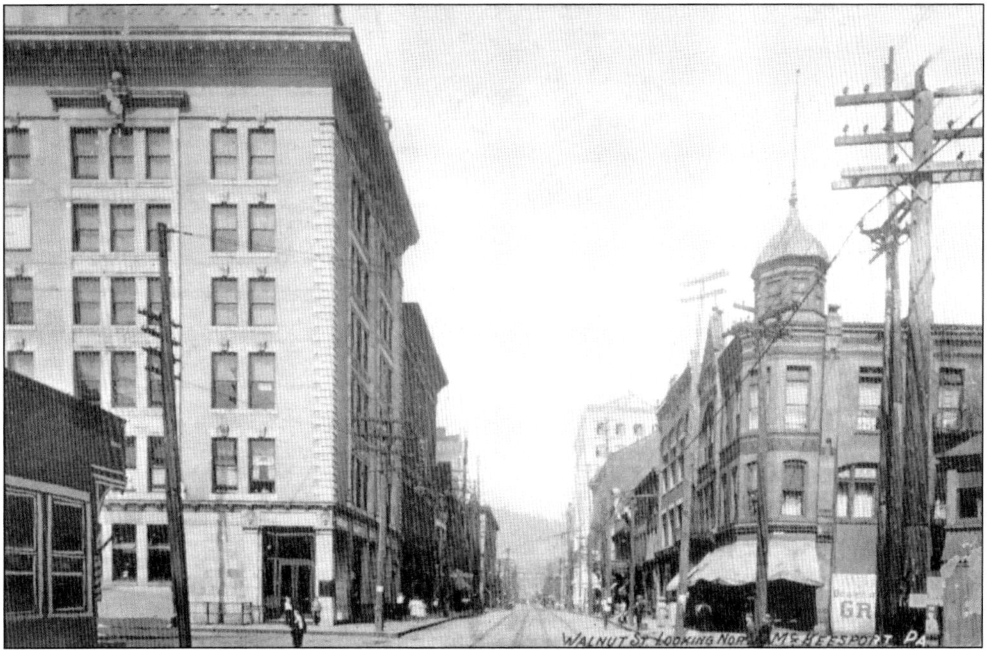

Looking north on Walnut Street from the railroad crossing, the Masonic Temple is on the left, and the Magnet Building is behind it. On the right is the Wood Building, erected in the 1880s. Knox Hill Dry Goods was in this building, followed by W.L. Sharples Grocery. At the extreme right is a corner of the railroad crossing tower. (Courtesy of Andrea [Luketic] Cartwright.)

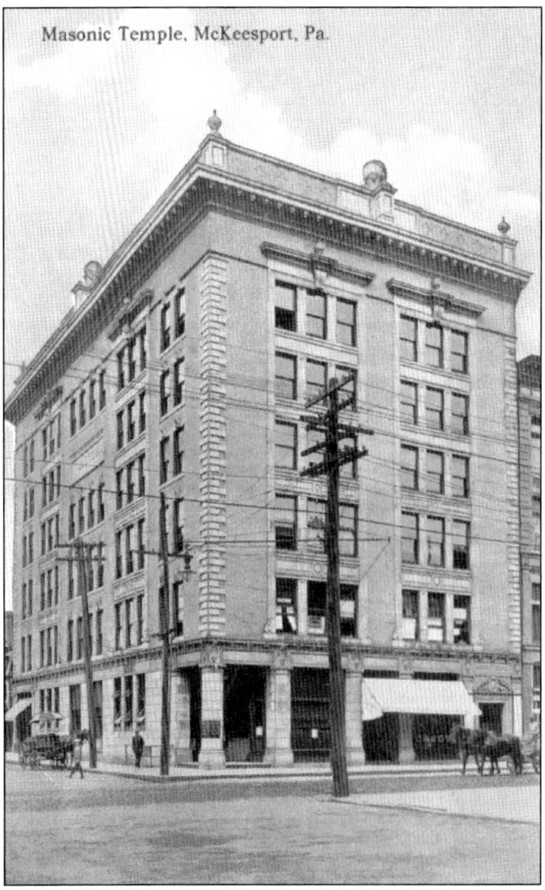

The Masonic Temple, at the northwest corner of Sixth Avenue and Walnut Street, was built on the site of the old First Baptist Church. The cornerstone was laid in 1905. The lodge moved here from its former quarters in the Wyant Building on Fifth Avenue. Harry Estep designed this building.

There were banking rooms on the first floor, a barbershop in the basement, numerous professional offices on the second and third floors, and lodge rooms on the fourth, fifth, and sixth floors. The Masonic tradition in McKeesport dated back to 1866, with the founding of Alliquippa Lodge No. 375. (Courtesy of Leonard Chemsak.)

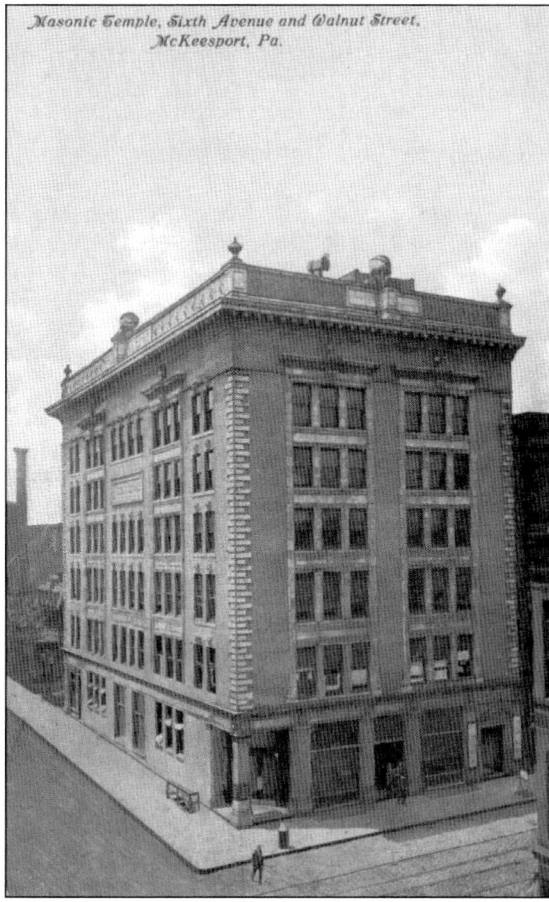

Looking north along Walnut Street from near Shaw Avenue, on the left are the railroad crossing gates, then the McKeesport Ice Company and the Masonic Temple. On the right is the Hotel Clifton. The Coliseum Building—where indoor sporting events, such as boxing matches, were held—is on the near side of the railroad crossing, and the building with the tower is the Wood Building.

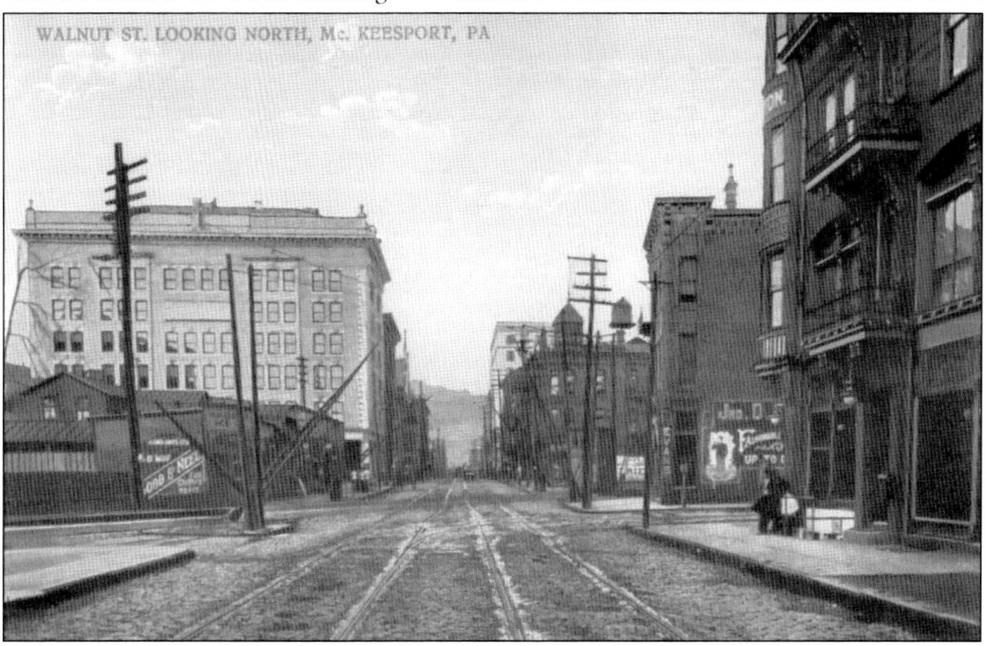

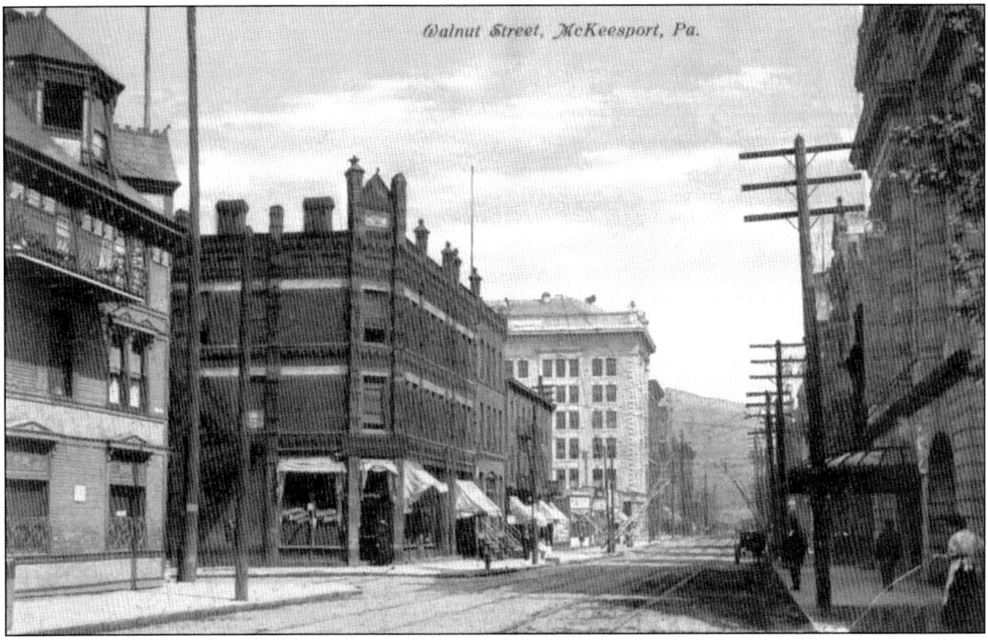

Looking north on Walnut Street from Seventh Avenue, at the extreme left is a home built by W.P. Wampler. Next is the Becker Block, built in 1892, which once housed the National Biscuit Company. The Pritchard Building, home of the McKeesport Times Company, is next. The Masonic Temple is in the background. On the right are the columns and canopy of Whites New Theater. (Courtesy of Andrea [Luketic] Cartwright.)

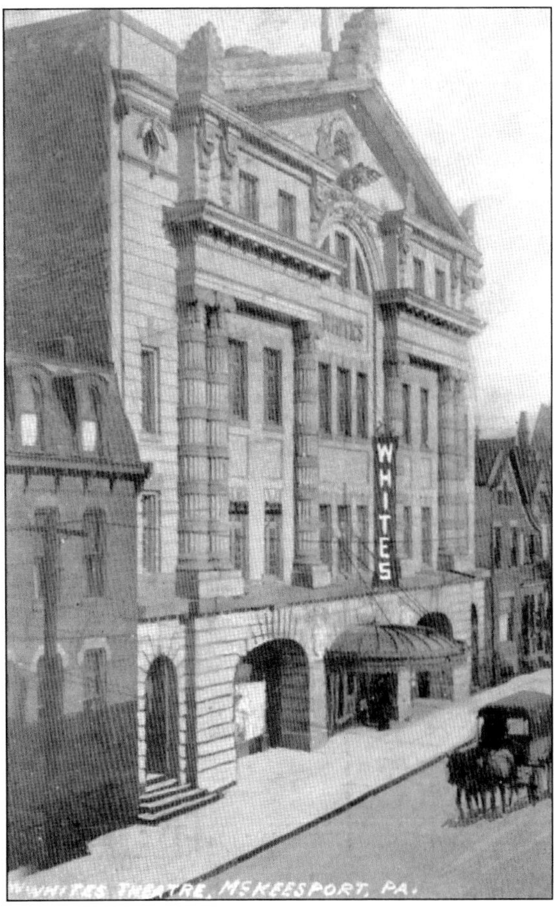

Whites New Theater opened in 1908. A very extravagant Beaux Arts facade of stone and terra-cotta with a copper and glass canopy opened into an equally lush interior. McKeesport architect Henry J. Lohman designed this theater, which seated 2,500 people and had 14 boxes. Jacob Langhart decorated the interior in olive green and gold, with a Japanese umbrella ceiling in the auditorium. (Courtesy of John Barna.)

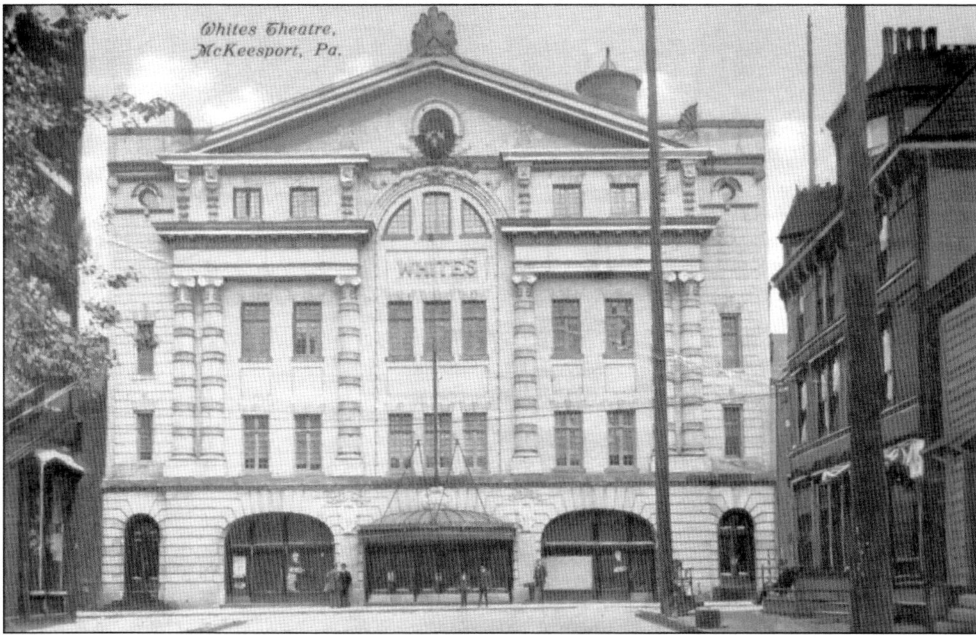

Whites New Theater opened with a performance by Julia Marlowe in the comedy *Gloria*. It was primarily a playhouse under the management of Dr. Thomas L. White. After it was sold to John P. Harris in 1920, it became a movie theater known as the Harris. On February 21, 1927, the first demonstration of Vitaphone in McKeesport premiered here. Whites New Theater was demolished in the late 1940s. (Courtesy of Andrea [Luketic] Cartwright.)

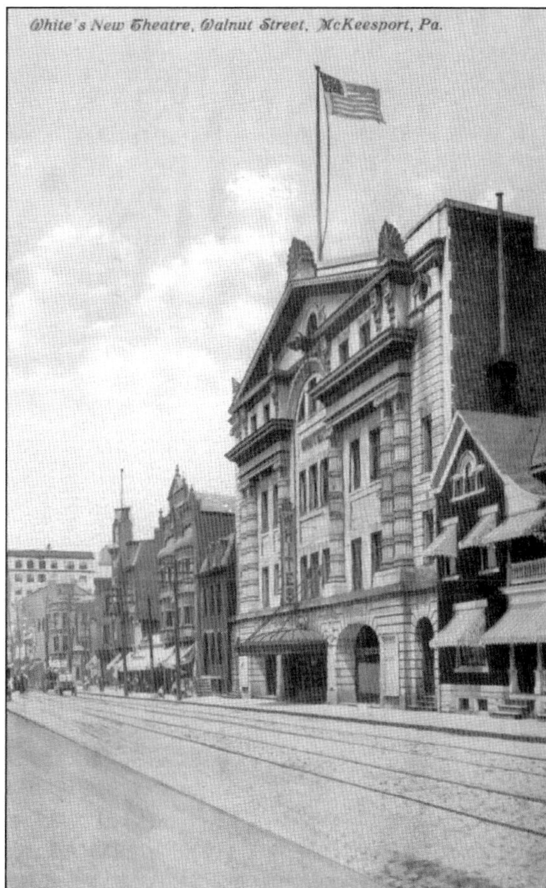

Along Walnut street, looking northeast from the corner of Seventh Avenue, Dr. Herbert Arthur's house is to the right. He was the mayor of McKeesport from 1909 to 1913. Two doors beyond Whites New Theater was the Manley Building with its two bay windows. The tower of the Clifton Hotel is seen in the distance at the corner of Shaw Avenue and Walnut Street.

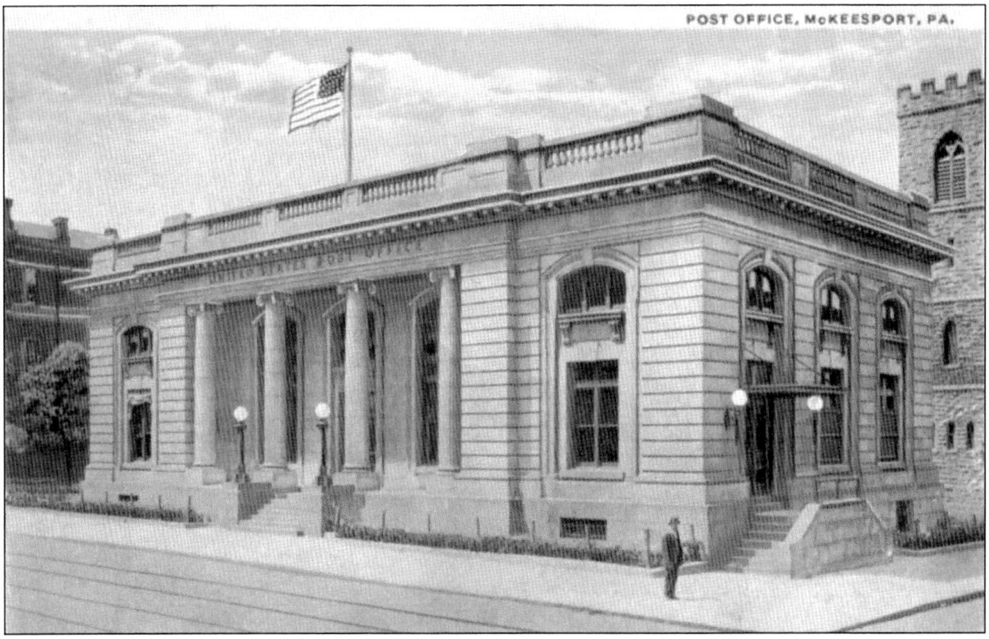

The McKeesport Post Office was established in 1827. From then until this building was completed in 1907, the post office had moved with each change of postmaster, totaling 20 relocations. Initially, mail arrived in McKeesport by horseback or packet boat from Pittsburgh, but in 1860, mail began to arrive by train. Post office boxes came into use in 1868, and in 1888, letter carriers began home delivery.

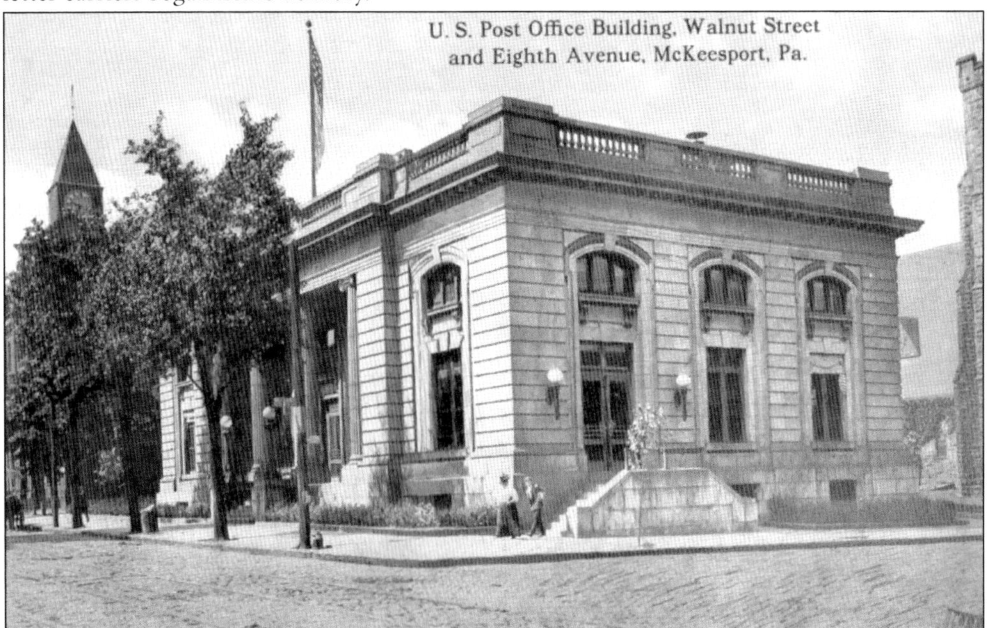

Under postmaster John Dersam, this site at the corner of Eighth Avenue and Walnut Street became the permanent home of the McKeesport Post Office. It opened in April 1907, was enlarged in 1932, and demolished in 1987. The columns from this building still exist, freestanding behind Striffler's Funeral Home in White Oak.

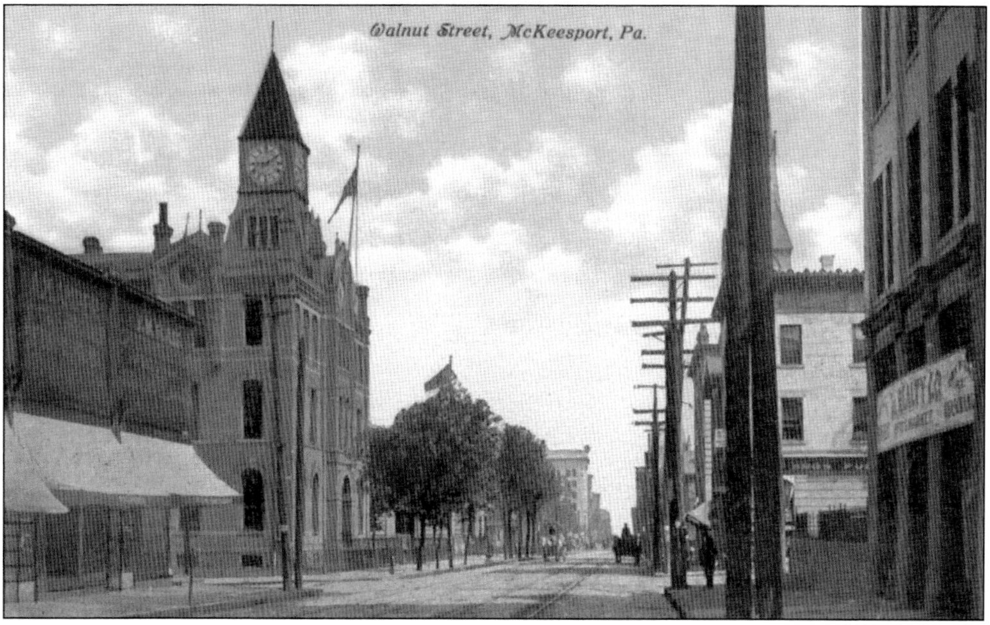

Looking north on Walnut Street from Ninth Avenue, on the left is Amsen M. Amper Hatter and Furnisher, with J.M. Glass Fruits, Tobacco, and Cigars next door. Across Ninth Avenue is the Walnut Street School, and behind the trees is the post office. On the right is the first David L. Clark Candy Company building, located at 907 Walnut Street. The next building is Kant Brother's Grocers. (Courtesy of Andrea [Luketic] Cartwright.)

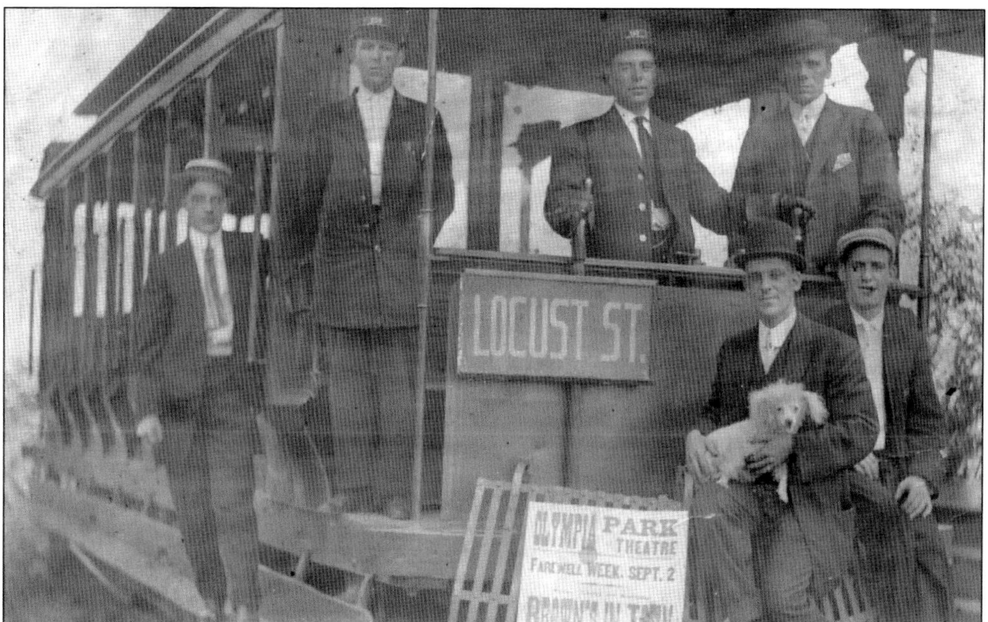

Car number 124 on Locust Street was part of the Pittsburgh, McKeesport & Connellsville Railway Company. This streetcar was built in 1899 and scrapped in the late 1920s. The open trolley was "the way to go" to the Olympia Park summer theater to catch a performance such as *Brown's In Town*, which is advertised on this car in 1912. (Courtesy of John Barna.)

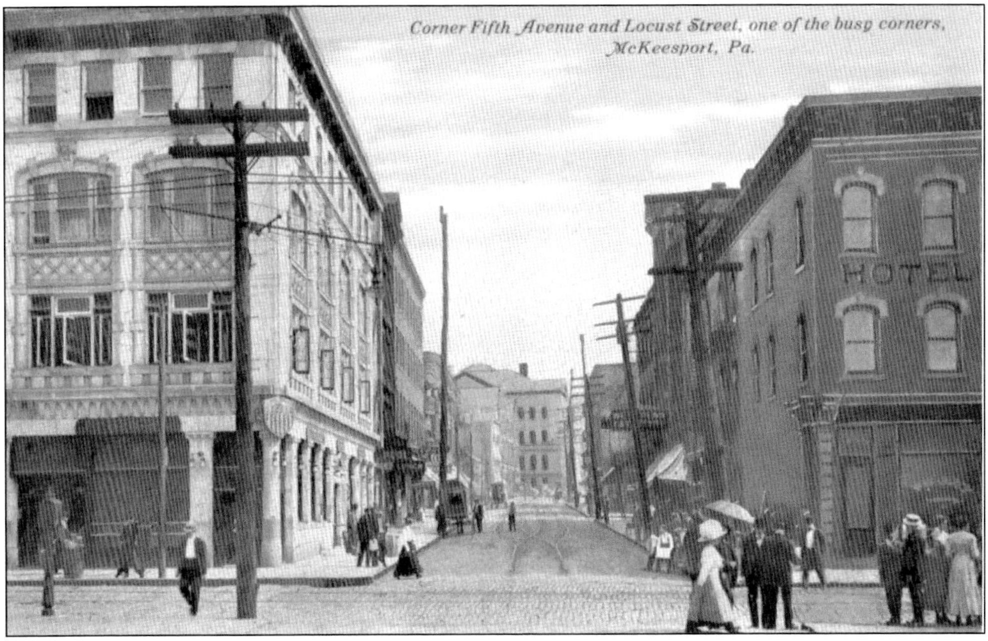

Looking south on Locust Street from the corner of Fifth Avenue, on the left is the Weiskircher Building. Behind it is the Walker Block, built in 1888. The Hotel Volk (right) housed a tavern, and in the late 1880s it held a six-cell jail in the basement. Behind Volk's is the sign for the West Penn trolley waiting room. (Courtesy of Chuck Jarrell.)

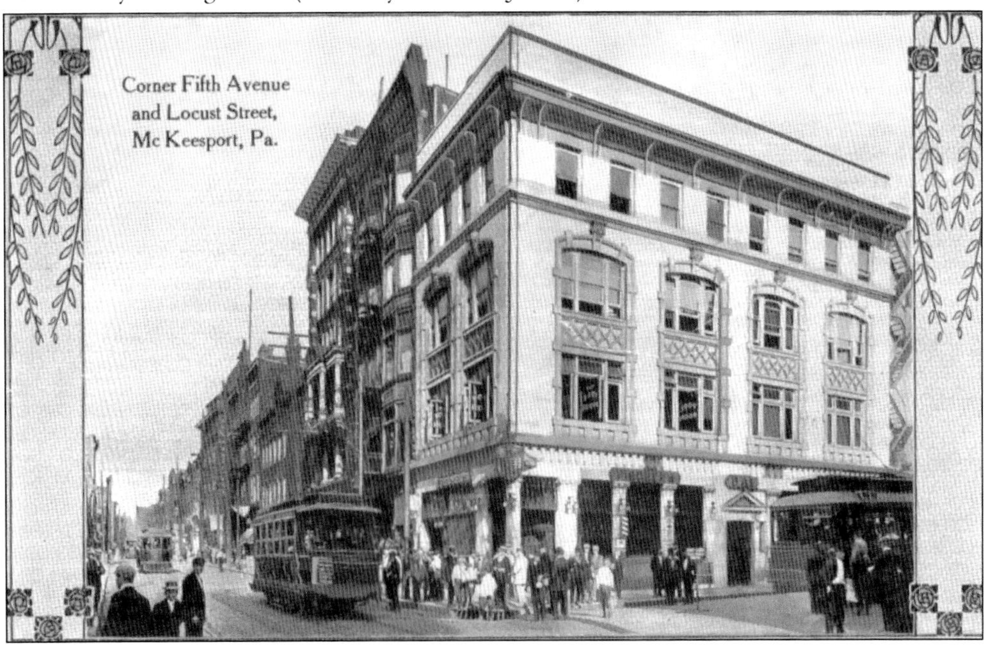

From the same intersection, now looking east up Fifth Avenue from Locust Street, the Weiskircher Building is at the foreground. This building replaced the Railroad House Hotel of the 1880s. On the first floor was Fischer's Café, with a bar entrance on the Locust Street side and a poolroom upstairs. Next door on Fifth Avenue was the Yester Building and then the Hotel White. (Courtesy of Leonard Chemsak.)

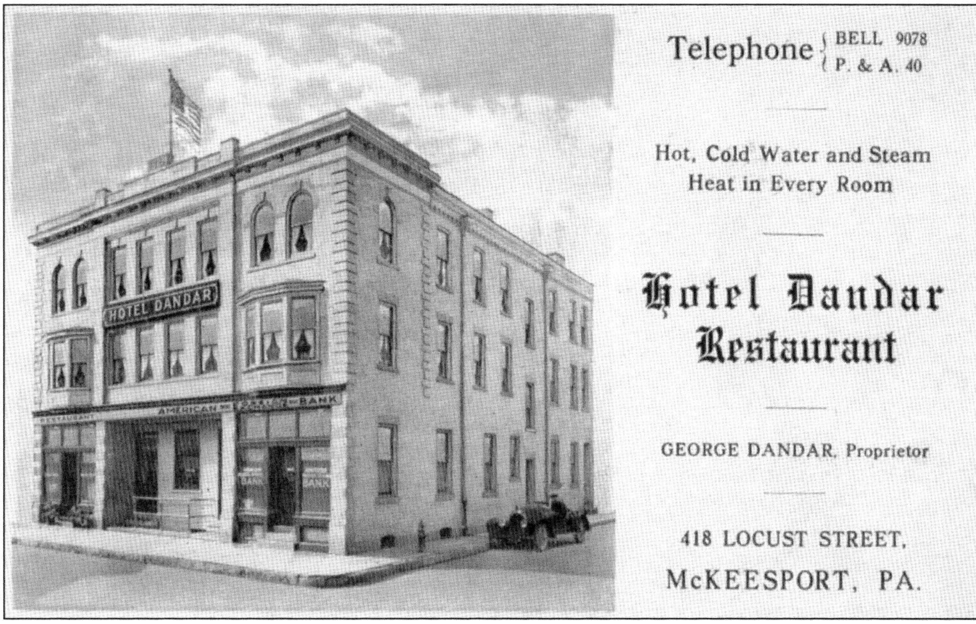

The Hotel Dandar was located at 418 Locust Street. Built in 1921, there were 36 hotel rooms. In addition, there was a barbershop in the basement and a foreign exchange bank, billiard room, and restaurant on the first floor. A previous building on this site housed the old Salvation Army barracks, then McKay's Restaurant, then the Harris Musee-Theater. (Courtesy of Leonard Chemsak.)

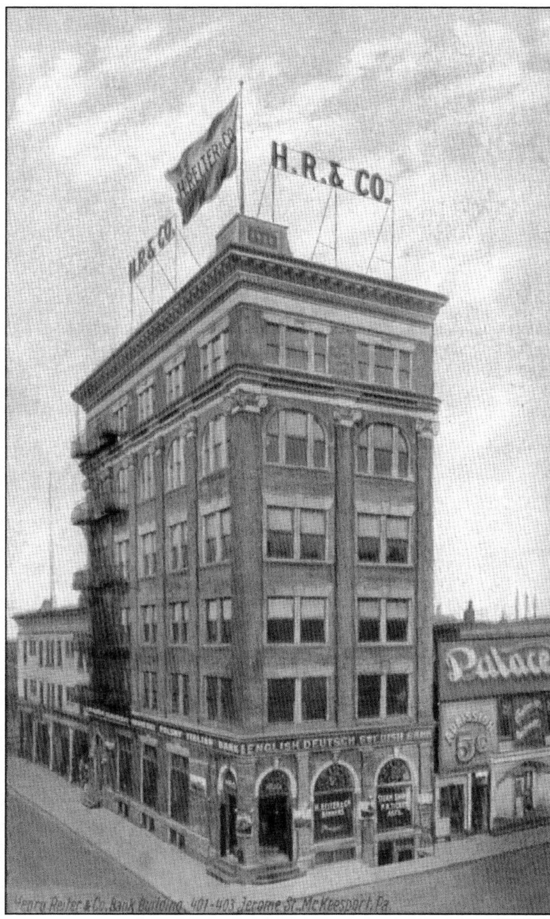

The Henry Reiter and Company bank building was erected in 1906 at 401 Jerome Street at the northeast corner of Locust Street. In 1908, it became Josef Roth and Son Foreign Bankers. Next door was the Palace Theater, featuring 5¢ admissions and continuous performances. Both buildings were removed to widen Jerome Street in the late 1930s. (Courtesy of Andrea [Luketic] Cartwright.)

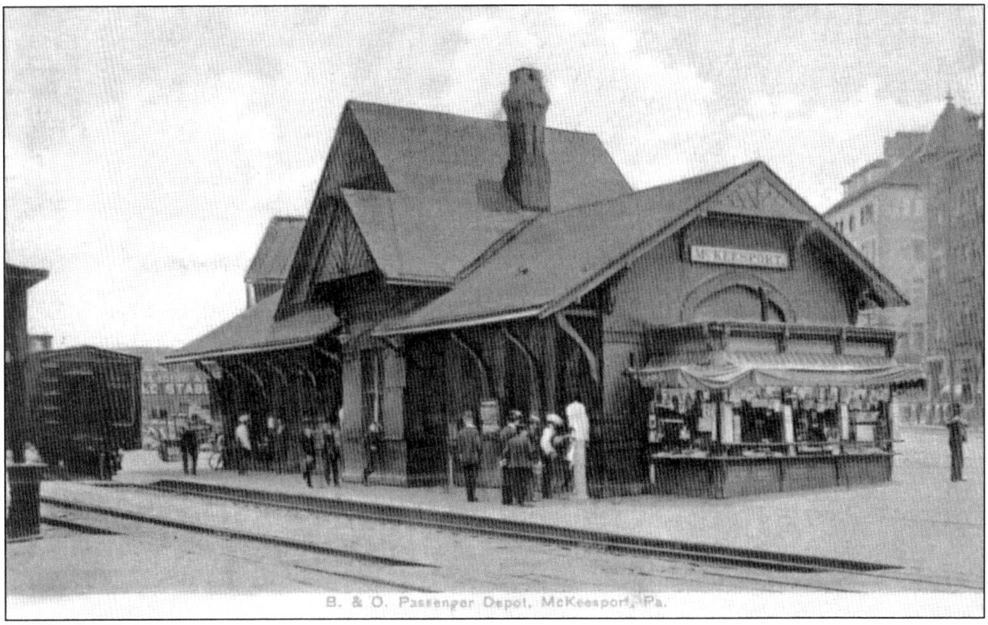

The Baltimore & Ohio passenger depot, built in 1883, was located between Locust Street, Sinclair Street, and Fifth Avenue. This brick building replaced an earlier wooden station. The roofline was changed in the 1940s, and the structure was torn down in 1970 after the relocation of the railroad tracks to Fourth Avenue.

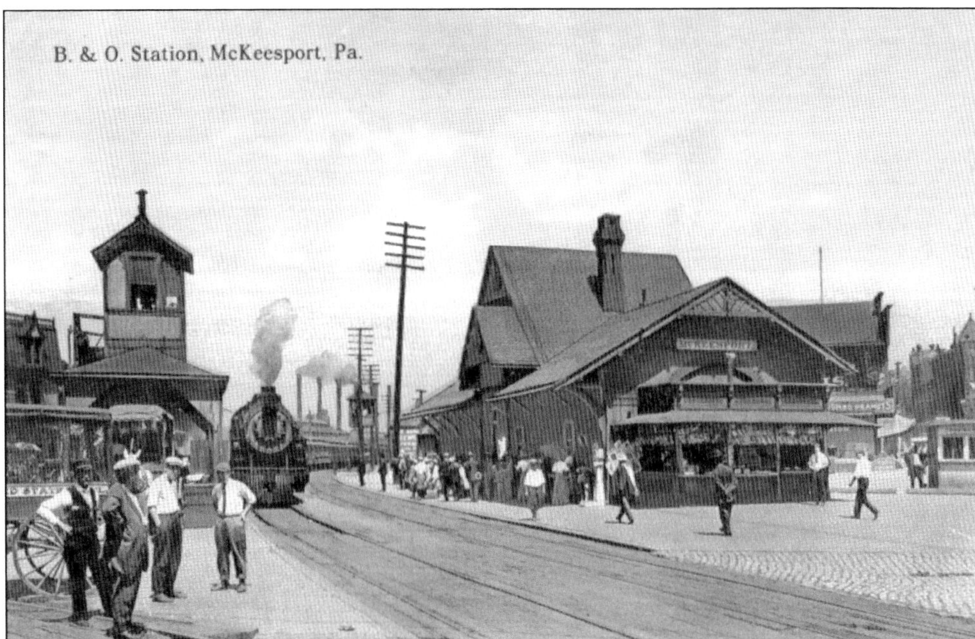

An eastbound passenger train is seen here pulling into the Baltimore & Ohio train station. At the end of the station was the Union News Stand. Drew's Feed Store is behind the station (right), with the "Jumbo Peanuts" sign visible. On the left is a horse-drawn US mail wagon, and the railroad watchtower is behind it. (Courtesy of Roger Reichenbach.)

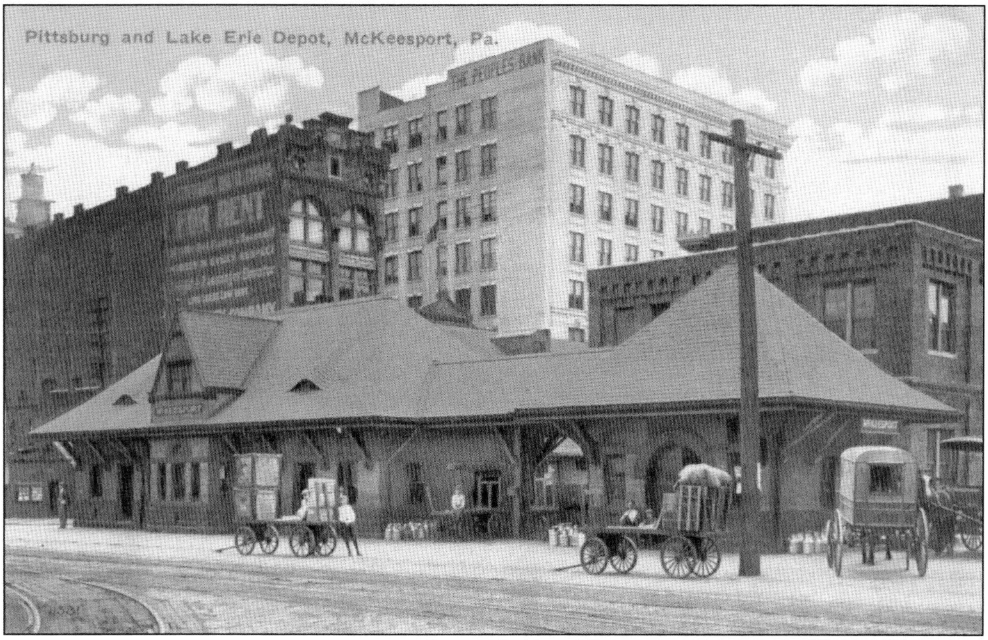

The Pittsburgh & Lake Erie passenger depot was built in 1895. Located at the southwest corner of Walnut Street and Fourth Avenue, it was later used as a freight station. The tall building at the left behind the station is the Leppig Building, erected in 1896. This was the home of the *Daily News* from 1918 until 1938, when the newspaper moved to its current home. (Courtesy of Andrea [Luketic] Cartwright.)

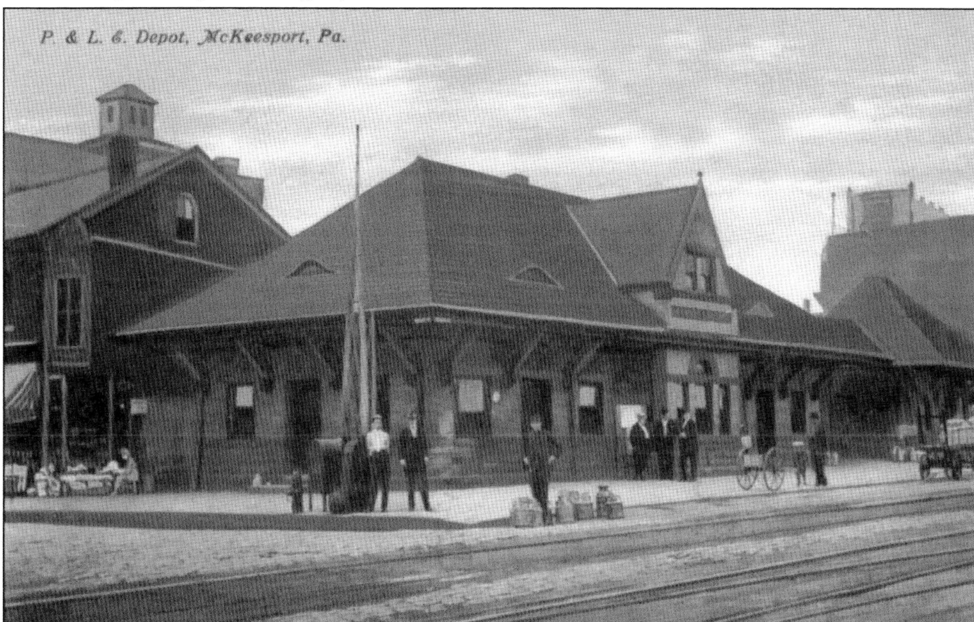

The Pittsburgh & Lake Erie Depot was torn down in 1960 as part of the First Ward redevelopment. Just to the left of the station was the Lake Erie House bar and restaurant, owned by Michael Lippert and later known as Lippert's Café. Marc Connelly, the Pulitzer Prize–winning playwright from McKeesport, was born in this building in 1891.

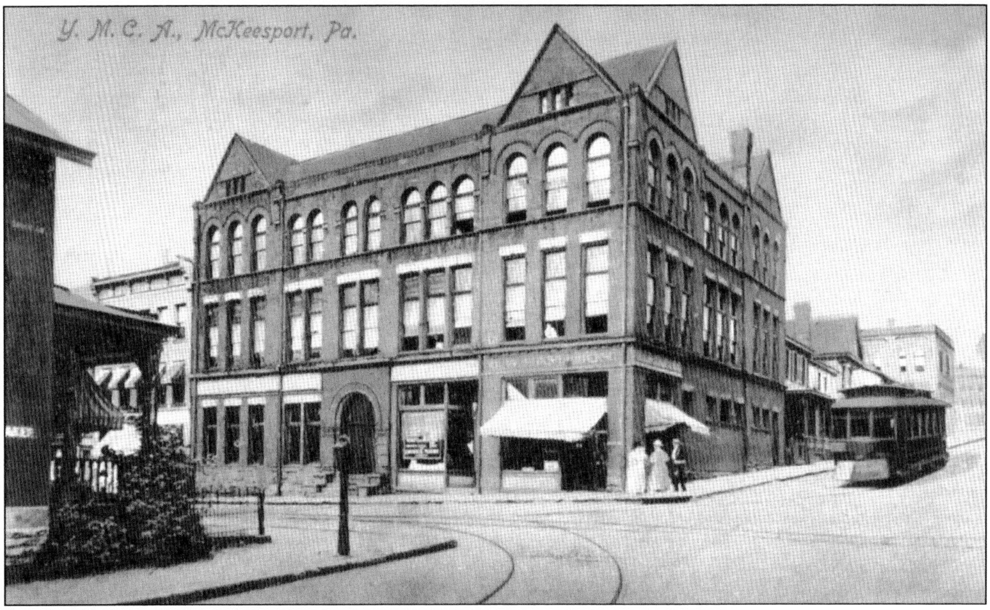

The Young Men's Christian Association (YMCA) had been a McKeesport institution since 1888. It was first located at 513 Walnut Street. This postcard is of the second site, located at the northeast corner of Shaw Avenue and Locust Street on the former Mehaffey property. It opened on May 10, 1894. (Courtesy of Leonard Chemsak.)

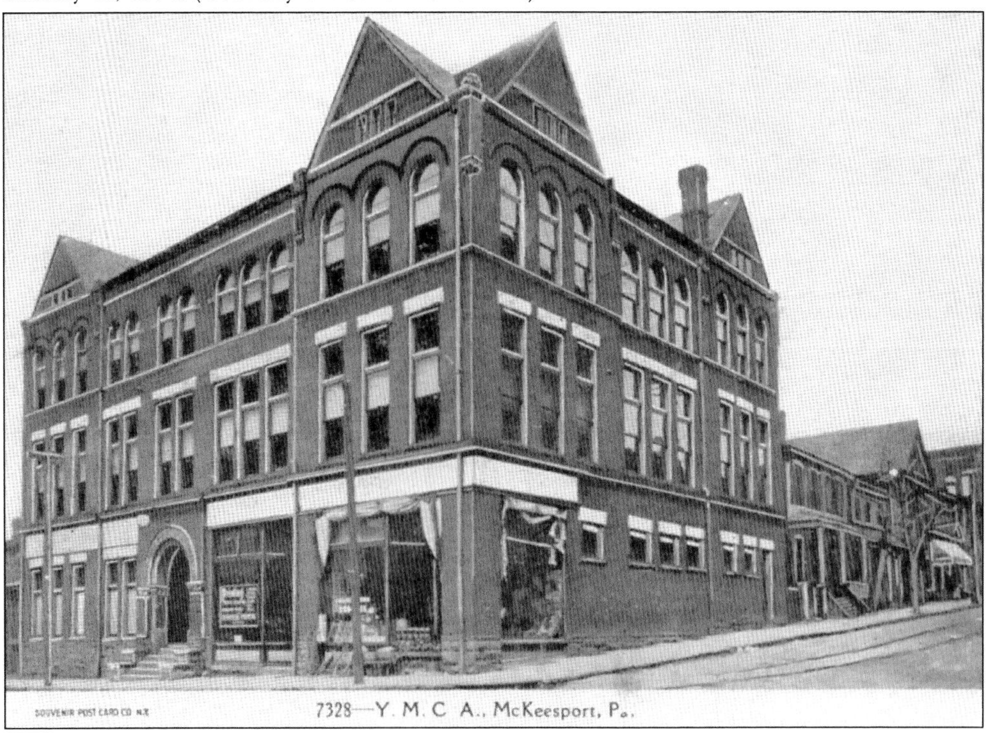

The YMCA's gymnasium and baths were located in the basement. Two storefronts were on the first floor. On the second floor were the offices, reading room, meeting room, ladies' parlor, and reception hall. The third floor contained a large hall, classrooms, and several sleeping apartments.

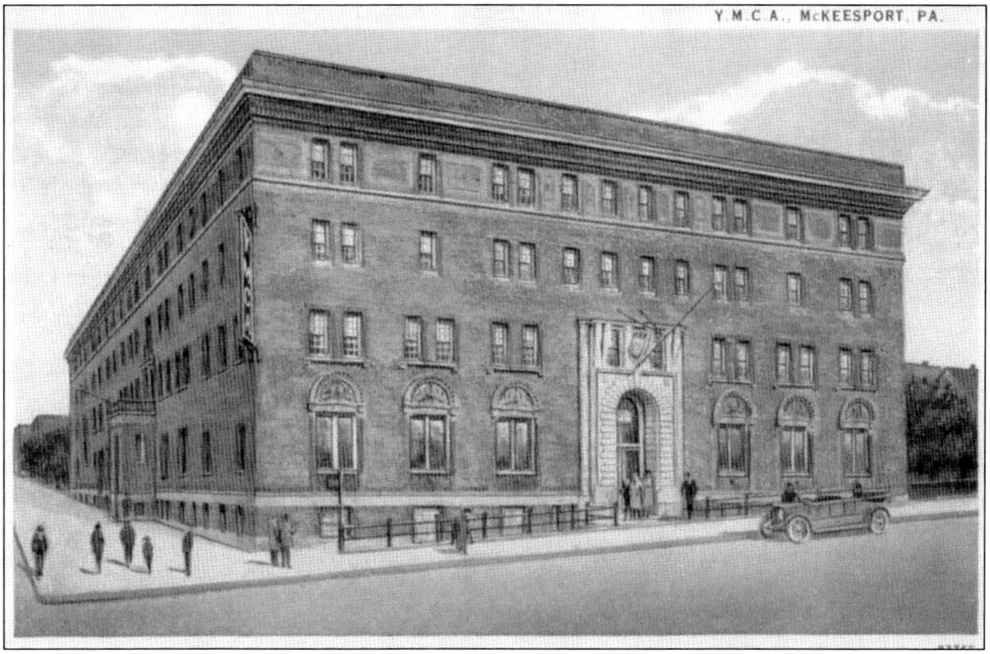

In 1922, the YMCA moved again, this time to a new building on the old Dunshee homestead, located at the southeast corner of Ringgold and Sinclair Streets. There was a swimming pool in the basement, two gymnasiums, locker rooms, bowling lanes, meeting rooms, a banquet room, and 104 dormitory rooms upstairs.

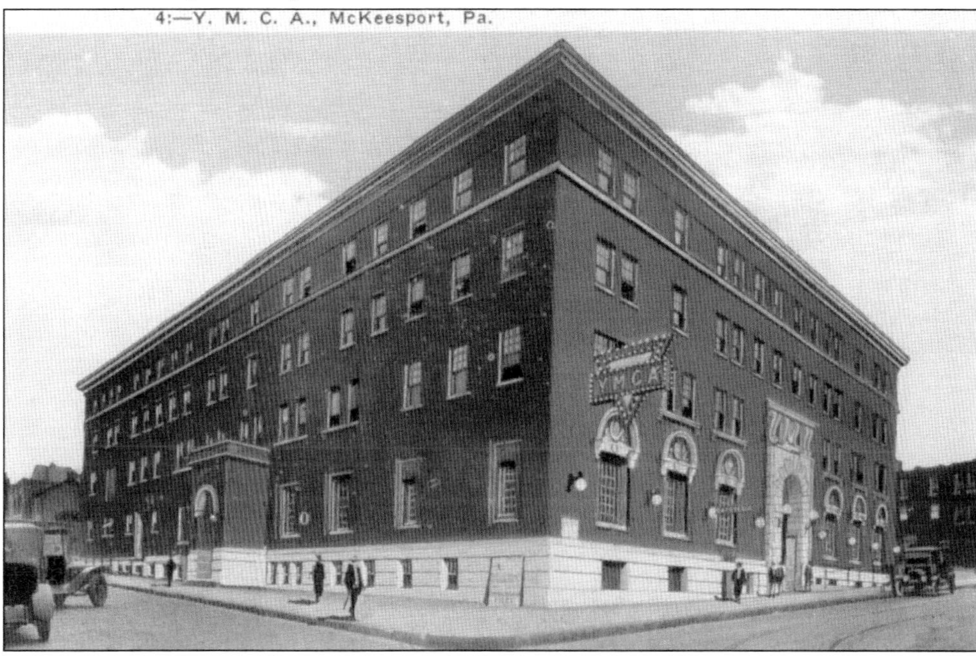

McKeesport's pioneer female aviator, Helen Richey, had her first close-up experience with an airplane here when an old biplane was set up in the lobby in 1925. The McKeesport YMCA also operated a camp in the Laurel Mountains—Camp T. Frank Soles—dedicated in 1955. (Courtesy of John Barna.)

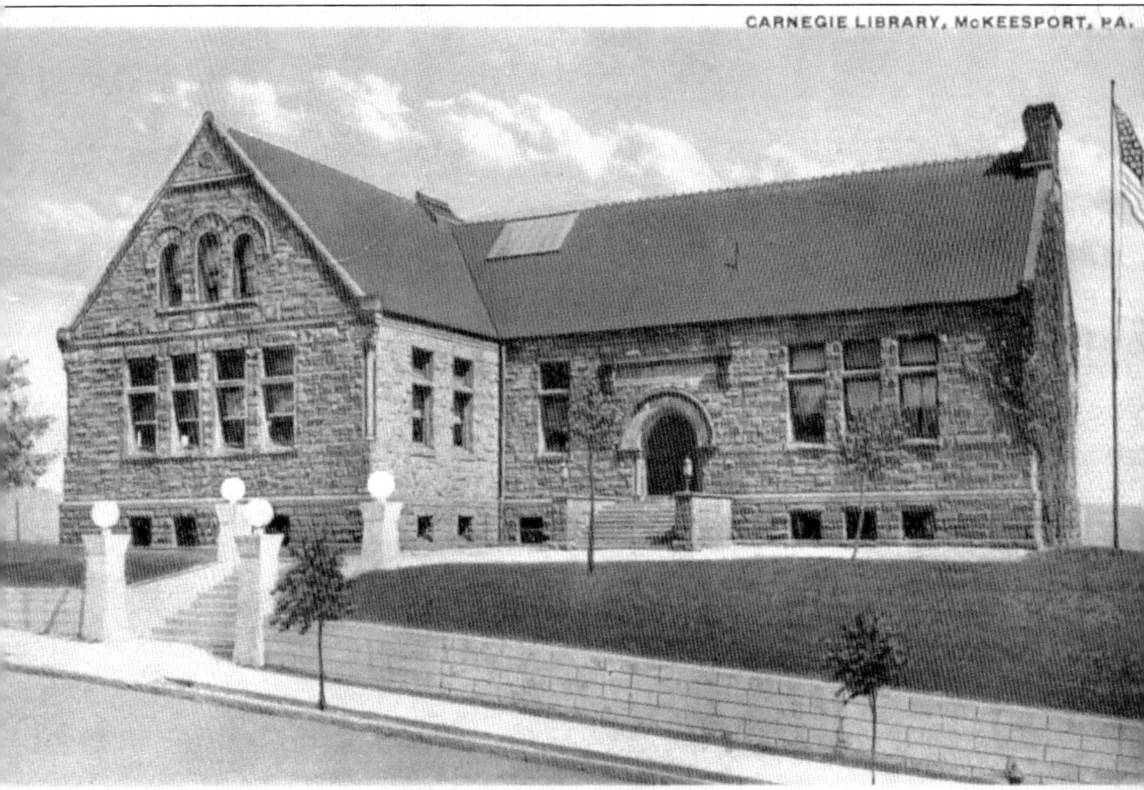

McKeesport's public library tradition dates back to 1875 with the founding of the McKeesport Library Association. Before disbanding, it went through several reorganizations because of financial troubles. In 1882, the short-lived Crooked Run Library Association was established in the Eighth Ward of McKeesport. Other early library associations also met with limited success. Then, in 1899, at the request of the Women's Club of McKeesport, Andrew Carnegie promised to donate $50,000 to build a public library if the city provided a site and an annual appropriation for maintenance. Many local citizens offered sites for the building. Ultimately, James Evans donated 1.5 acres that were bordered by Union Street and Carnegie and Library Avenues in a new residential development. William J. East designed the building, which was dedicated July 15, 1902. It contained 3,000 volumes when opened. In the new library building, there was a room set aside for the women's club meetings. The Carnegie Library of McKeesport continues to operate out of this building today.

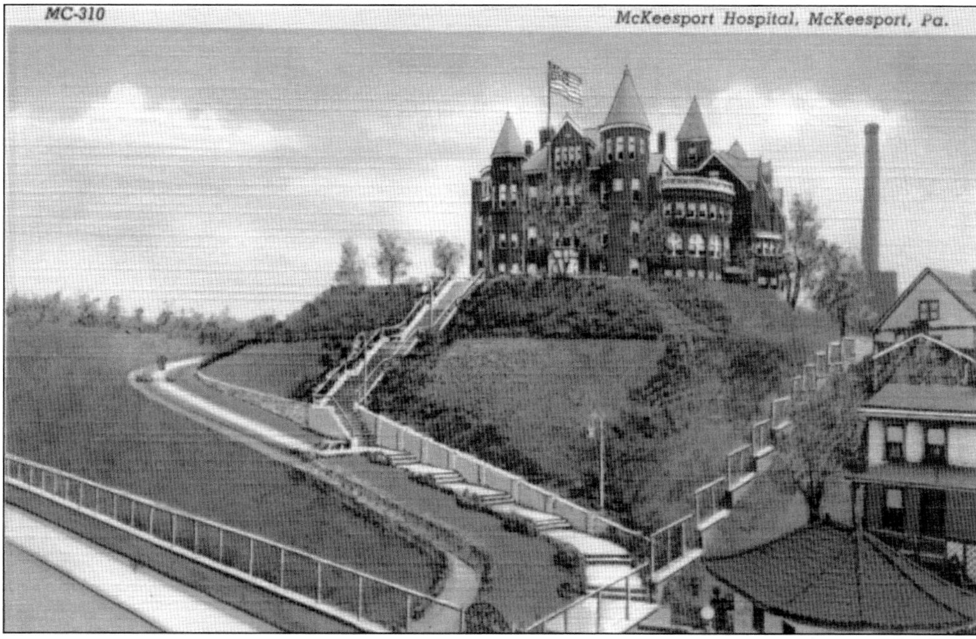

Perhaps no other building in McKeesport appears on postcards as often as the McKeesport Hospital. This "castle on the hill" was designed by Pittsburgh architects Hodgson & Thomas and was built by McKeesport contractor Daniel Stratton. Over the years, the building became known by the affectionate term "Old Main."

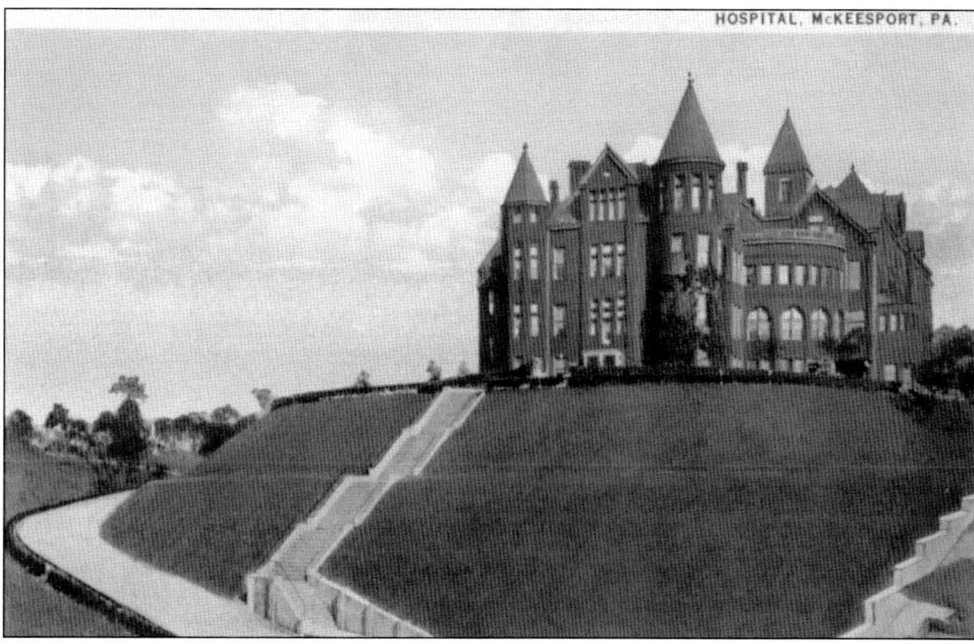

In 1890, McKeesport attorney Magnus Pflaum introduced a resolution to the board of trade to build a hospital, and a charter was granted in January 1891. Banker James Evans donated three acres, and he also became the first president of the hospital board. The cornerstone was laid on October 31, 1891, and the building was dedicated April 18, 1894. It opened with 20 beds and 39 medical staff.

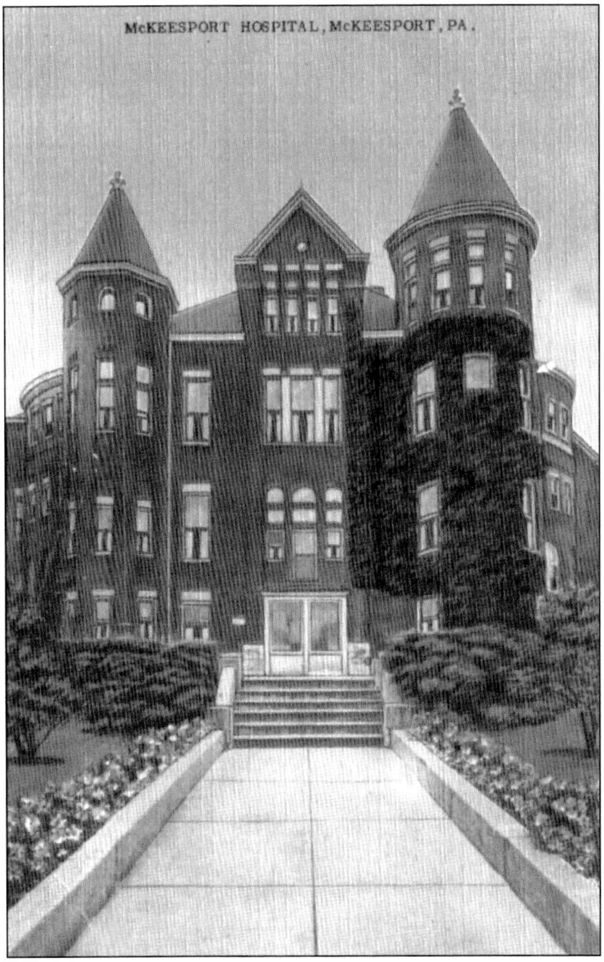

After opening in 1894, on April 25, the first patient admitted was David Hardy. He had leg injuries as a result of an accident with a runaway horse. The first baby was born in the hospital on July 13. John Alderin had the first operation here, an appendectomy. That first year, 604 patients were treated.

Estella Faust established the McKeesport Hospital Nurses Training School, and the first class of three students graduated in 1896. During their two-year (later three-year) training program, student nurses had to live in the nurses' quarters at the hospital and wear the school uniform and cap.

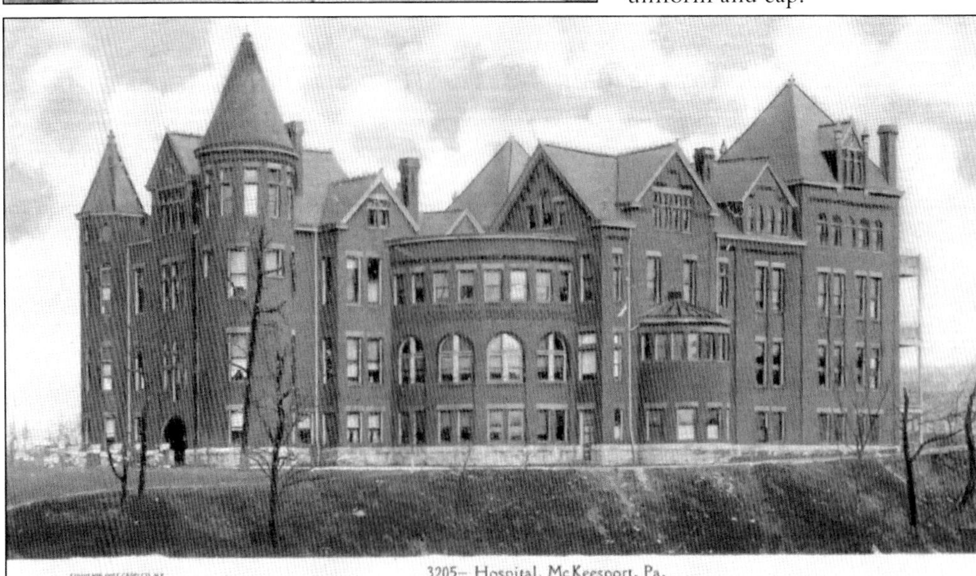

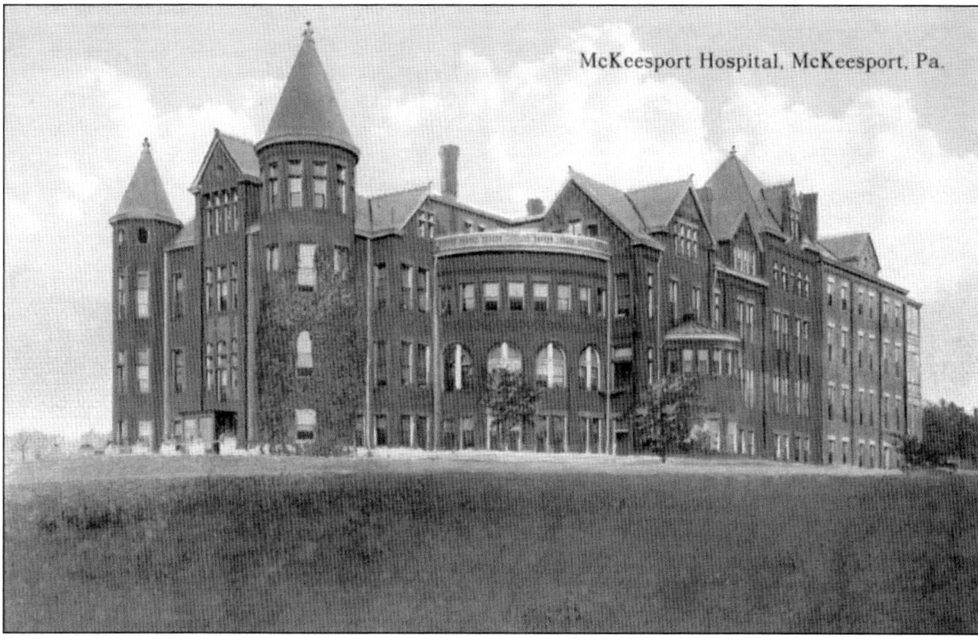

Construction of the hospital continued in phases as the necessary financing was procured. In 1896, the Ladies Aid Society began fundraising to help finish the construction of the building and to finish the interior. By 1898, the entire building was complete and in use. The hospital could accommodate between 75 and 100 patients.

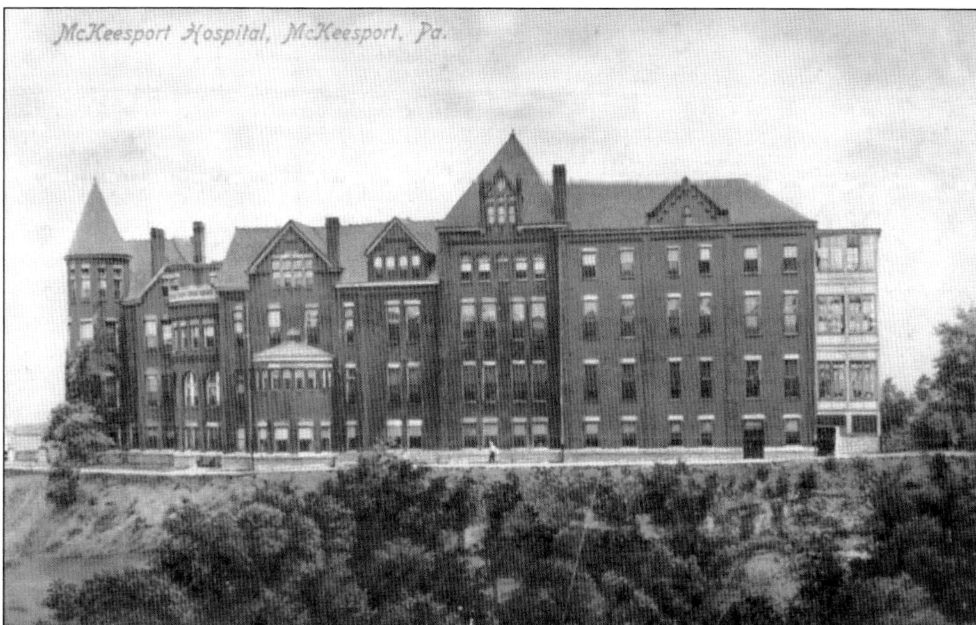

The hospital continued to be used, despite increasingly crowded conditions and outdated facilities, until a new hospital was built adjacent to it. The Shaw Building opened in 1953, followed by the Crawford Building in 1959. With these two new wings complete, demolition of the old hospital began in August 1959.

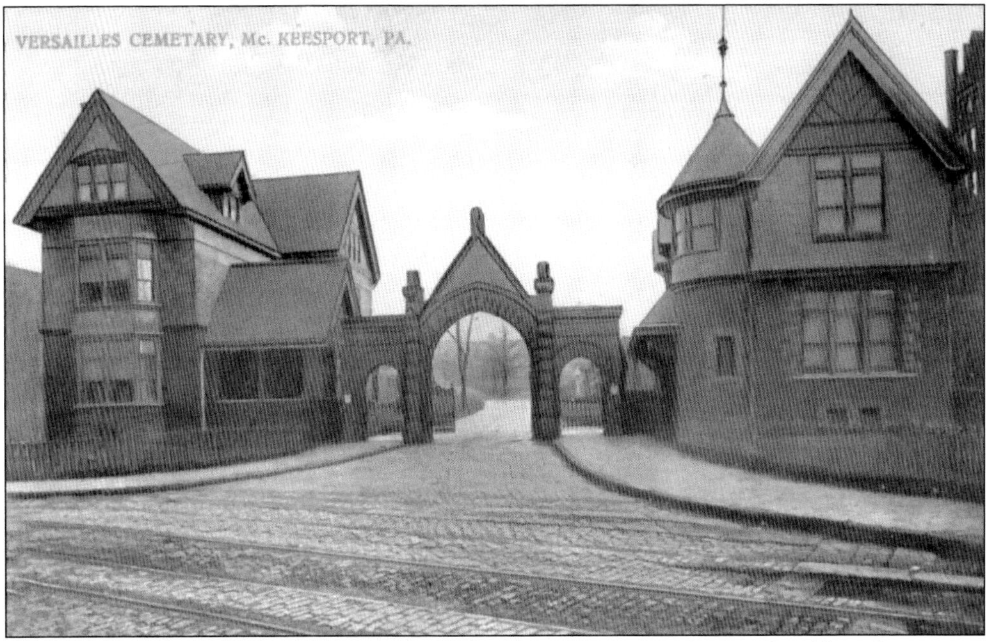

In 1856, the McKeesport and Versailles Cemetery Company was chartered and bought 26 acres from the Huey Estate. This cemetery was dedicated in November 1856, and the first burial was of Jordan Blair on November 15. In 1892, the cemetery company built a residence (left) for the superintendent and an office building (right) connected by an arched gateway. (Courtesy of Leonard Chemsak.)

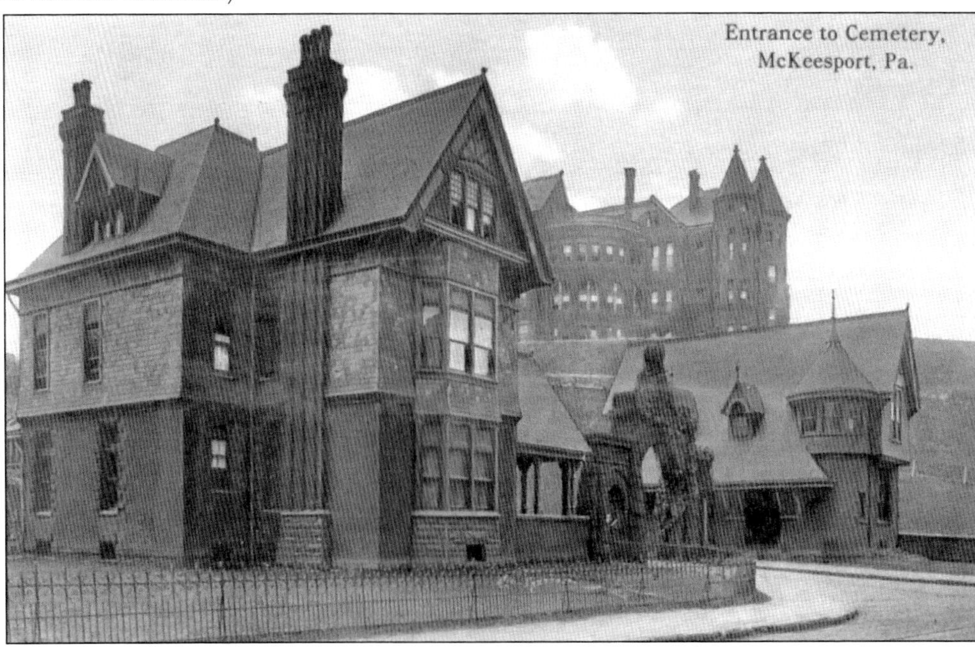

The residence was torn down in the 1960s but the office building remains. This was not the first cemetery in McKeesport. The first cemetery was the old Ninth Street Cemetery, laid out by David McKee. In 1874, the Ninth Street Cemetery was removed, with some of the bodies being reinterred at the McKeesport and Versailles Cemetery. (Courtesy of Andrea [Luketic] Cartwright.)

Five

Schools

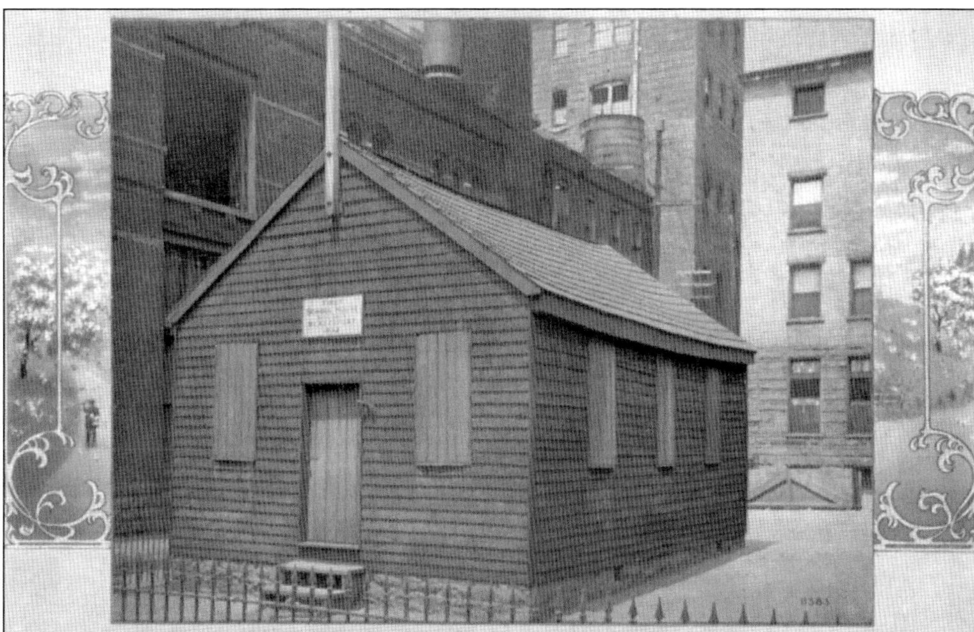

This was McKeesport's first schoolhouse, built in 1832 by private subscription and located on the Diamond at Fourth Avenue. Prior to this, classes had been conducted in private homes. Mr. Higly (or Higby) taught the first classes in this one-room schoolhouses. Tuition was $1 per month, and students were expected to buy their own books. (Courtesy of Leonard Chemsak.)

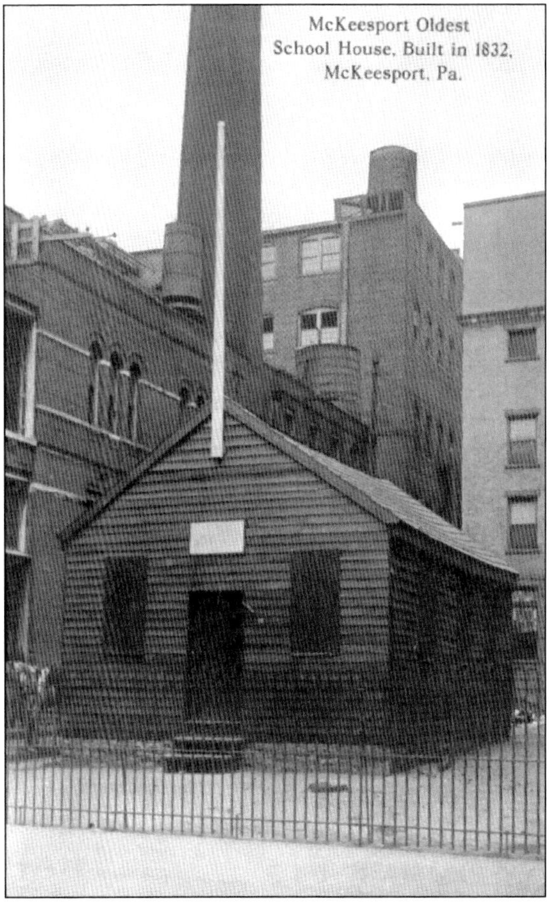

This schoolhouse was used until sometime in the late 1840s. In 1841, the first public school was built on Walnut Street near the corner of Ninth Avenue, and in 1849, a three-story brick schoolhouse was constructed at the corner of Sixth Avenue and Market Street. The Market Street School was replaced in 1863 by a new school on the same site (see page 50). (Courtesy of Leonard Chemsak.)

The schoolhouse was moved in 1849 to the First Presbyterian Church lot, where it was used for storage and as a bake house. In 1908, it was moved to the Market Street School lot and restored by the school district. It was threatened by demolition in 1925 and moved to its original location on the Diamond. In 1942, it was moved one last time, to Renziehausen Park. (Courtesy of Roger Reichenbach.)

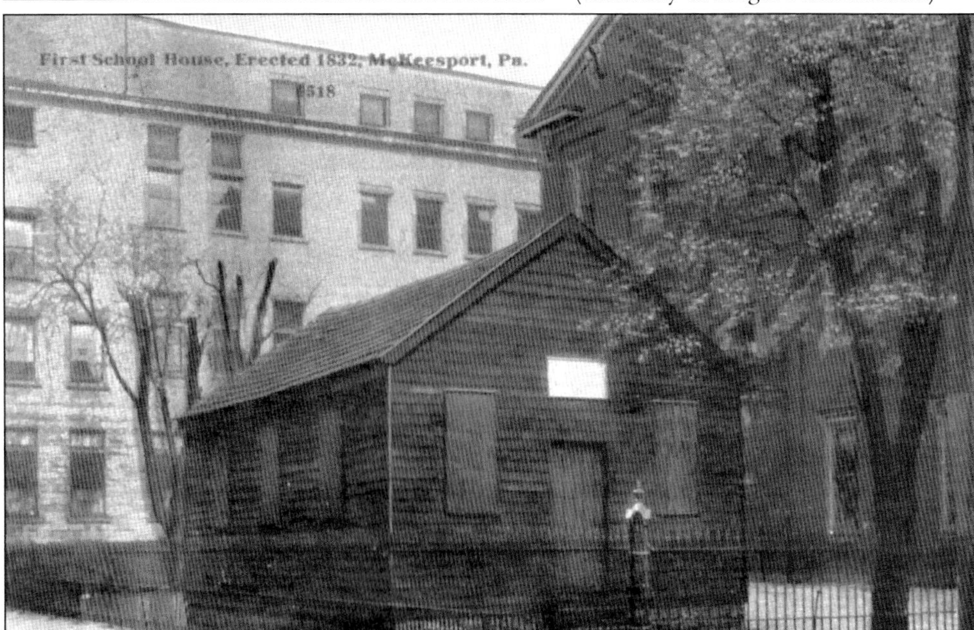

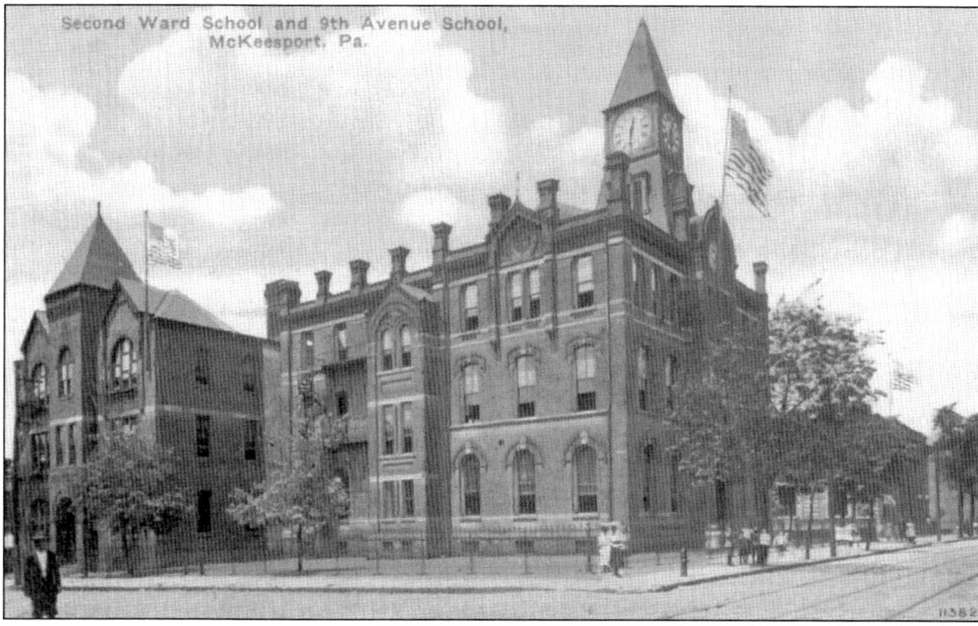

The Walnut Street School, or Second Ward School (right), was built in 1880. It housed McKeesport's first high school. In 1884, ten students made up the first graduating class. The clock was added in 1882, financed by James Neel. It measured eight feet and four inches in diameter and was electrically illuminated in 1908. The school was razed in 1963, and the post office was built on its site.

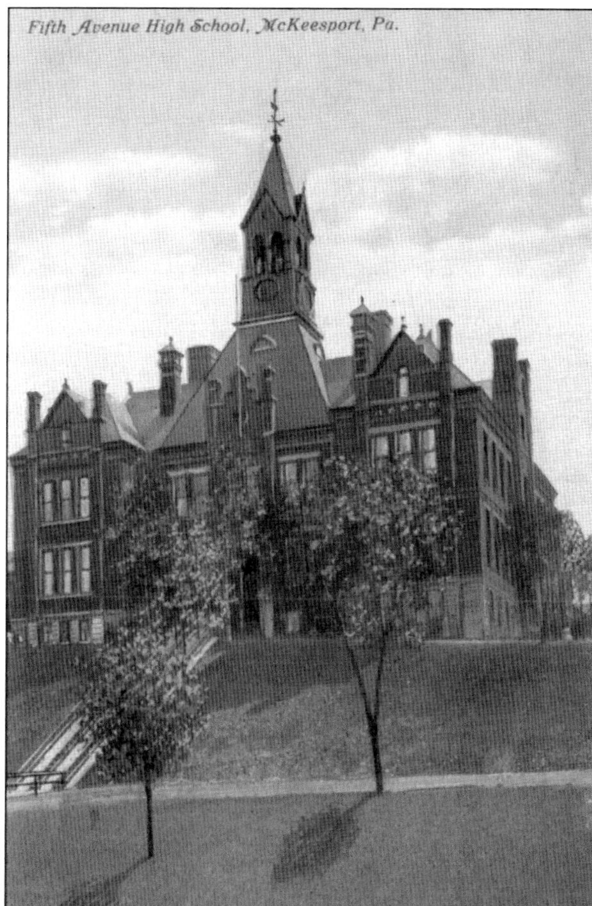

The Fifth Avenue School was located on the hill overlooking Fifth Avenue, between Coursin and Hazel Streets. This was the first brick schoolhouse in the old Third Ward. It was designed by architect Henry Mosier and had 13 classrooms and a 120-foot belfry. It was replaced in 1952. (Courtesy of Chuck Jarrell.)

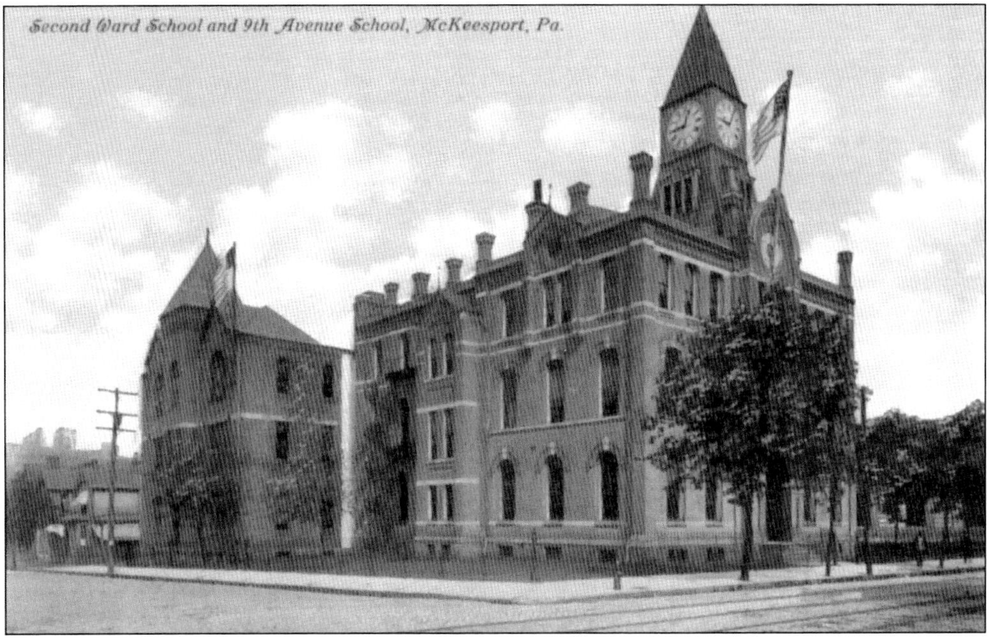

Second Ward School and 9th Avenue School, McKeesport, Pa.

The Ninth Avenue School, seen on the left next to Walnut Street School, was built in 1890 to relieve overcrowding at the Walnut Street School. J.C. Fulton of Uniontown was the architect. The building contained 12 classrooms and had a large hall on the third floor. In 1931, it was remodeled, and in 1963, it was demolished.

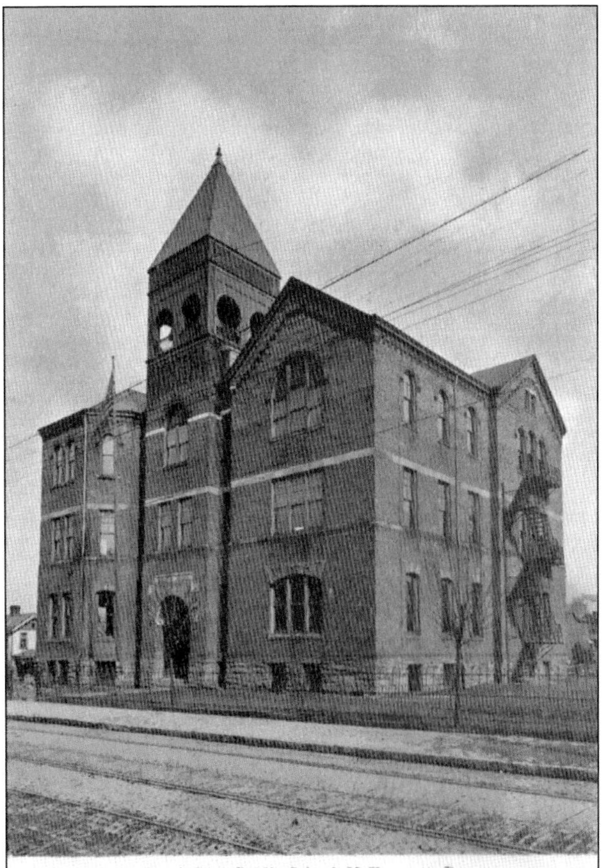

South Park Public School, McKeesport, Pa.

South Park School faced Evans Avenue between Oak and Bridge Avenues. Residents in what was called the "Point Breeze" section of the city had been petitioning for a school since 1888. In response, this school was dedicated in 1891. Like the Ninth Avenue School, it was designed by J.C Fulton. The school was remodeled in 1928 and razed in 1962. In its final year, 362 students attended. (Courtesy of Leonard Chemsak.)

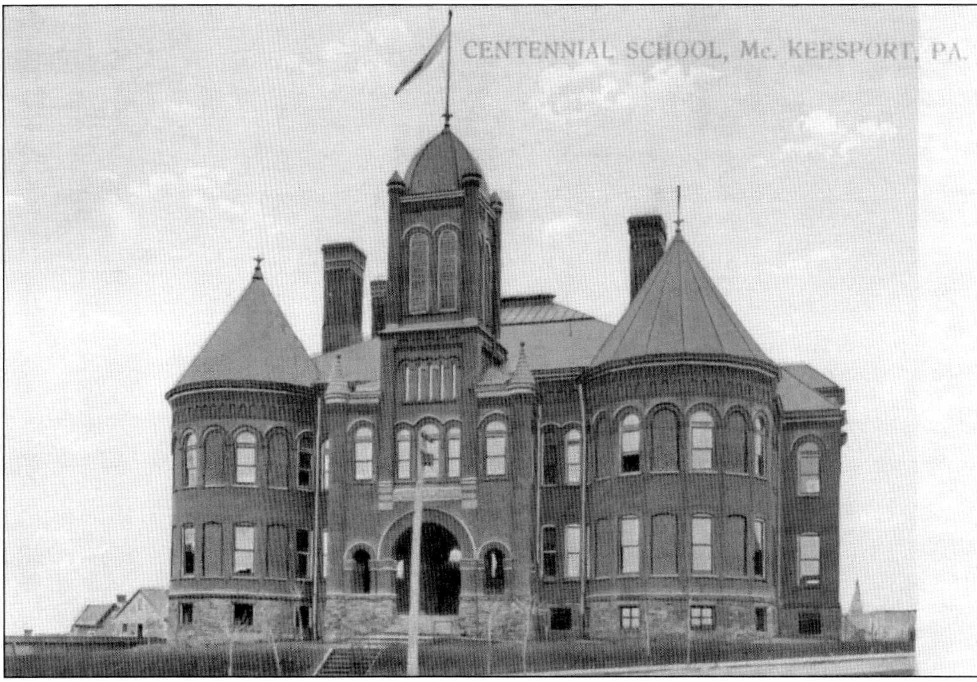

Overcrowding at the public schools continued to be a problem. In 1894, because of the increasing residential development in the Riverview Park section of the Seventh Ward, Centennial School was built. It was located at the corner of Union and Beaver Avenues.

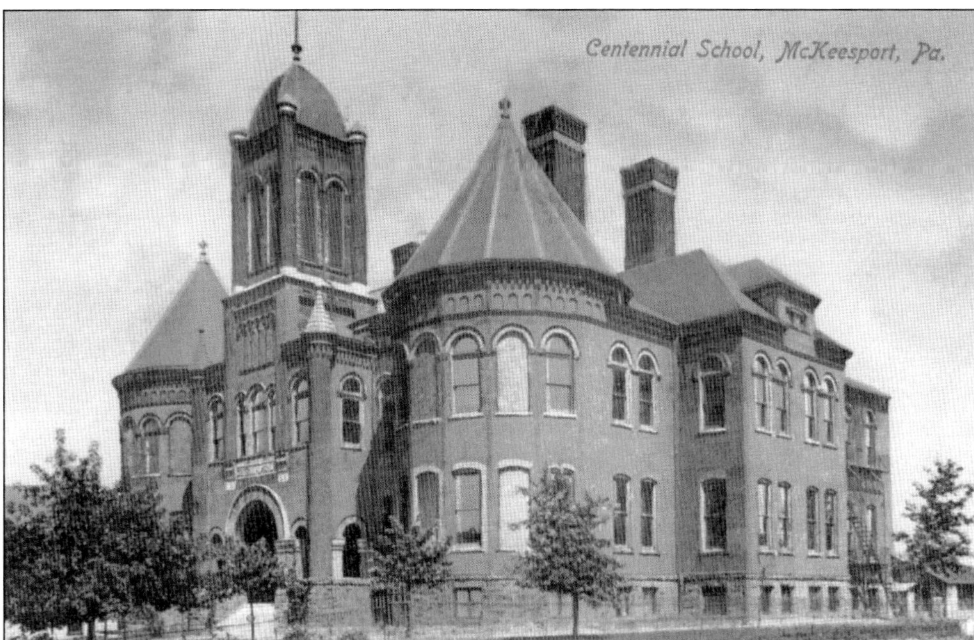

Henry J. Lohman, McKeesport architect, designed Centennial School. It contained 16 rooms. This first building was destroyed by fire on December 29, 1919, and replaced on the same site in 1921 with the current Centennial School building. (Courtesy of Roger Reichenbach.)

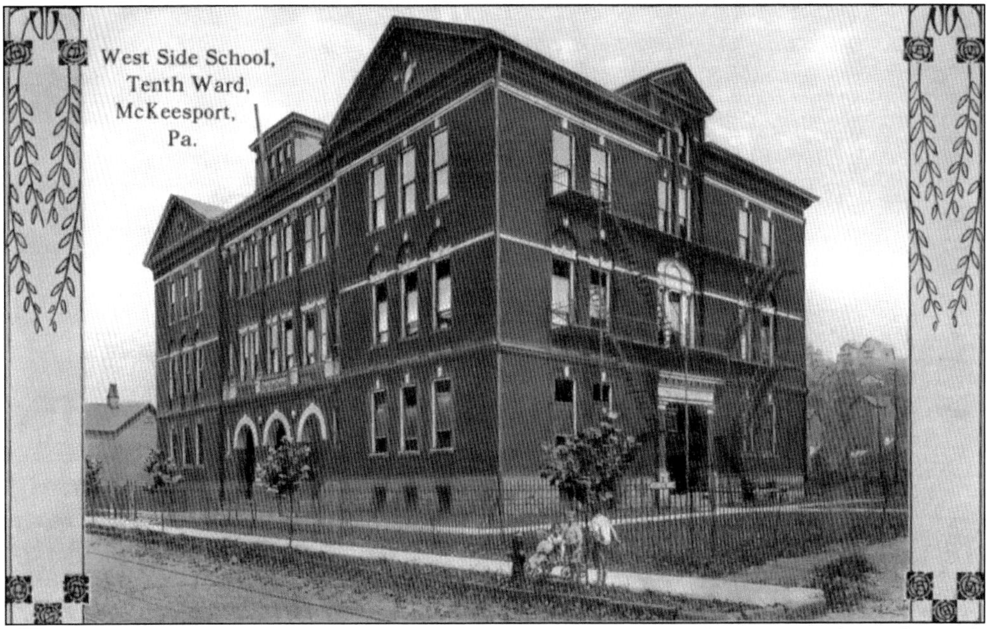

The West Side School, at the corner of Atlantic Avenue and Roanoke Street in the 10th Ward, was built in 1902. It was dedicated on Thanksgiving Day, 1903, after numerous construction delays prevented it from opening at the start of the school year. Opening enrollment was 361 students.

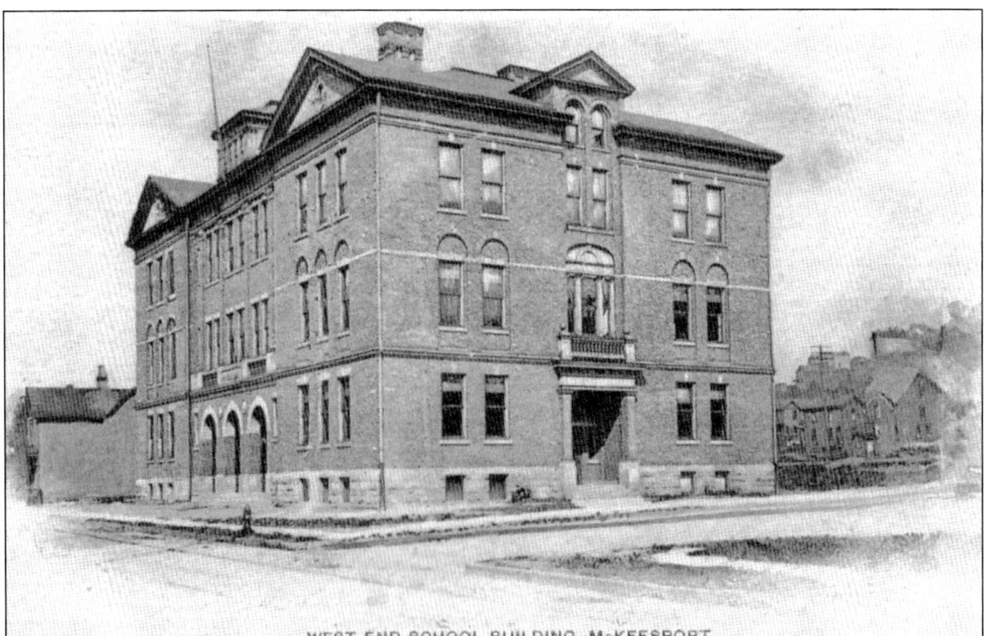

The architect for West Side School was William F. Wilson from McKeesport. A second architect, T.J. Herron, was hired to design a bell tower that was never constructed. From 1956 to 1957, the Penn State University Center used five rooms in this building for its classes and offices. The building was demolished in 1978. (Courtesy of Leonard Chemsak.)

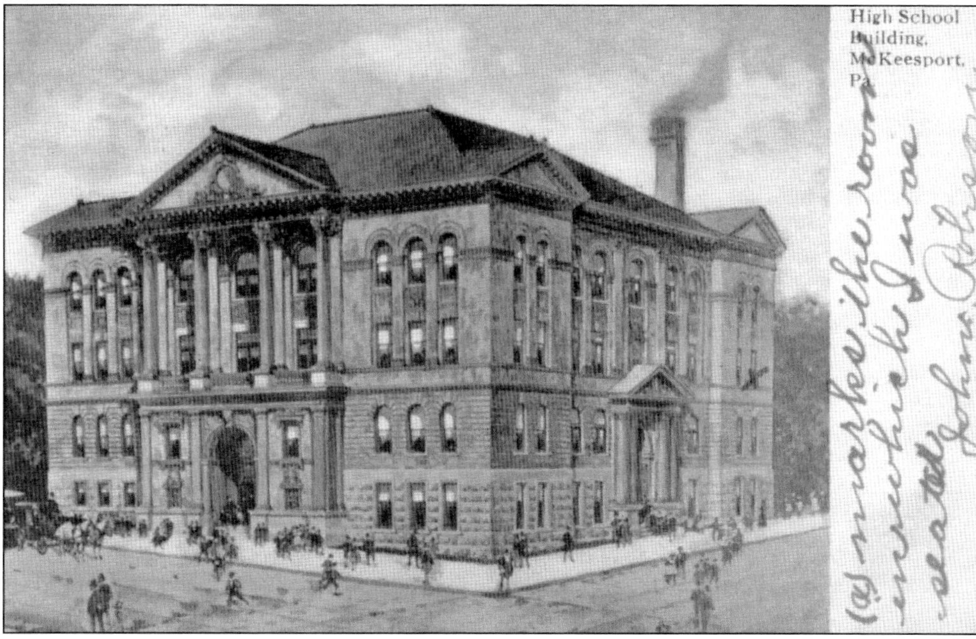

In December 1898, an architectural competition was held for the design of the Shaw Avenue High School. Of the 10 firms competing, McCollum and Ely from Washington, Pennsylvania, won the $80,000 bid. The foundation stone for the school was to be quarried at the McKeesport Versailles Cemetery.

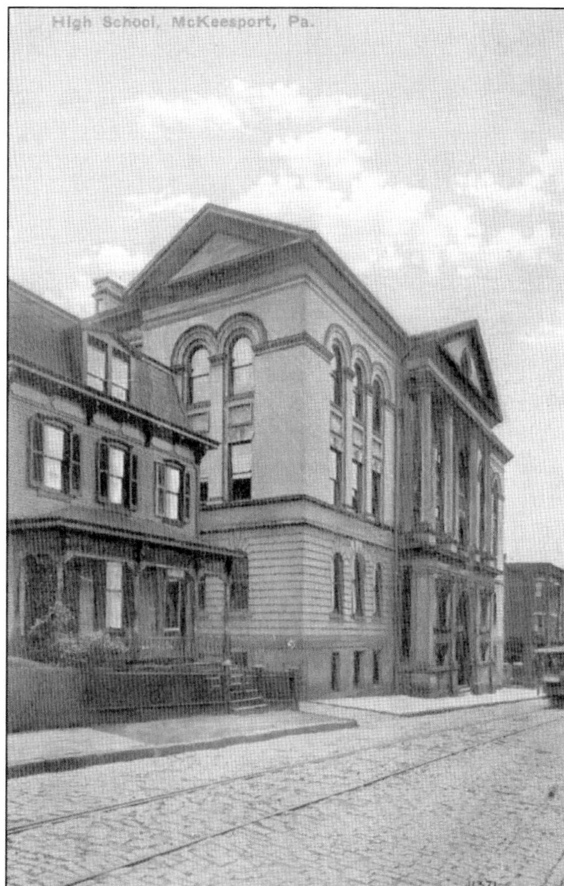

Shaw Avenue High School opened for the 1900–1901 school year. Through 1909, graduating classes averaged 35 students. In 1916, a new high school was built, and Shaw Avenue School became a grade school.

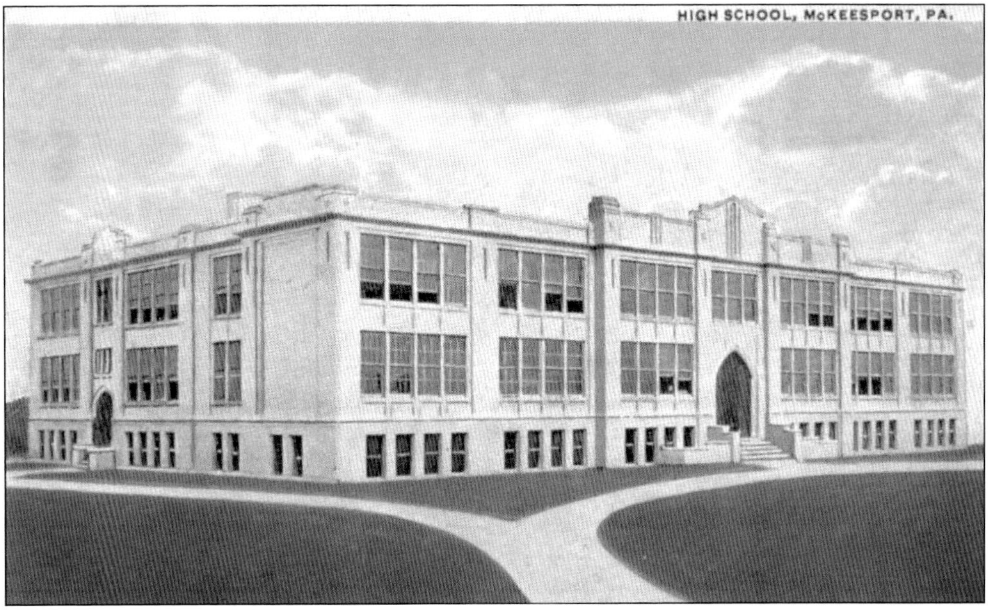

In 1915, five acres of Rebecca Evans's property along Huey Street, now Cornell Street, was purchased for a new high school. The architectural firm Vrydaugh and Wolfe of Pittsburgh was hired. The new school contained 82 rooms, including 20 classrooms, an auditorium, a gymnasium, laboratories, and a kitchen. Opening in October 1916, it could accommodate up to 800 students. It was named Technical High School.

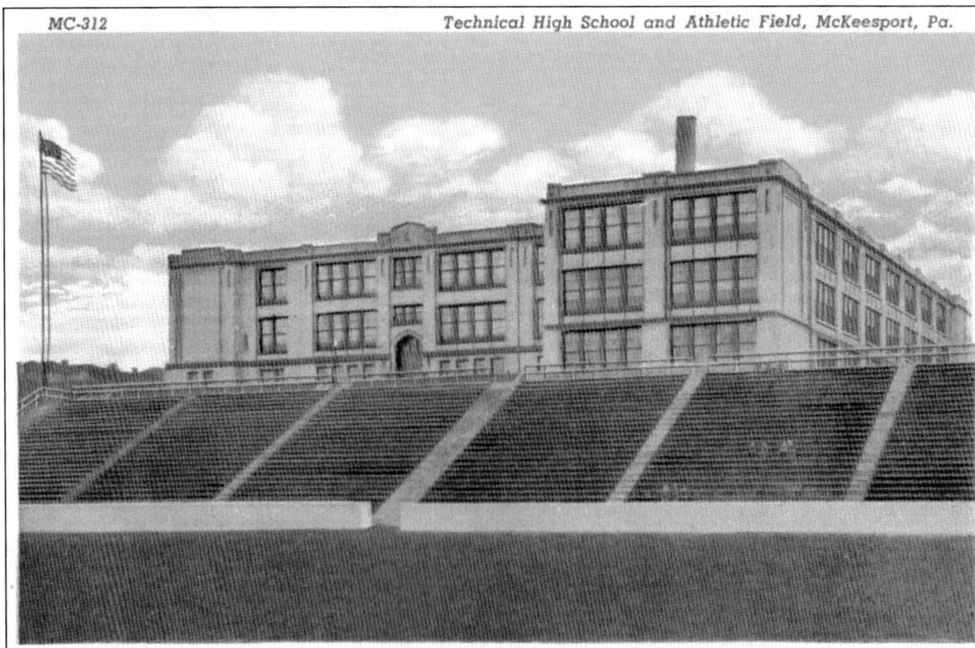

An addition (right) was designed with the original plans and was constructed in 1924. The War Memorial Field in the foreground was dedicated on November 11, 1927, and the first football game was played the following day, with McKeesport losing to Homestead 27-0. Prior to this, the football team played at Cycler Park in the 10th Ward.

Six

Churches

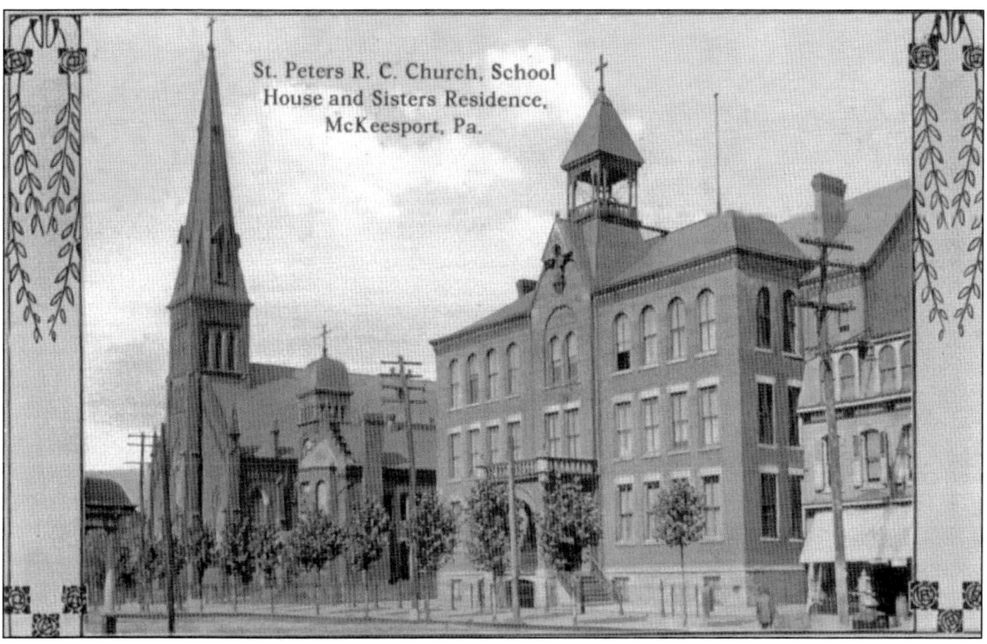

St. Peter's Roman Catholic Church (left), convent (center), and school (right), were located along the 700 block of Market Street. The convent and school were built c. 1887 through the generosity of the White family. The school had classrooms on the first and second floors and a hall on the third. In 1927, classes expanded to include a four-year high school. It closed in 1970 and was demolished in 1971. (Courtesy of Chuck Jarrell.)

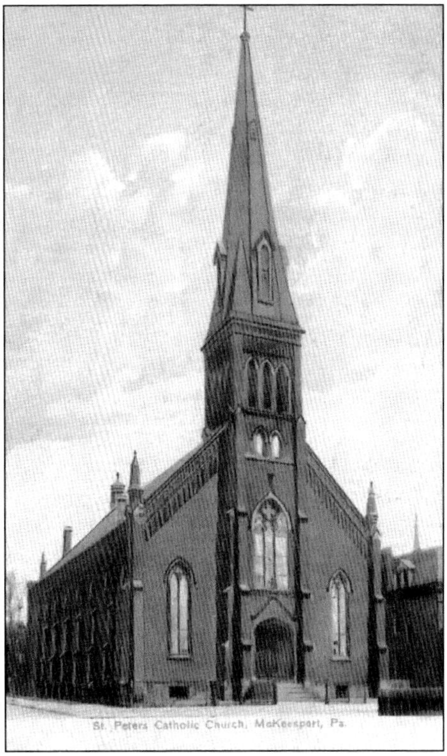

St. Peter's Roman Catholic Church was built in 1874 at the corner of Seventh Avenue and Market Street. This was the second church on the site. The first church was built in 1846, and it was there that Rev. John Neumann (now St. John Neumann) preached as a visiting priest. The church seen here, designed by Charles M. Bartberger, had a capacity of 725 people and a steeple 175 feet high. (Courtesy of Chuck Jarrell.)

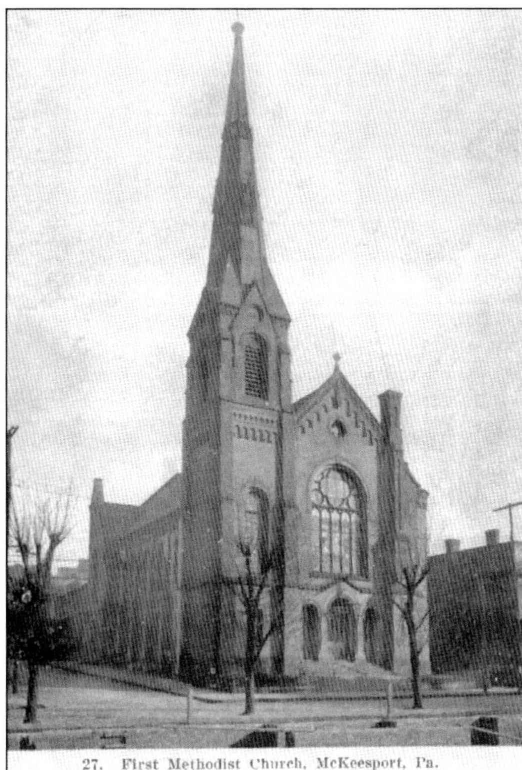

The First Methodist Church, built in 1876, was the fourth home of the Methodist congregation in McKeesport. D.K. Miller designed this church, located at the corner of Walnut Street and Penny Avenue. Its spire was 183 feet high, and in the 1880s, this steeple was the location of the local fire alarm bell. The congregation was initially organized in 1840.

The First Methodist Church had Sunday school rooms on the first floor, and the main auditorium was on the second floor. The seating capacity was 800 people. On July 11, 1924, the church burned down, necessitating the move to a new location.

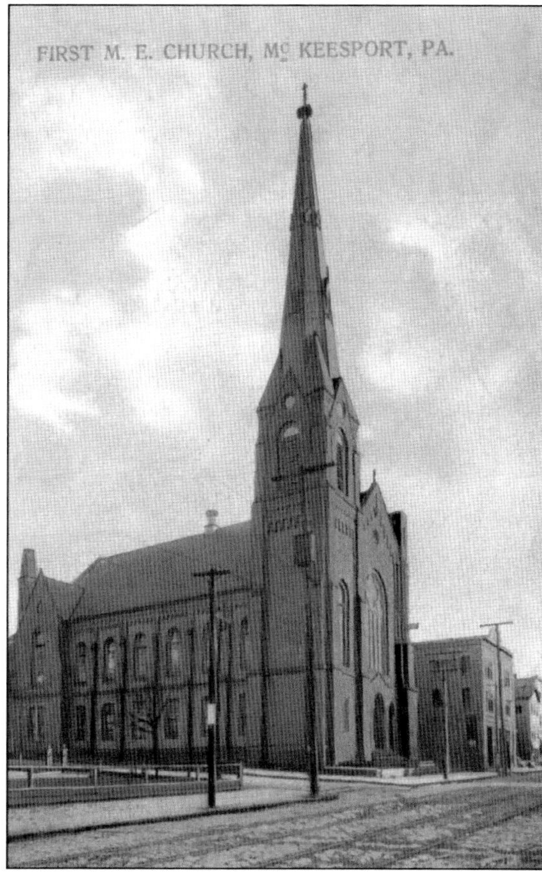

The First Methodist Church purchased a new site at Cornell Street and Versailles Avenue, formerly home to the YMCA athletic field. The cornerstone for this Gothic-style church was laid in 1925, and the building was dedicated in 1926.

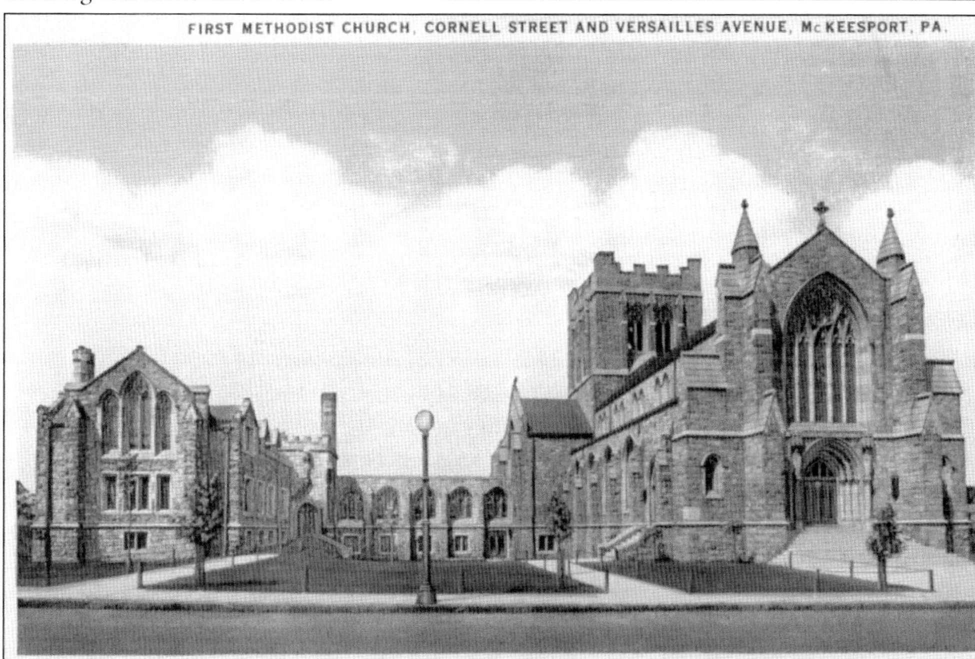

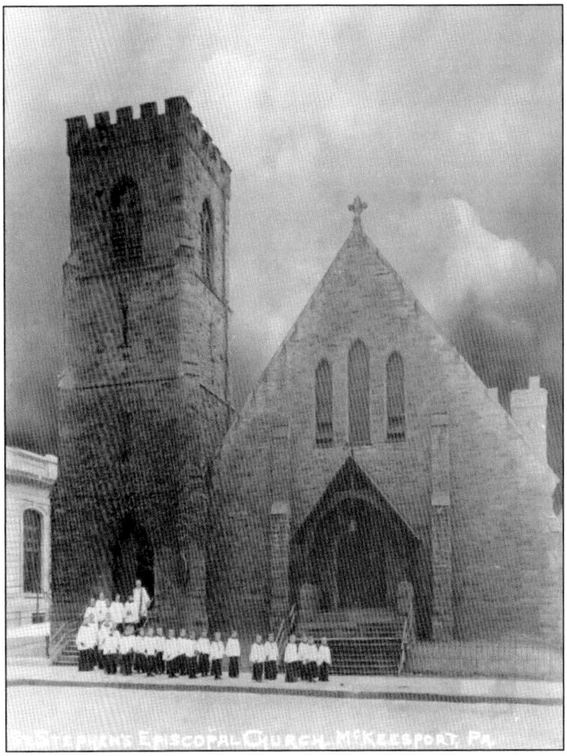

St. Stephen's Episcopal Church was built in 1888 on Eighth Avenue between Market and Walnut Streets. This was the first stone nonresidential structure in McKeesport, replacing an earlier frame church built in 1874 on the same site. C.M. Burns Jr. of Philadelphia was the architect of this 1888 building. (Courtesy of Leonard Chemsak.)

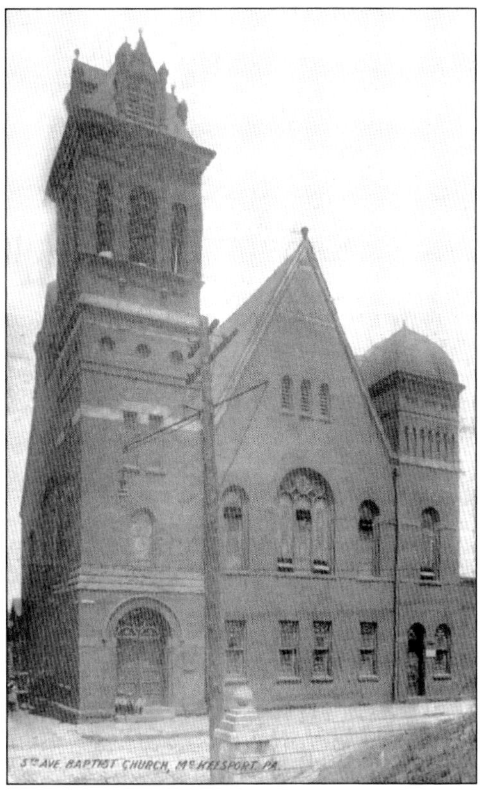

The Fifth Avenue Baptist Church, located at the corner of Fifth Avenue and Faith Alley, was built in 1899. A lecture room was on the first floor, and the main auditorium was on the second floor. Andrew Carnegie donated the organ. This church grew out of a mission Bible school that dated back to 1887. The congregation moved to Versailles Avenue in 1922.

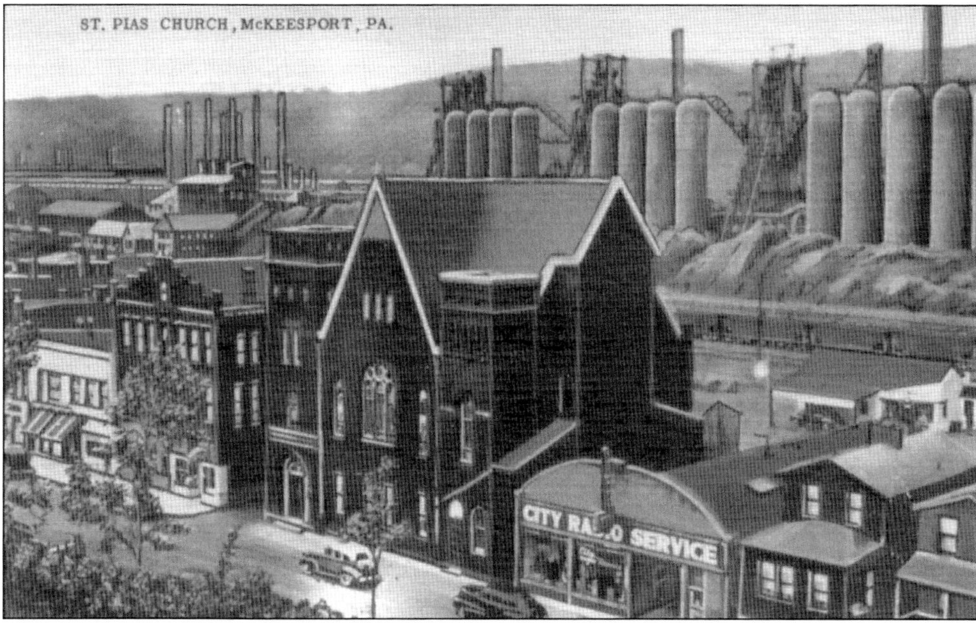

St. Pius V Church was organized in 1903 as an offshoot of St. Peter's Church. Its first frame church, built at the corner of Evans Street and Ninth Avenue, was dedicated November 6, 1904, and destroyed by fire in 1919. The congregation then bought the former Fifth Avenue Baptist Church (pictured) and used it through the 1950s. In 1928, a new church was built for St. Pius V at Boyd and Freemont Streets.

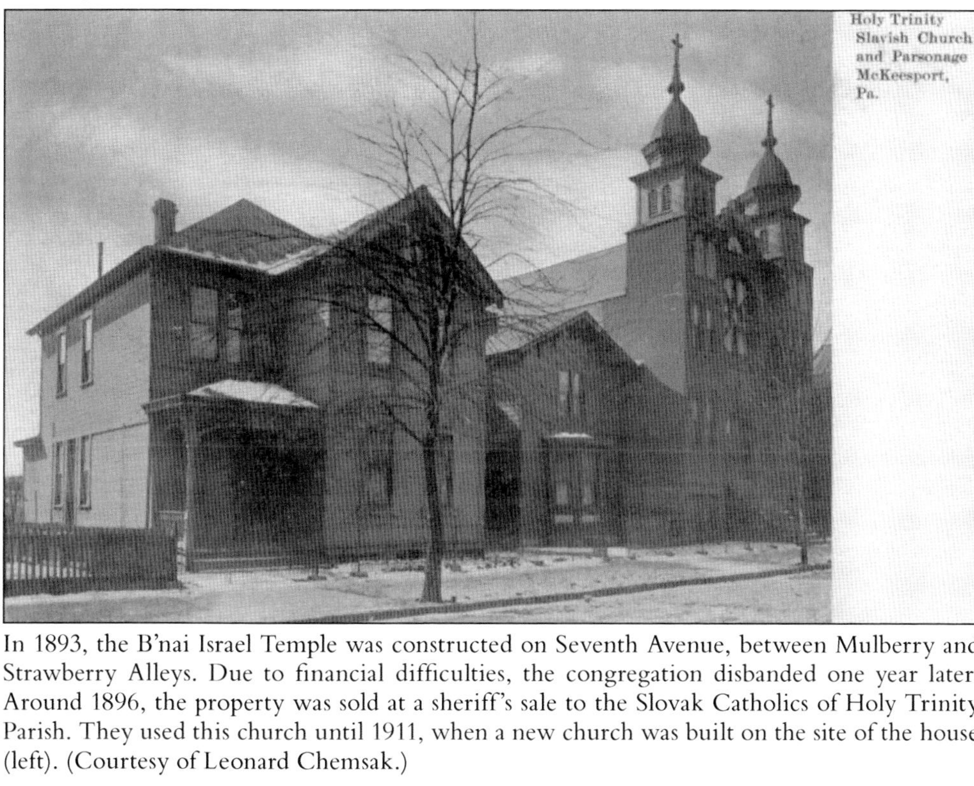

In 1893, the B'nai Israel Temple was constructed on Seventh Avenue, between Mulberry and Strawberry Alleys. Due to financial difficulties, the congregation disbanded one year later. Around 1896, the property was sold at a sheriff's sale to the Slovak Catholics of Holy Trinity Parish. They used this church until 1911, when a new church was built on the site of the house (left). (Courtesy of Leonard Chemsak.)

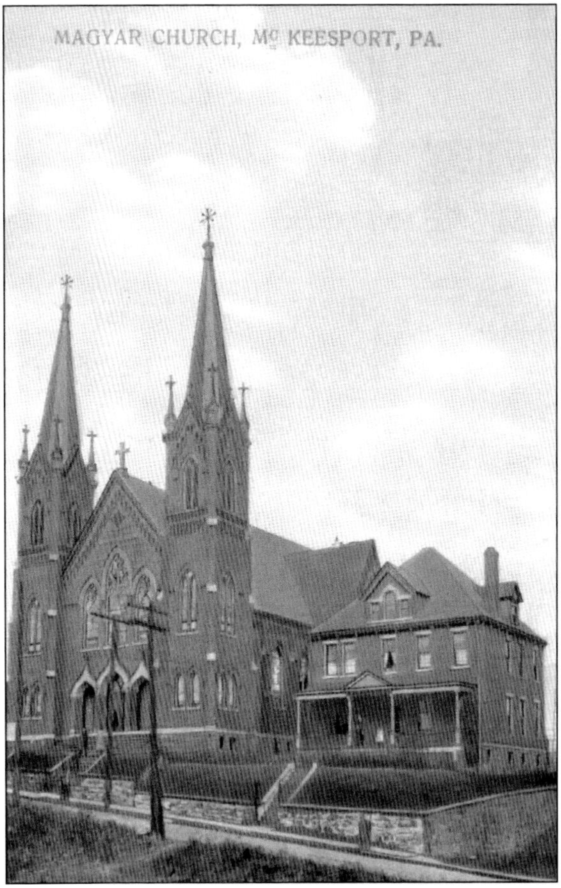

St. Stephen's Roman Catholic Magyar Church, dedicated in 1901, was on Beacon Street near Evans Avenue. This was the first Hungarian Roman Catholic Church in Pennsylvania and the fifth in the United States. The parish house is on the right. (Courtesy of Andrea [Luketic] Cartwright.)

Inside St. Stephen's, the main altar was constructed from the wood of trees grown in Hungary. The Bishop of Hungary donated it. Over the main altar was a painting of St. Stephen that was donated by Franz Jozef, emperor of Austria-Hungary. Andrew Carnegie donated the organ.

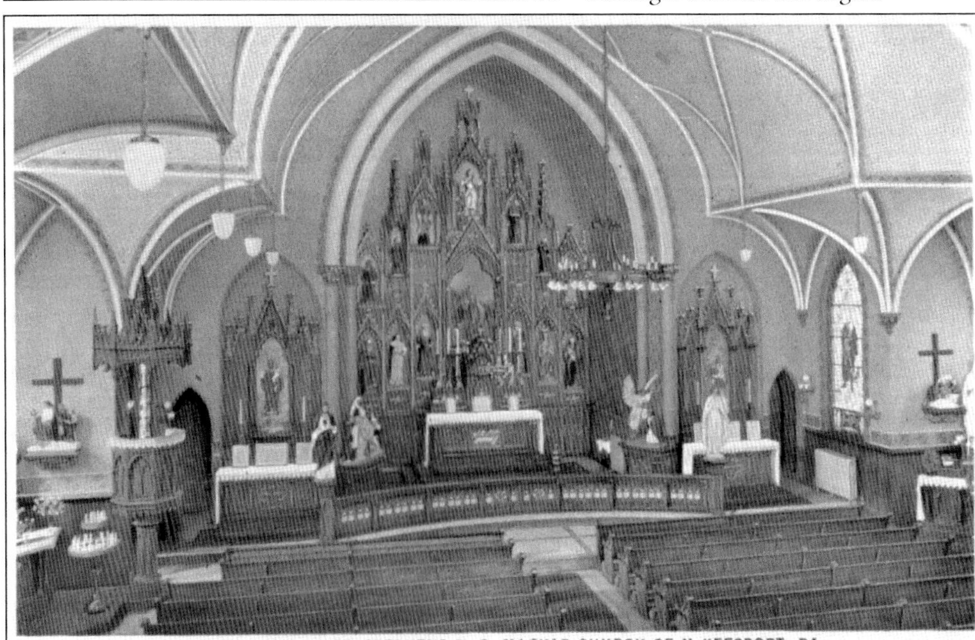

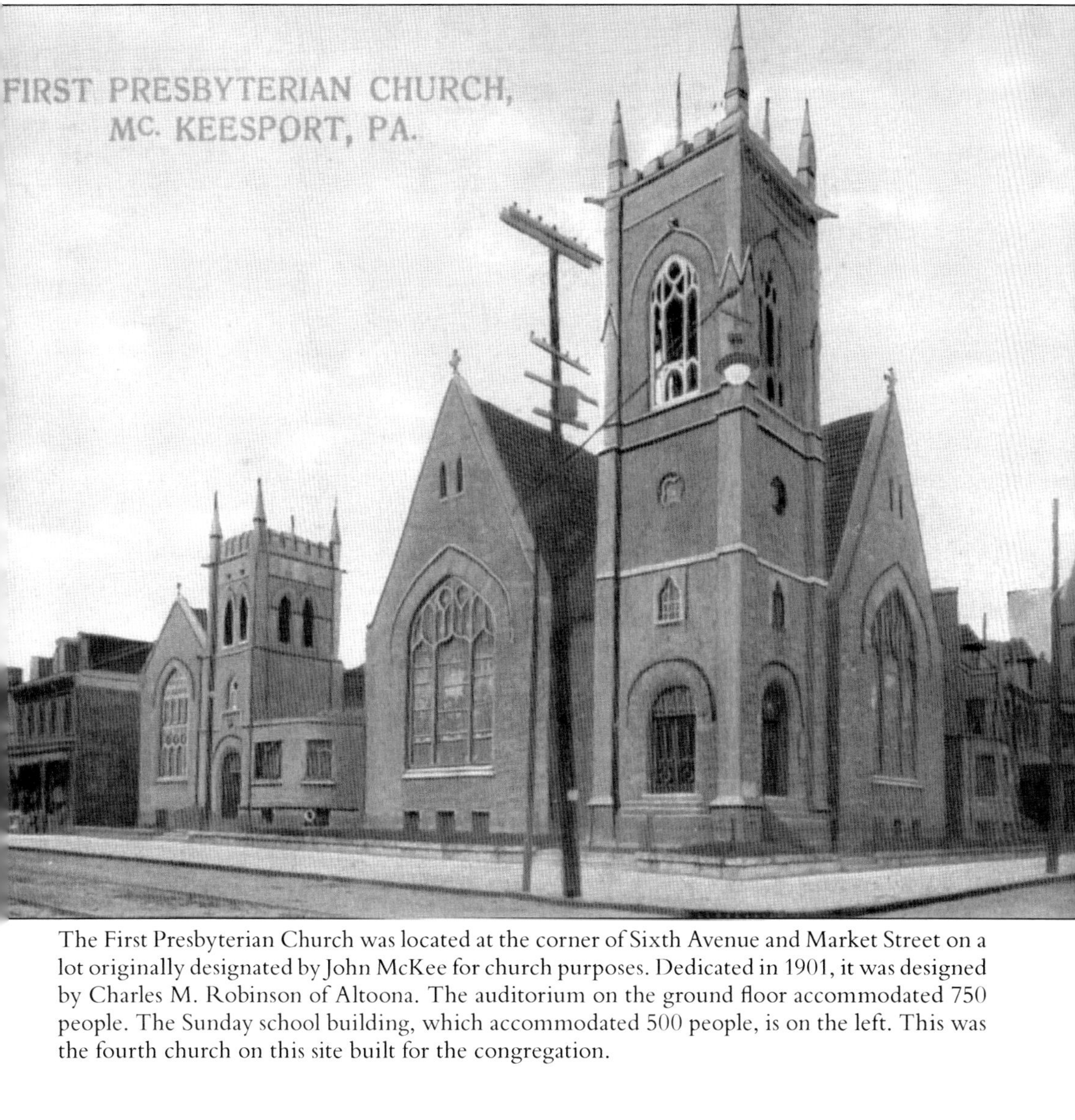

The First Presbyterian Church was located at the corner of Sixth Avenue and Market Street on a lot originally designated by John McKee for church purposes. Dedicated in 1901, it was designed by Charles M. Robinson of Altoona. The auditorium on the ground floor accommodated 750 people. The Sunday school building, which accommodated 500 people, is on the left. This was the fourth church on this site built for the congregation.

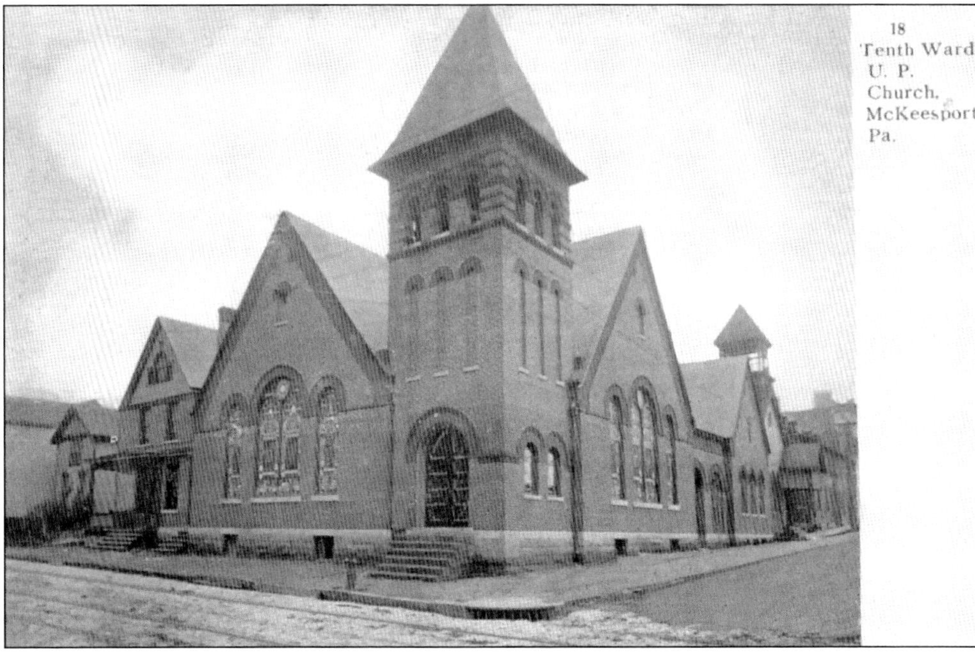

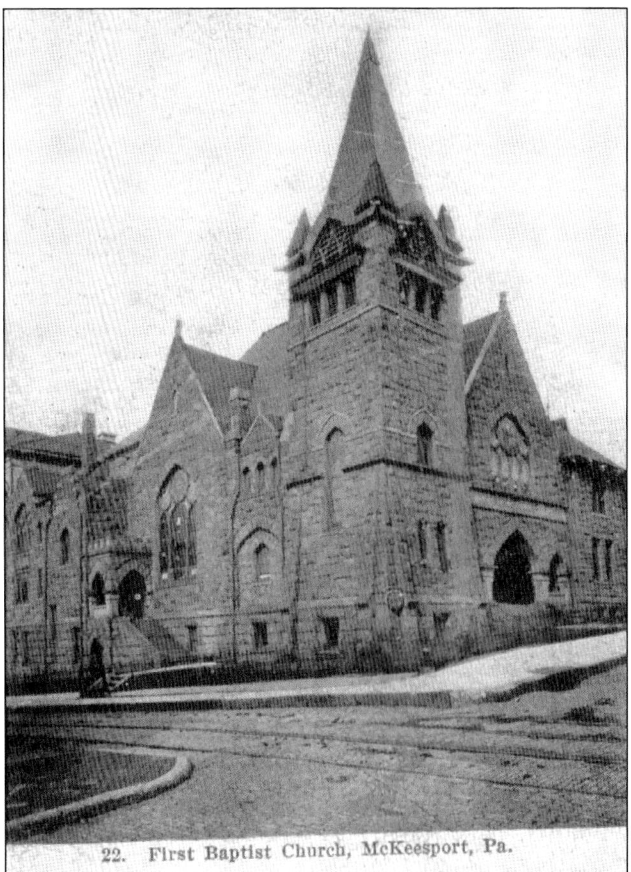

The Tenth Ward United Presbyterian Church, better known as the Atlantic Avenue United Presbyterian Church, was dedicated in 1902. Located at the corner of Atlantic Avenue and Perry Street, this was the second church on the site. The congregation originated as a mission that was organized in 1892.

The First Baptist Church cornerstone was laid in 1903, and the building was dedicated in 1904. The congregation dated back to 1820. In 1837, a church was built on Blackberry Alley, below the Diamond. This was followed by a church built in 1867, located at Sixth Avenue and Walnut Street.

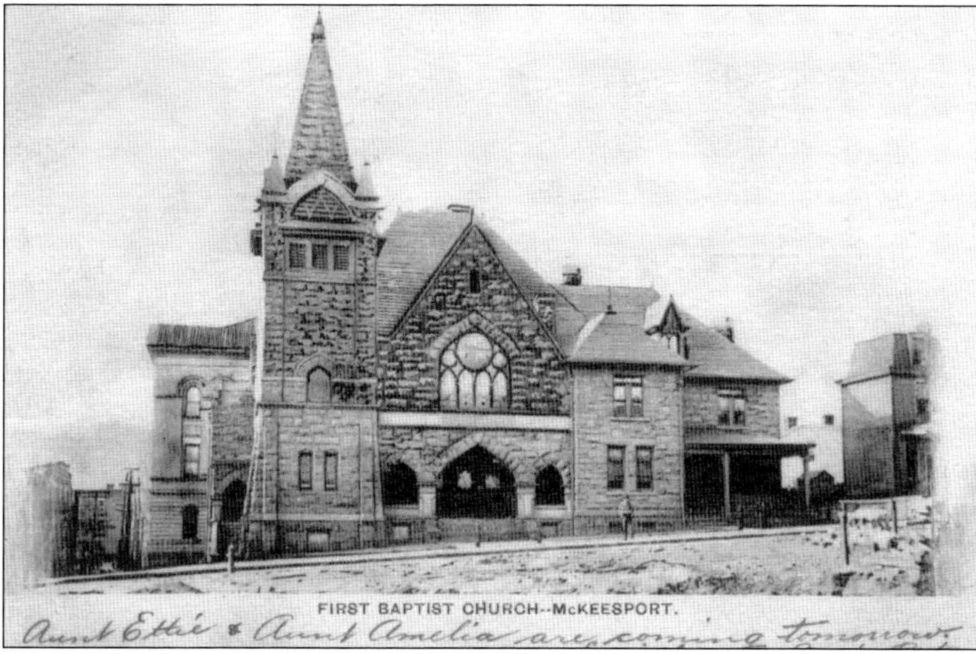

The building seen here was located at the northeast corner of Locust and Olive Streets. J.C. Fulton of Uniontown, Pennsylvania, was the architect. It was a brownstone structure that seated 900 people. Andrew Carnegie donated half the cost of the pipe organ.

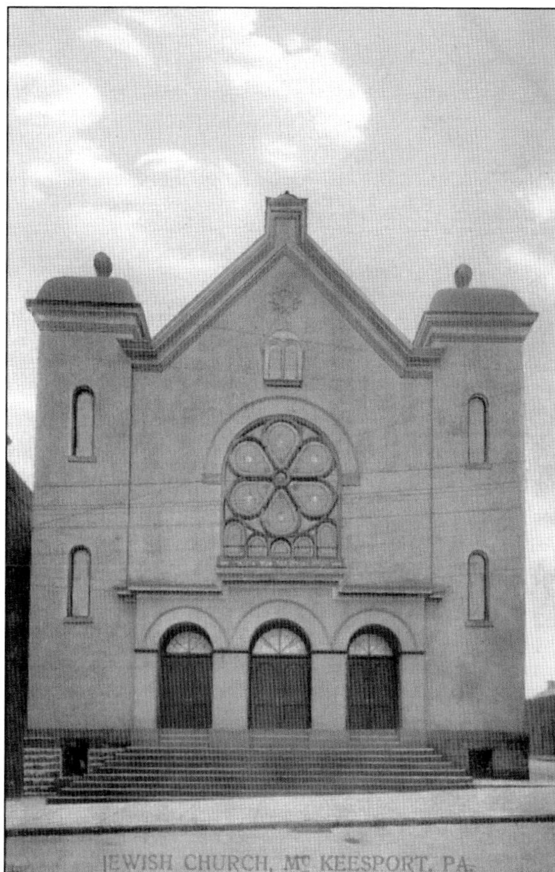

The Austrian Hungarian Hebrew congregation Gemulas Chesed of McKeesport was organized in 1886. In 1905, this new synagogue at the corner of Market Street and Third Avenue was dedicated. The architect was McKeesport's Henry J. Lohman. The main auditorium was on the first floor, along with a gallery. It was torn down as part of the First Ward redevelopment. (Courtesy of Leonard Chemsak.)

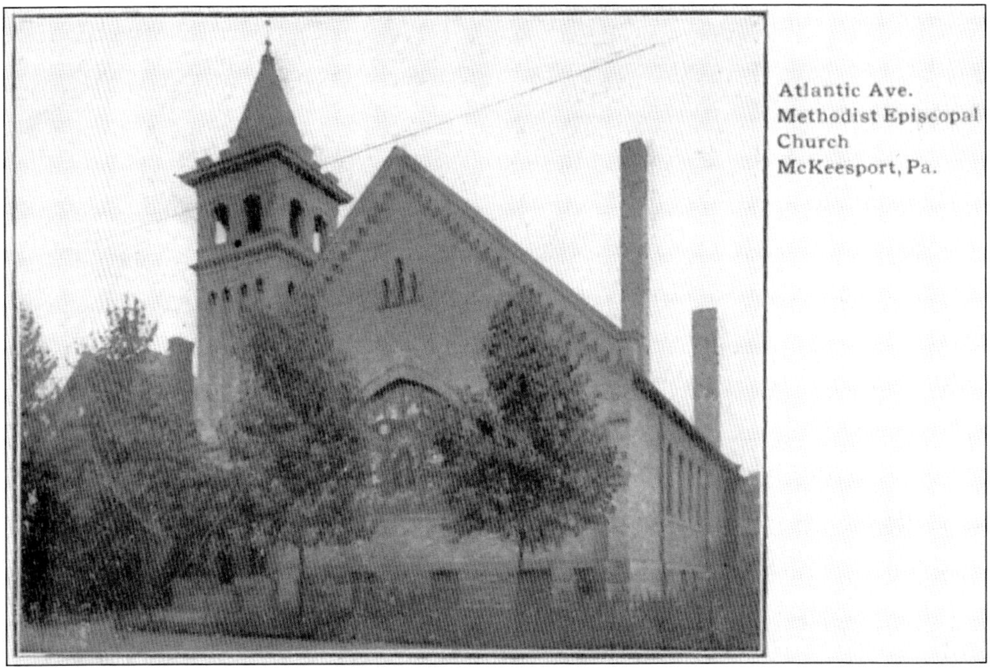

The Atlantic Avenue Methodist Episcopal Church was built between 1905 and 1906. The congregation began as a mission in 1880, and the first church was built two years later. The church seen here replaced the first church and was built on the same lot. Clepper and Moffitt of Pittsburgh were the architects, and Signor Moiou of Uniontown painted the frescoes. Andrew Carnegie donated half the cost of the pipe organ. (Courtesy of Leonard Chemsak.)

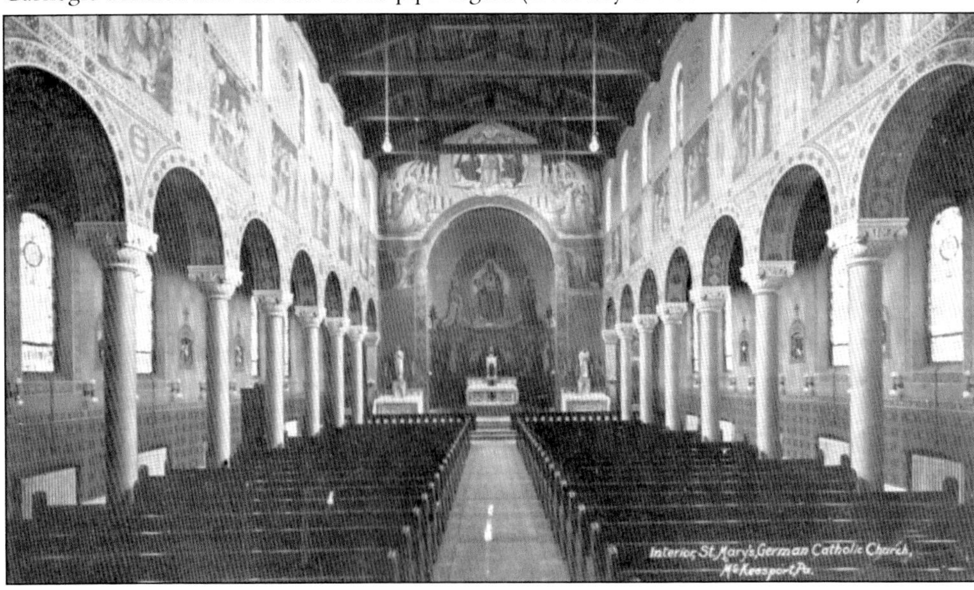

St. Mary's German Catholic Church, dedicated in April 1908, was located at the corner of Locust and Olive Streets. It was designed in the Roman basilica style, unique in the United States. The interior paintings were executed by Fathers Bonaventure and Raphael of St. Anselm's College in Manchester, New Hampshire, and the remaining decoration was completed by Jacob Langhart of McKeesport. (Courtesy of Leonard Chemsak.)

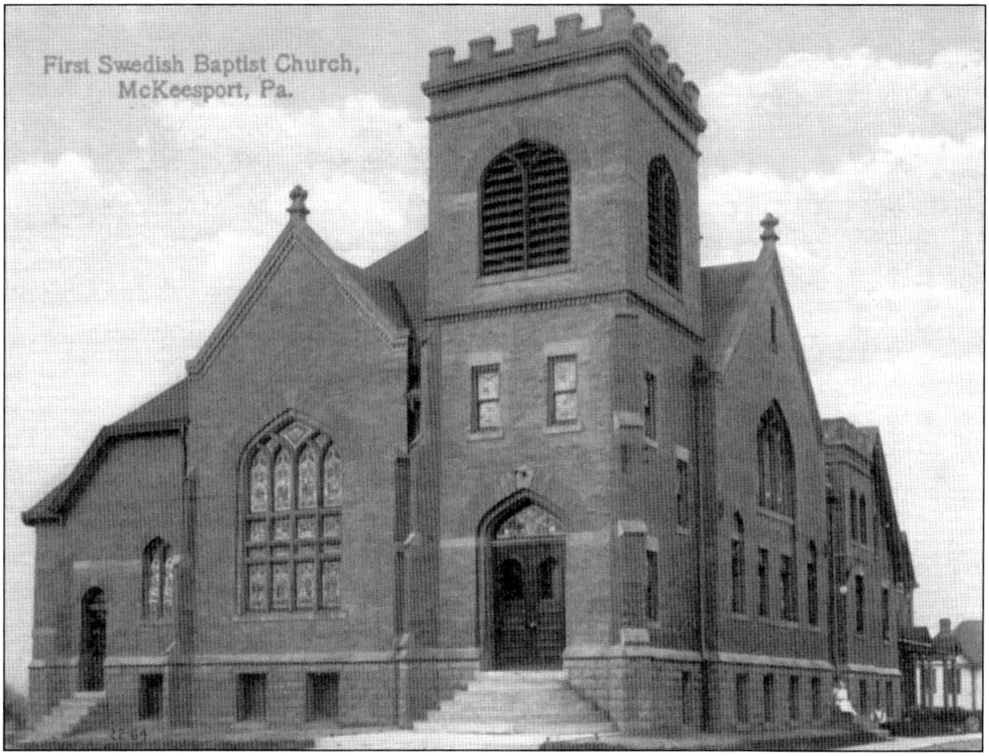

The First Swedish Baptist Church, dedicated in April 1908, was located at the corner of Soles and Riverview Streets. The congregation organized in 1884 and worshipped at various locations until this church was built. John Coxhead of Buffalo, New York, was the architect. (Courtesy of Leonard Chemsak.)

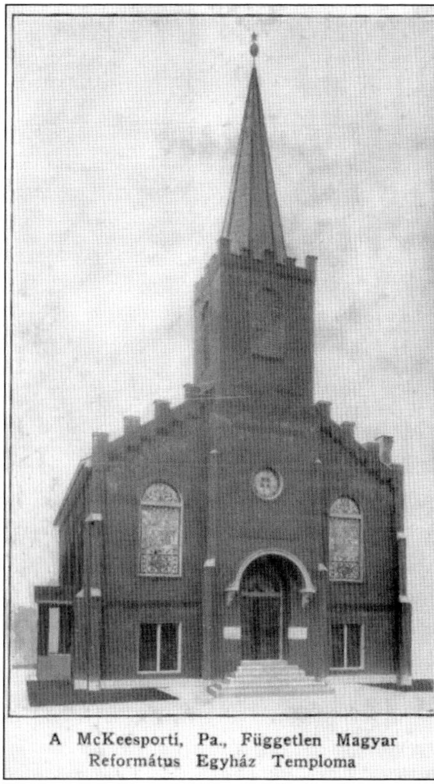

A McKeesporti, Pa., Független Magyar Református Egyház Temploma

The Free Magyar Reformed Church was founded in 1922. From 1923 through 1926, the congregation worshiped in a remodeled house on this site at the corner of Mulberry Alley and Seventh Avenue. The new church was built in 1926 and used until 1972. Bertl F. Hermann was the architect and contractor. (Courtesy of Roger Reichenbach.)

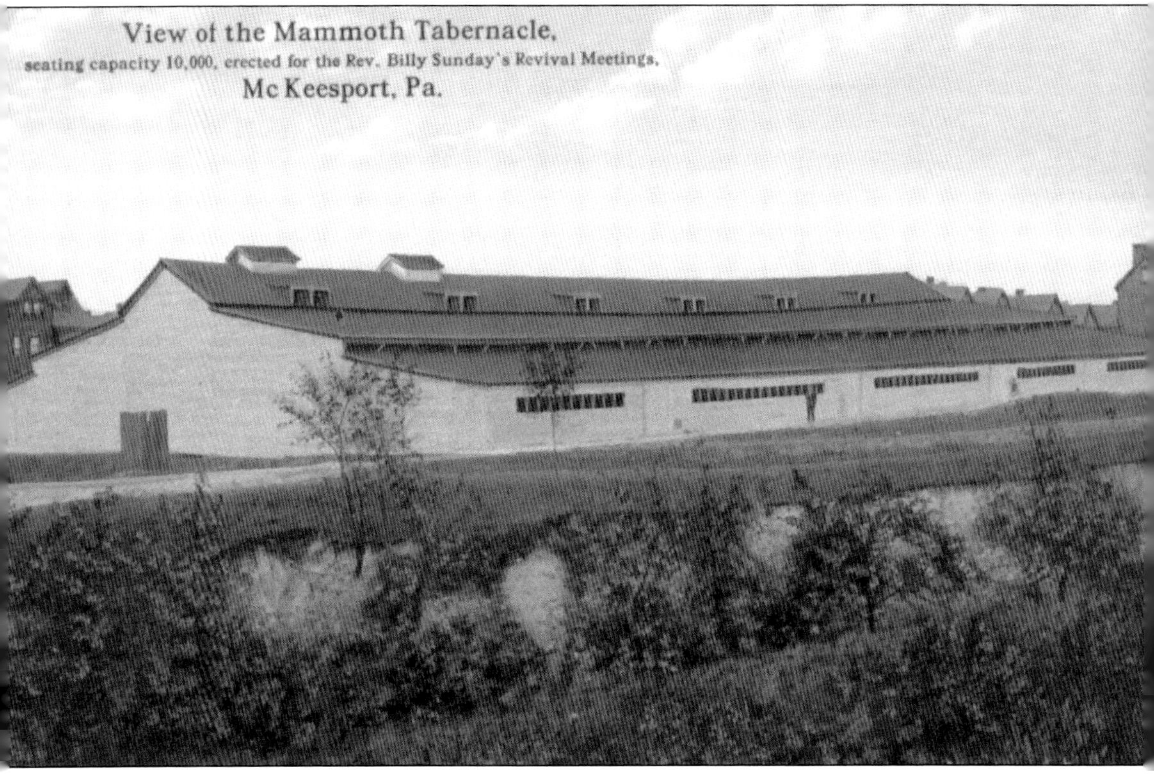

In 1912, Billy Sunday, the former baseball player who became a firebrand evangelist, came to McKeesport. This tabernacle, seating 12,000, was built as a temporary structure to accommodate the crowd. It was constructed at the corner of Versailles Avenue and Cornell Street, where the current First Methodist Church sits. Sunday was in McKeesport for a six-week stay, preaching three sermons on Sundays and two on weekdays. He hosted separate meetings for men and women. People traveled more than 100 miles to hear him. On the last day, 1,571 converts marched down the aisle. The building was then torn down and the lumber salvaged for other uses.

Seven

Residential and Recreational

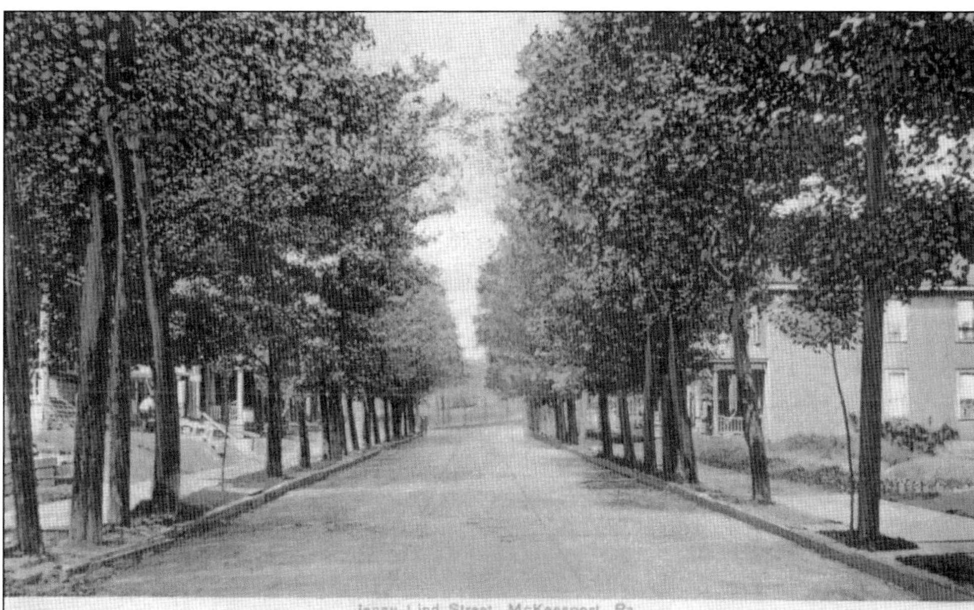

As McKeesport grew, residential neighborhoods developed in the hill district. In the late 19th century, lots were laid out in the Seventh Ward in what was called Riverview Park. New streets opened, and hundreds of homes were built for the rapidly expanding population.

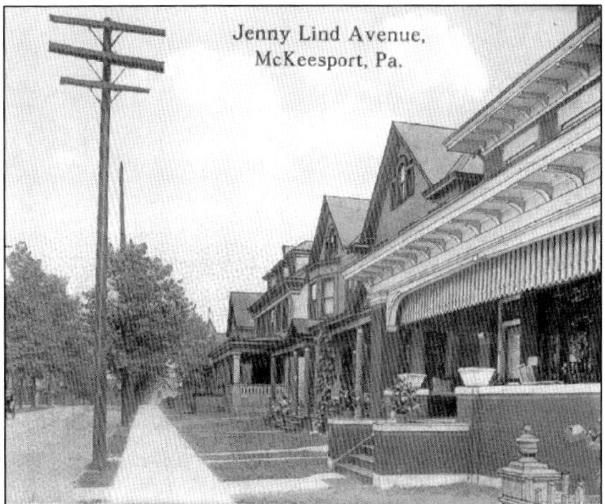

Jenny Lind Street was named after the famous Swedish singer. She was promoted by P.T. Barnum and was so popular that during a concert in Pittsburgh, those who could not get tickets caused a riot, and Lind had to be evacuated from the building. Developers named this street Jenny Lind to entice new Scandinavian immigrants to buy houses there. (Courtesy of Chuck Jarrell.)

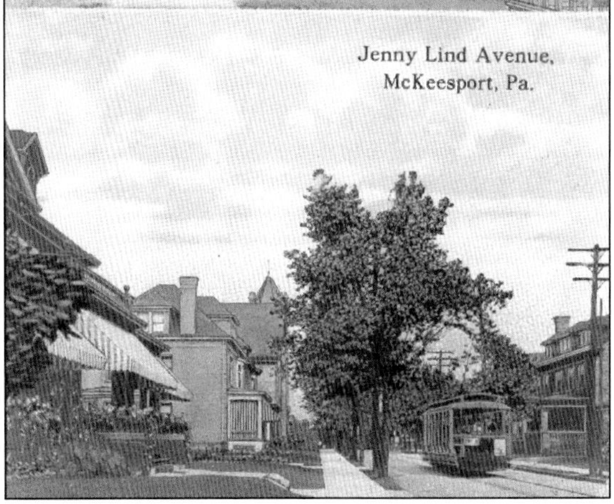

In this view at the corner of Union and Jenny Lind Streets, the trolley track is visible on the right. Built by Citizens Passenger Railway Company in 1892, this single-track trolley line extended from downtown to Rogena Street at the southern end of Jenny Lind Street. (Courtesy of Leonard Chemsak.)

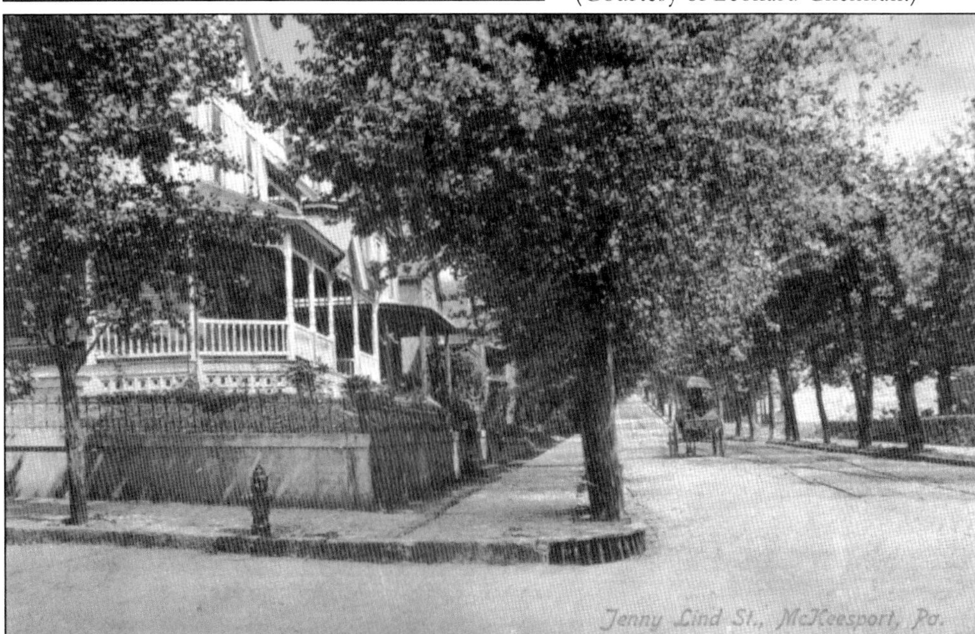

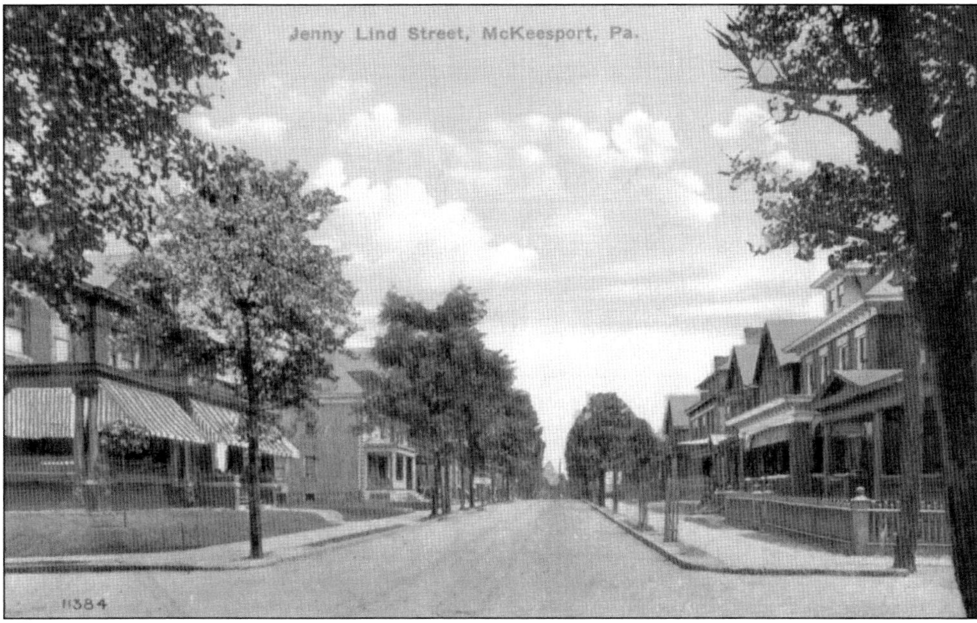

This view from the corner of Federal and Jenny Lind Streets includes the Elisha P. Douglass residence (on the left, with the striped awnings). Douglass was a prominent McKeesport attorney. Some of the more substantial homes built during this prosperous era in McKeesport are visible in this image. (Courtesy of Andrea [Luketic] Cartwright.)

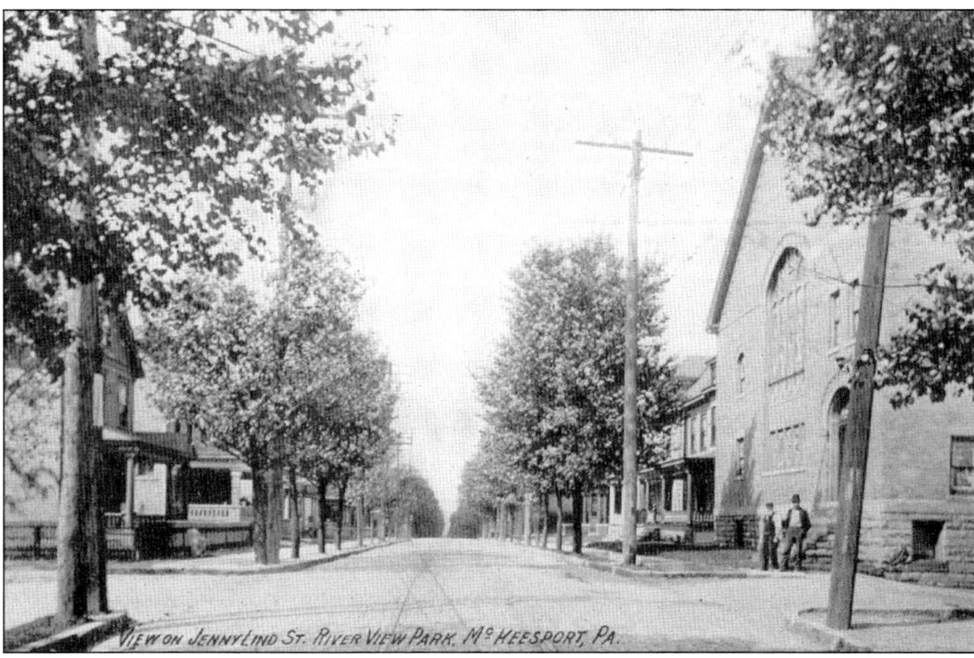

This part of town was predominantly Swedish. The First Swedish Evangelical Church (right), dedicated in 1907, was built to meet the religious needs of that growing ethnic population. It stood at the corner of Butler and Jenny Lind Streets. (Courtesy of Chuck Jarrell.)

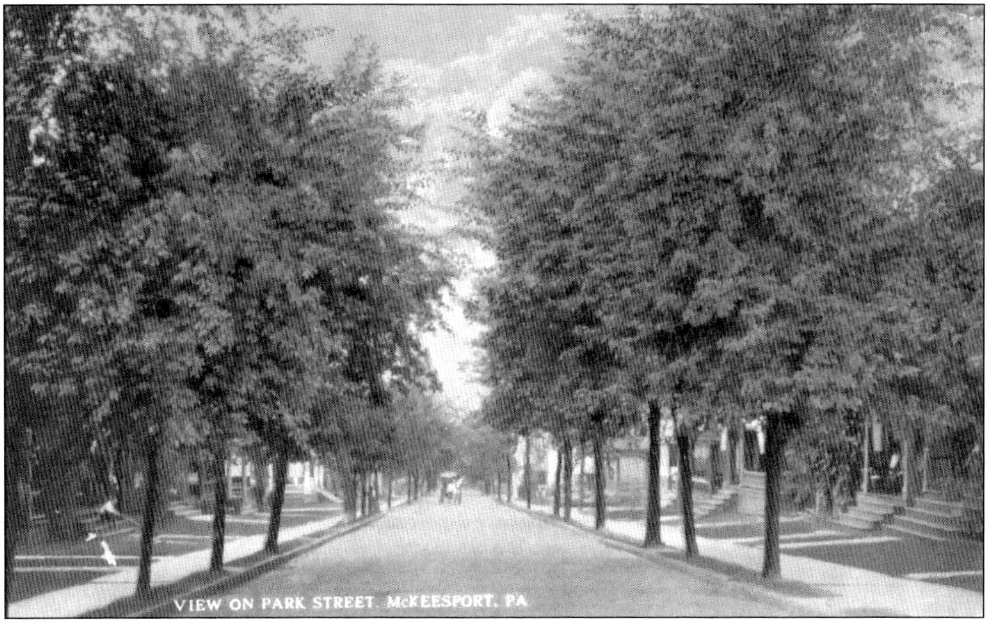

The East Park development was planned by James Evans on his family's land. Beginning in 1888, roads were laid out and houses were built there through the early 1900s. Land was set aside in the development for a community park. (Courtesy of Andrea [Luketic] Cartwright.)

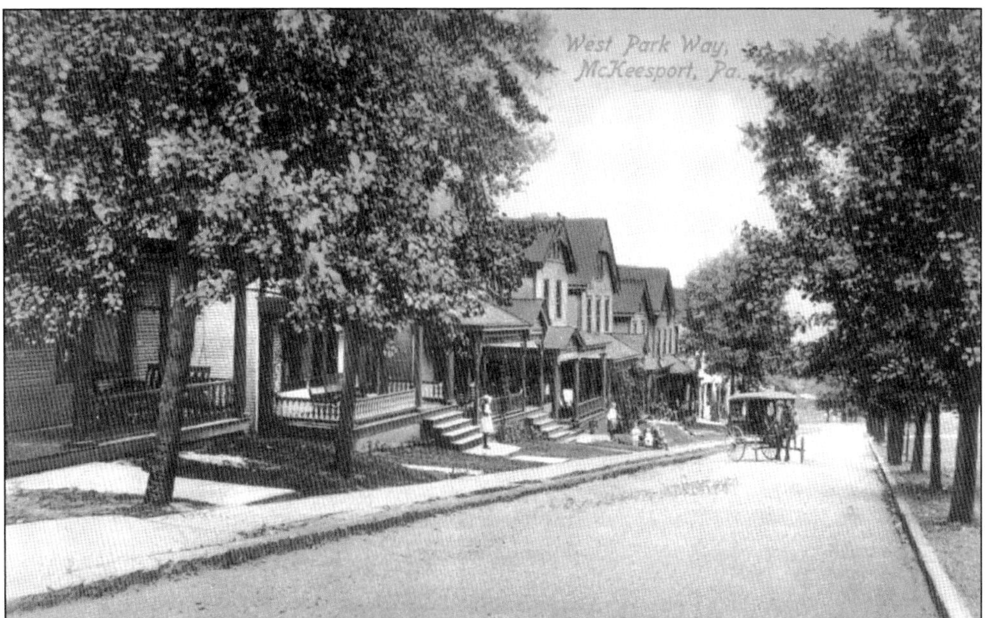

West Park Way, part of the East Park development, bordered the community park. This image was taken from the corner of Colfax Avenue and West Park Way, looking north. Expansion of National Tube into the old Bowery District spurred residential development in this eastern part of the city. (Courtesy of Andrea [Luketic] Cartwright.)

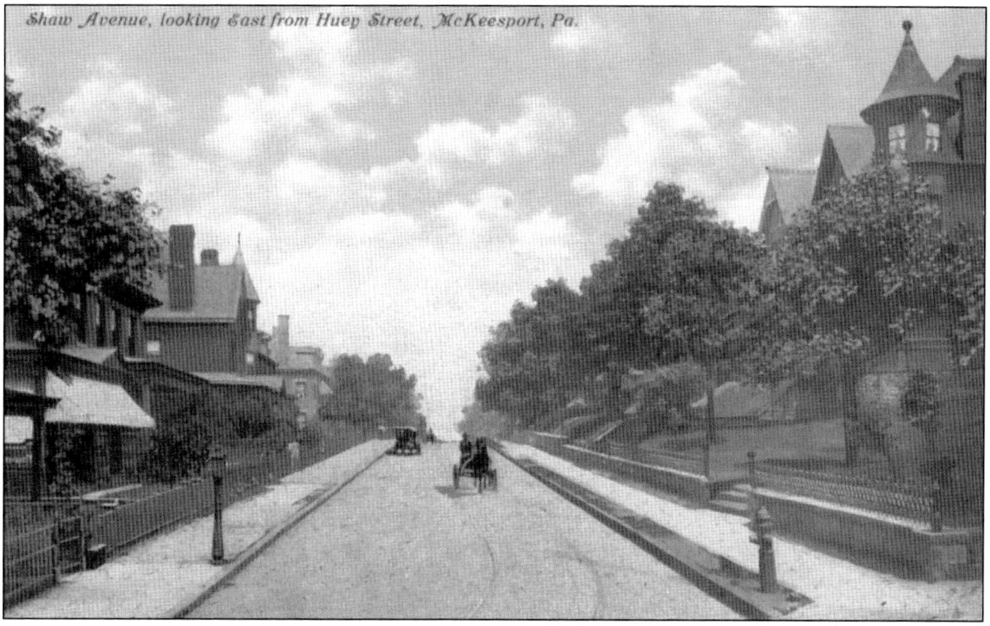

Shaw Avenue was originally Shaw's Lane. It ran through the property of Robert Shaw, who operated a tannery near the corner of Huey Street. Seen here, the 600 block of Shaw Avenue developed during the building boom of the early to mid-1890s. The Citizens Railway Company track ran to Union Avenue and then to Versailles Avenue.

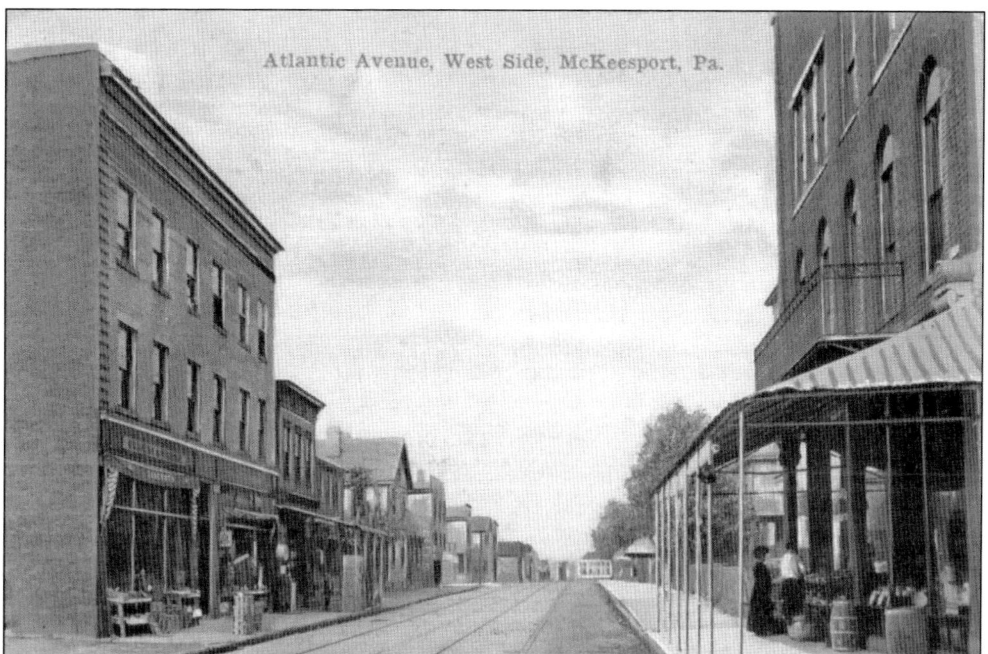

Atlantic Avenue was in Reynoldton, a borough chartered in 1886 and then annexed to McKeesport in 1898 as the 10th Ward. Looking east from the corner of Dale Street, the Gross Building (right) was erected in 1893 and housed a grocery store. Rodgers and Vincents Dry Goods (left) was built in 1905. (Courtesy of Leonard Chemsak.)

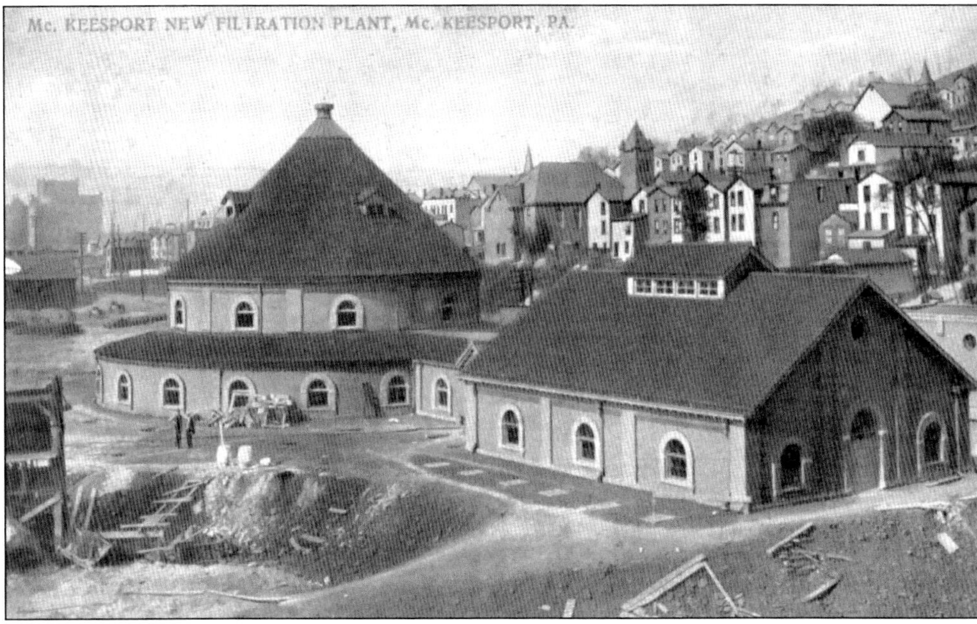

On October 11, 1908, a new water-processing plant opened in McKeesport. The round building was used for municipal water softening, and the rectangular building was used for water filtration. Designed by Alexander Potter, the water softening building was described as resembling an early Christian round church. Prior to the construction of this facility, numerous waterborne diseases were prevalent throughout the city. (Courtesy of Leonard Chemsak.)

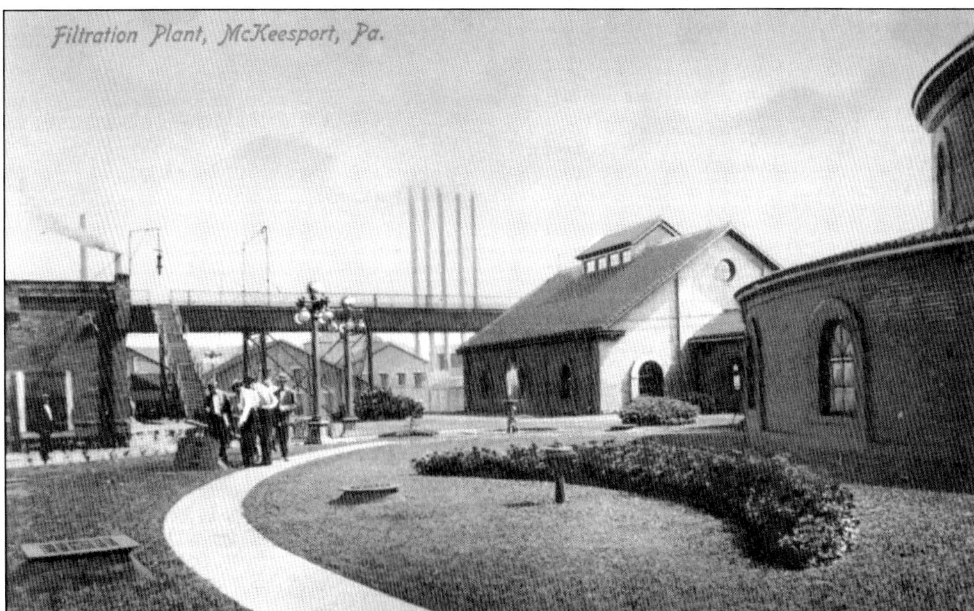

The new water filtration plant was built along the Youghiogheny riverbank north of the Fifteenth Avenue Bridge. This replaced an earlier water plant. McKeesport went from having the worst water in the country, according to a US Geological Survey, to having what McKeesporters considered the finest water in the country. Cases of typhoid fever, which had been numerous, virtually disappeared after this plant was built. (Courtesy of Chuck Jarrell.)

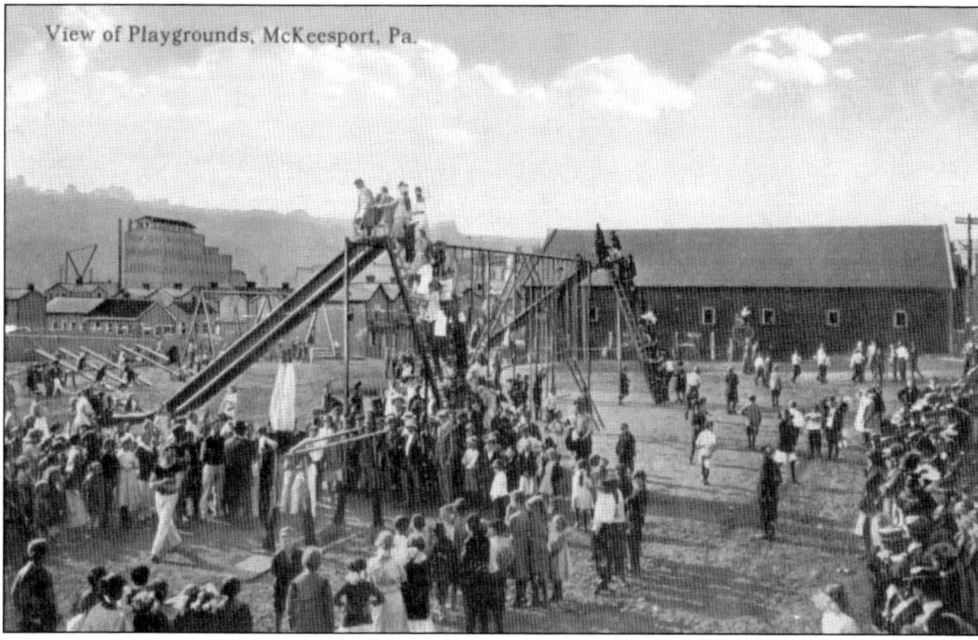

Between the filtration plant and the city stables (on the right) was a city playground. It was established around 1909 and frequented by the children living in the Third Ward. The tall building in the background on the left was part of the Thomas Moore Distillery, maker of Old Possum Hollow Whiskey. (Courtesy of Roger Reichenbach.)

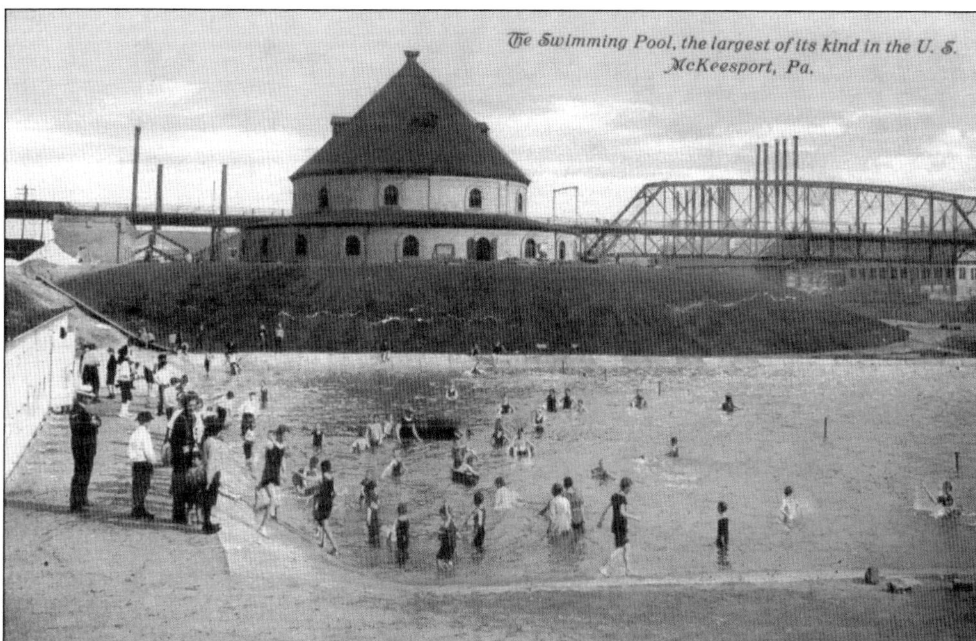

The municipal swimming pool was built next to the playground and filtration plant around 1909. At the time, it was boasted to be the largest artificial pool in the state, covering nearly an acre. The Fifteenth Avenue Bridge is seen in the background. (Courtesy of Chuck Jarrell.)

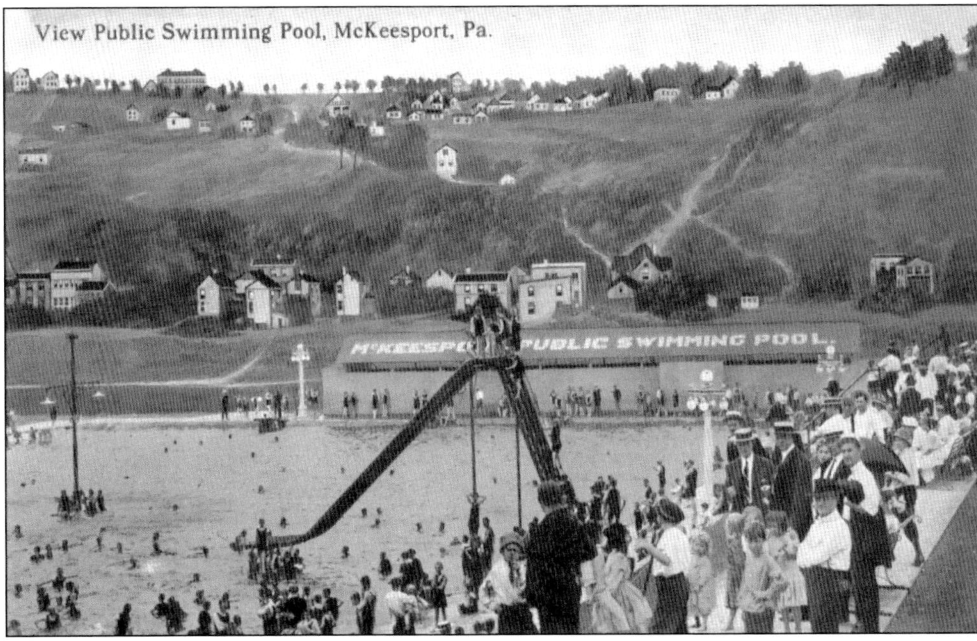

This view, looking southwest across the river, shows the bathhouse. In the distance, across the Youghiogheny River, the borough of Port Vue is visible. The section of Port Vue along the riverbank was nicknamed "Merry England." (Courtesy of Leonard Chemsak.)

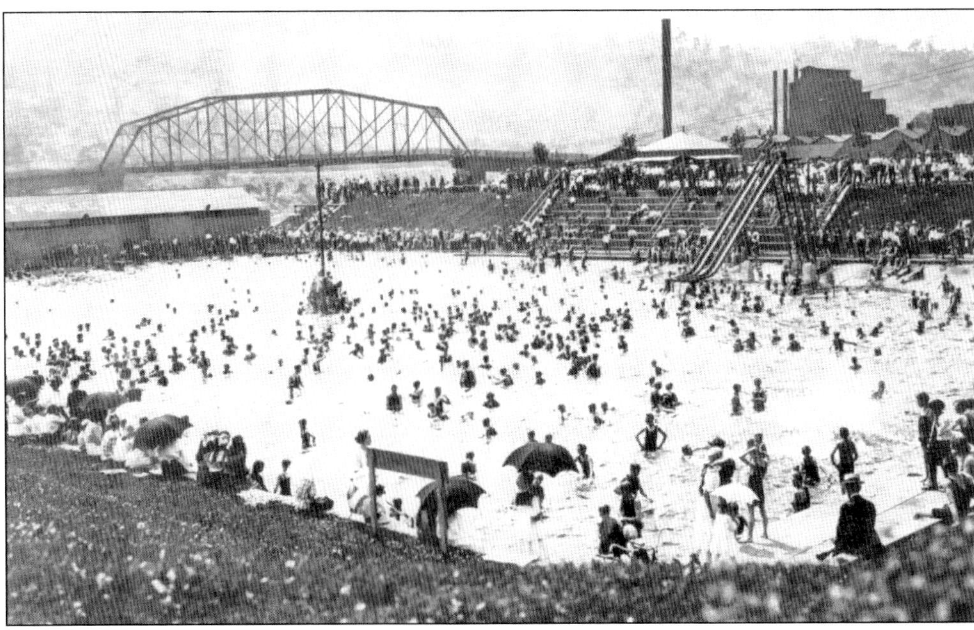

The Thirteenth Avenue Bridge is seen in this view, along with the distillery in the background to the right. The swimming pool contained more than one million gallons of treated water that was continually replenished from the filtration plant.

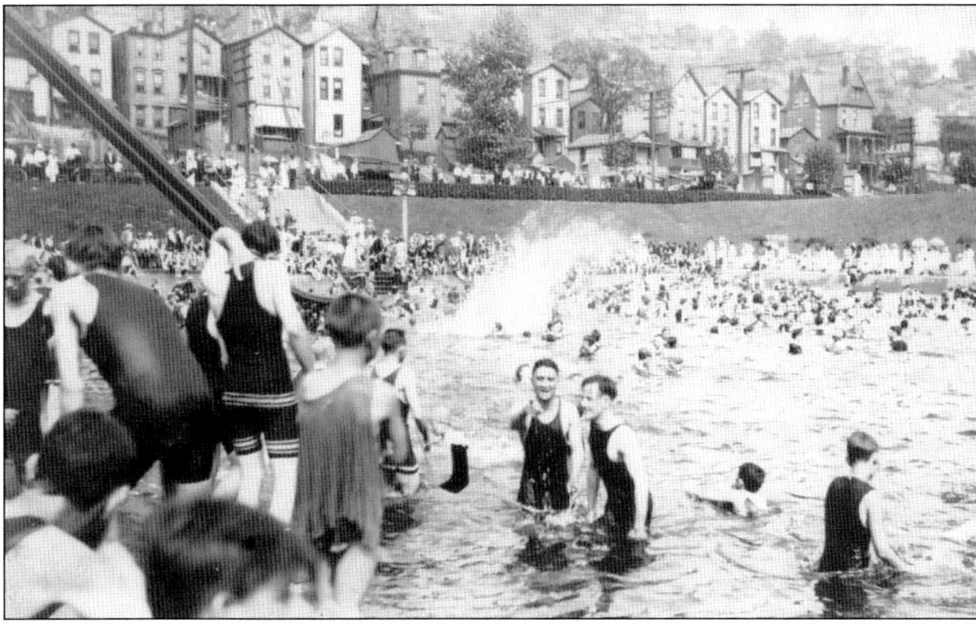

The building of the pool, under the supervision of the chamber of commerce, was made possible by donations of money and materials from local businessmen. To the left is the pool slide, and in the background are the houses along the 1400 block of Walnut Street. (Courtesy of Roger Reichenbach.)

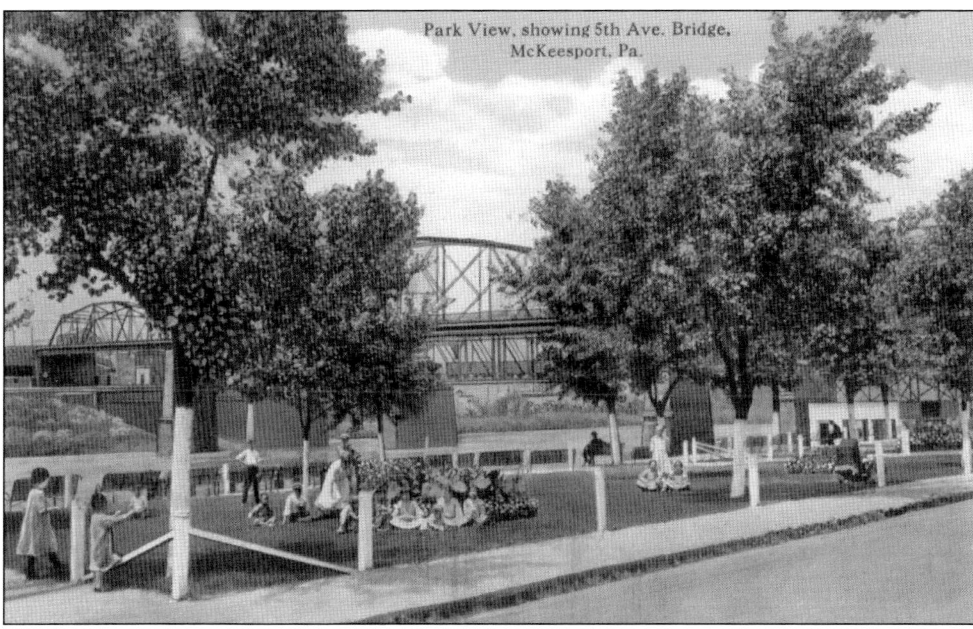

The park along the Youghiogheny riverbank, between Fifth and Ninth Avenues, is seen here. In 1908, the Chamber of Commerce Playground opened in this park. The old Fifth Avenue Bridge is in the background. (Courtesy of Chuck Jarrell.)

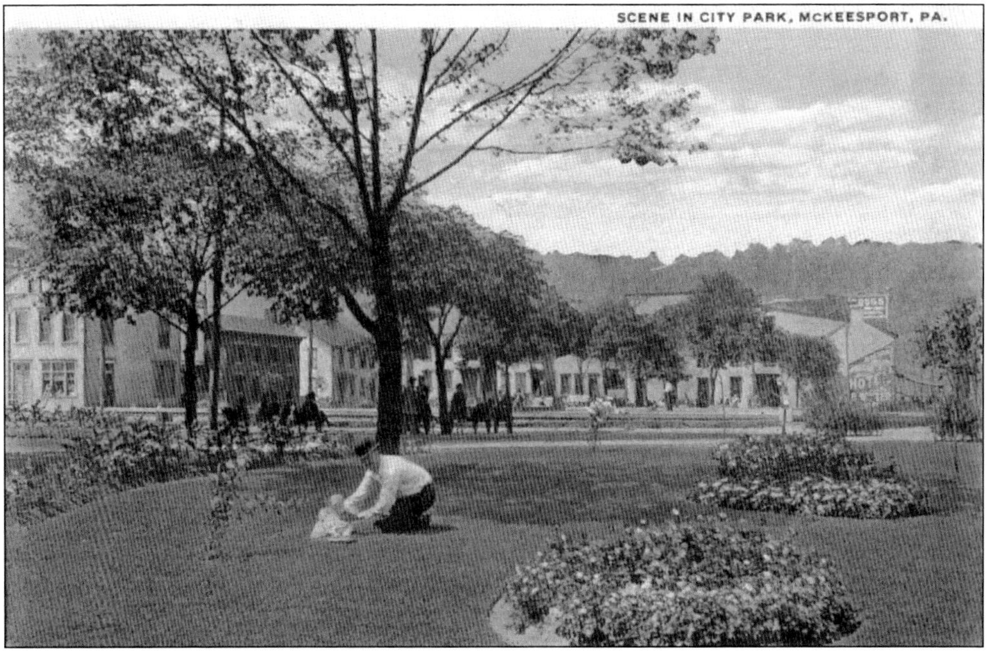

The southwest section of Diamond Park at Fourth Avenue and Market Street is pictured here. The Diamond was dedicated for public use by John McKee when he planned the town. Originally laid out as a park with four quadrants, by the mid-1890s, two of the four sections of the park were occupied by the Central Fire Station and the Market House.

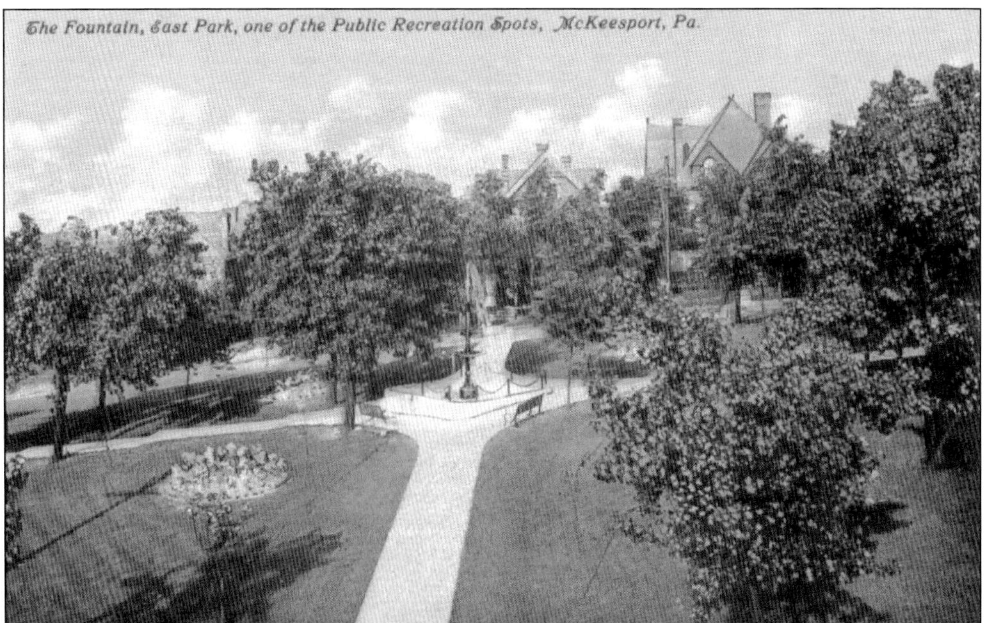

The East Park plan was developed by James Evans as part of his real estate promotion (see page 94). Located at the center of his housing development, it was first called East Park and is now known as North Park. It provided a space measuring 170 by 536 feet for public use and was publicized as having "one of the finest views in the valley."

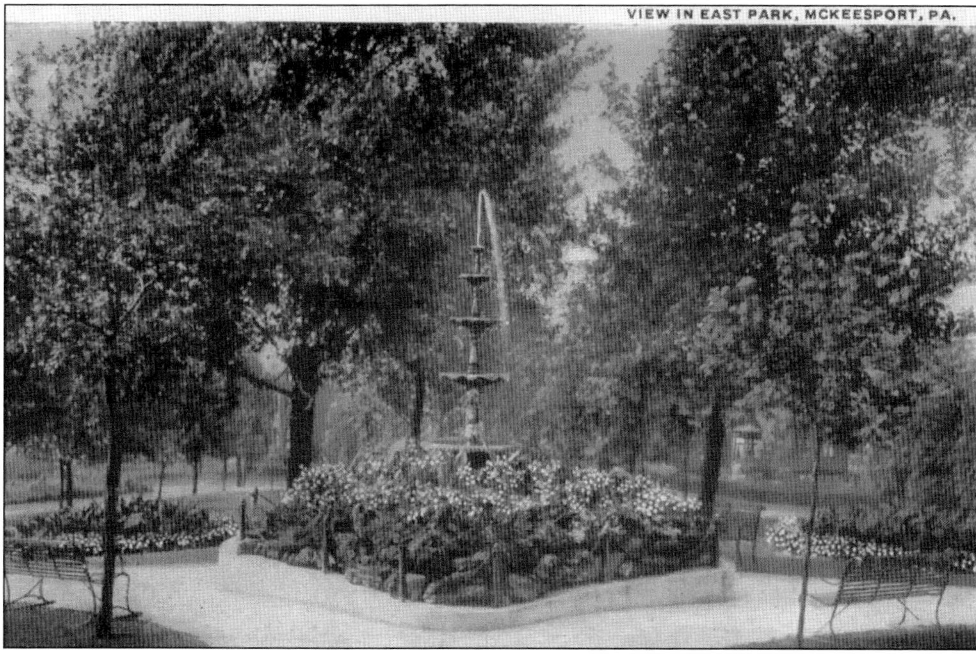

This fountain stood at the center of East Park, at the junction of its two sidewalks. Once developed, this park was donated to the city, which maintained the landscaping, providing a peaceful retreat for residents in the Sixth Ward. Some of the trees in the park were planted as memorials. (Courtesy of Leonard Chemsak.)

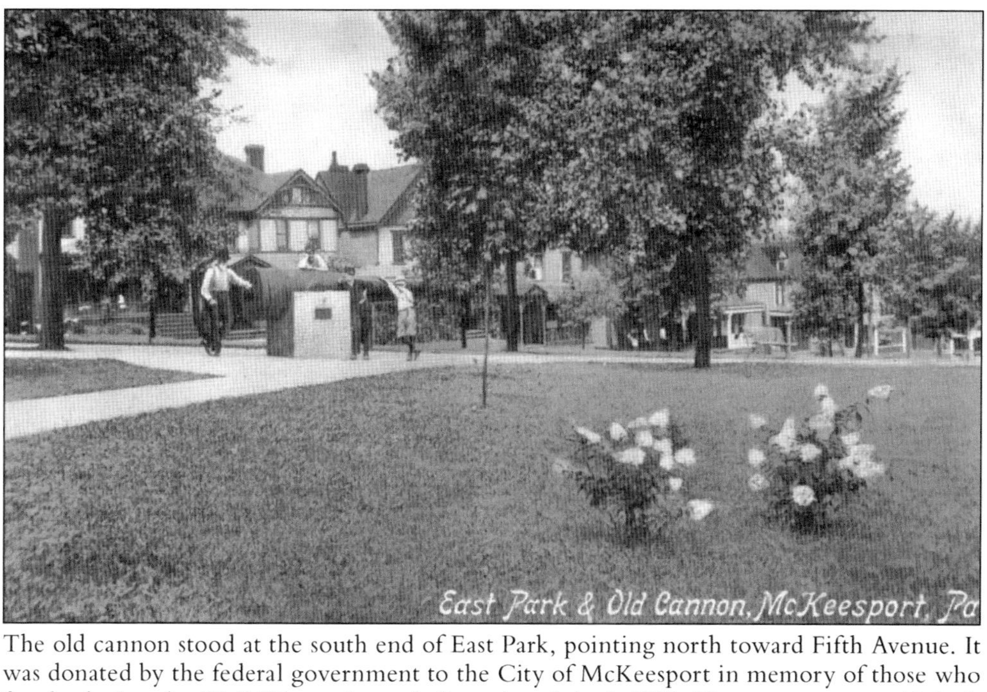

The old cannon stood at the south end of East Park, pointing north toward Fifth Avenue. It was donated by the federal government to the City of McKeesport in memory of those who fought during the Civil War and was dedicated on July 4, 1910. The cannon was a 10-inch Rodman gun dating from 1861 and weighed 15,500 pounds. (Courtesy of the Edith Greaves Barrowcliff collection.)

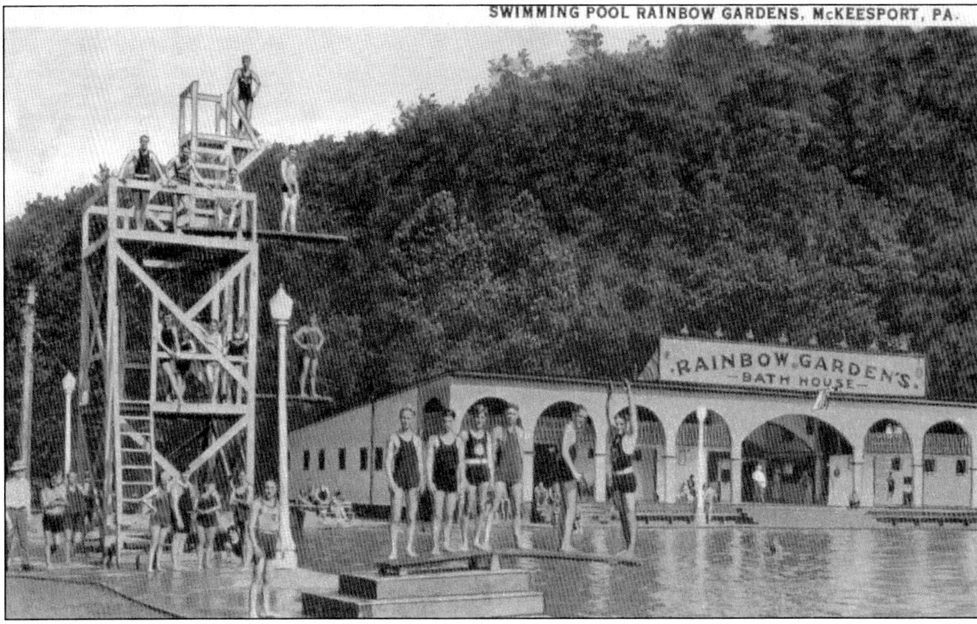

Rainbow Gardens was located just outside of McKeesport, at the northeast corner of Lincoln Way and Jack's Run Road, in what was then Versailles Township. Developed in 1926, the park had a swimming pool and bathhouse (pictured), a playground, picnic grounds, a dance hall, a miniature railroad, and a lake. McKeesporters could take the McKeesport-Irwin trolley line to get there.

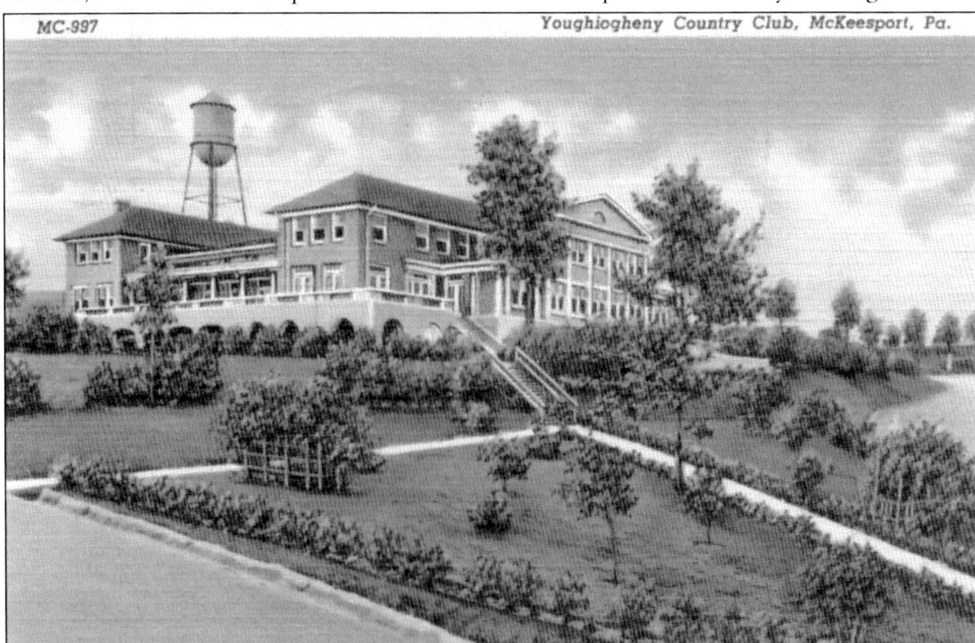

The Youghiogheny Country Club was also located just outside McKeesport, in Elizabeth Township on Greenock-Buena Vista Road. Founded by McKeesporters, the country club opened on May 30, 1911. The Col. William Douglass homestead became the clubhouse, and over the years, the original farmhouse was enclosed by the building seen here. The golf course originally had only nine holes, but it was expanded to 18 holes in 1922.

Eight

Olympia Park

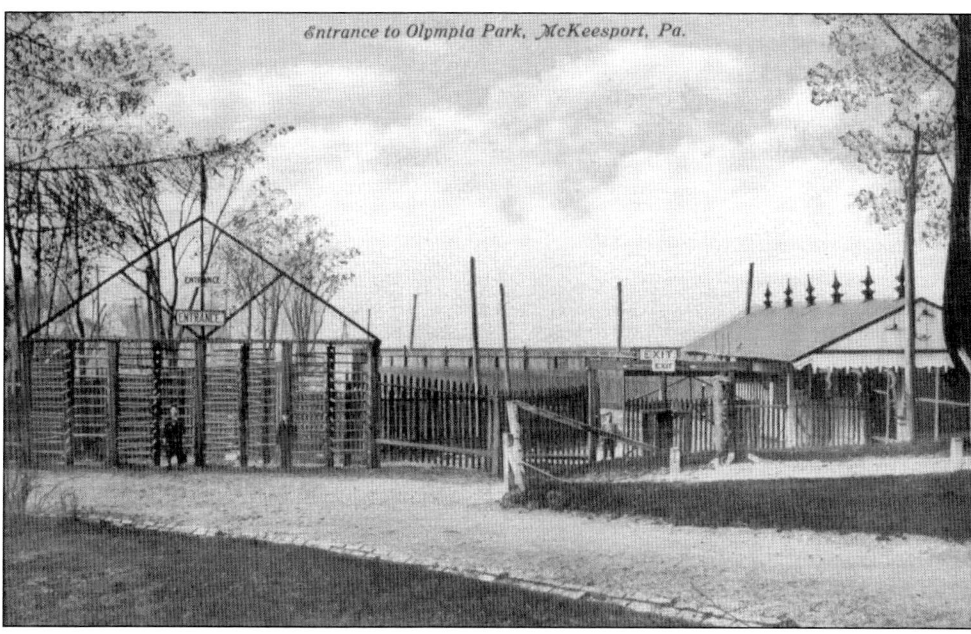

Olympia Park, located in Versailles Borough, was a popular recreational destination for many McKeesporters. In 1901, the Pittsburgh, McKeesport & Connellsville Railway Company purchased the Bissell farm to create this amusement park along its trolley line. This image includes the turnstiles at the main entrance, located off Walnut Street. (Courtesy of Leonard Chemsak.)

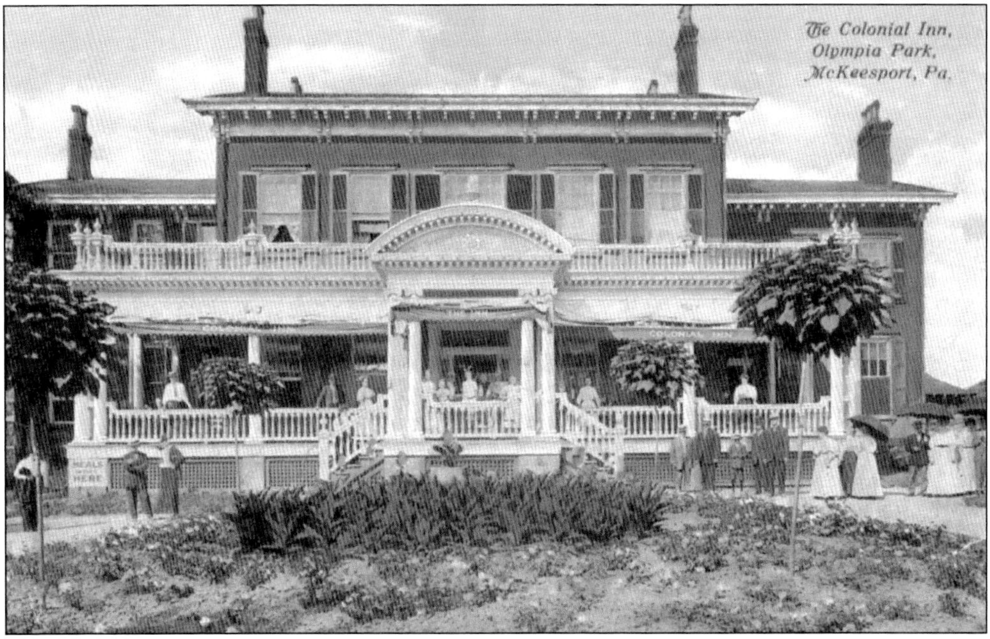

Olympia Park was originally part of a grant of 515 acres that was given to Fauntley Muse by the Commonwealth of Pennsylvania in the late 1700s. The Muse family sold 76 acres to George Bayard, who built the Colonial Inn in 1857 from brick made on the property. Later, the house was sold to William Bissell.

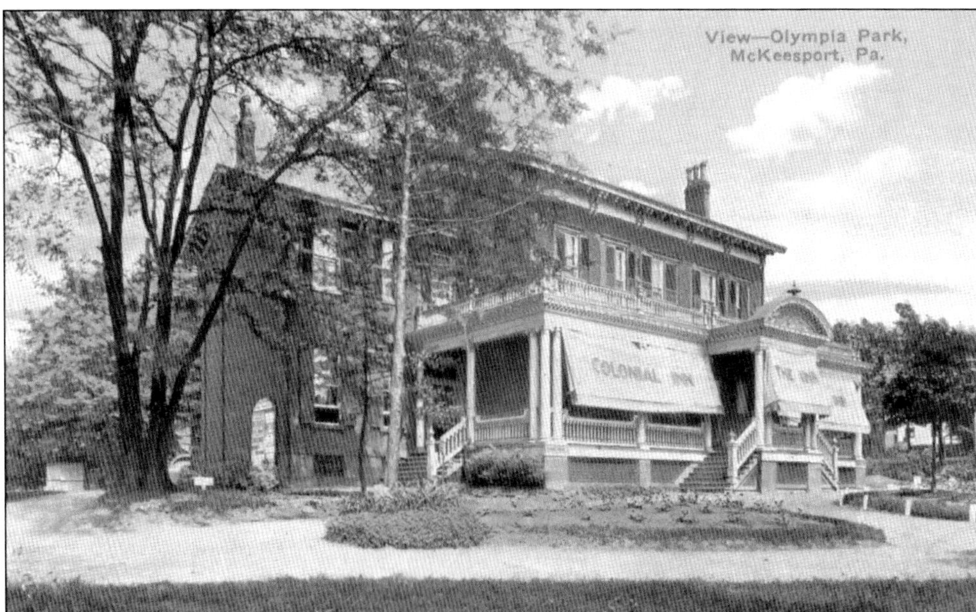

Prior to its purchase by the trolley company, the National Tube Works Company used the Colonial Inn as a club for company officials and guests. As the centerpiece of Olympia Park, the Colonial Inn was used as hotel and restaurant and as a residence for the park manager. (Courtesy of Leonard Chemsak.)

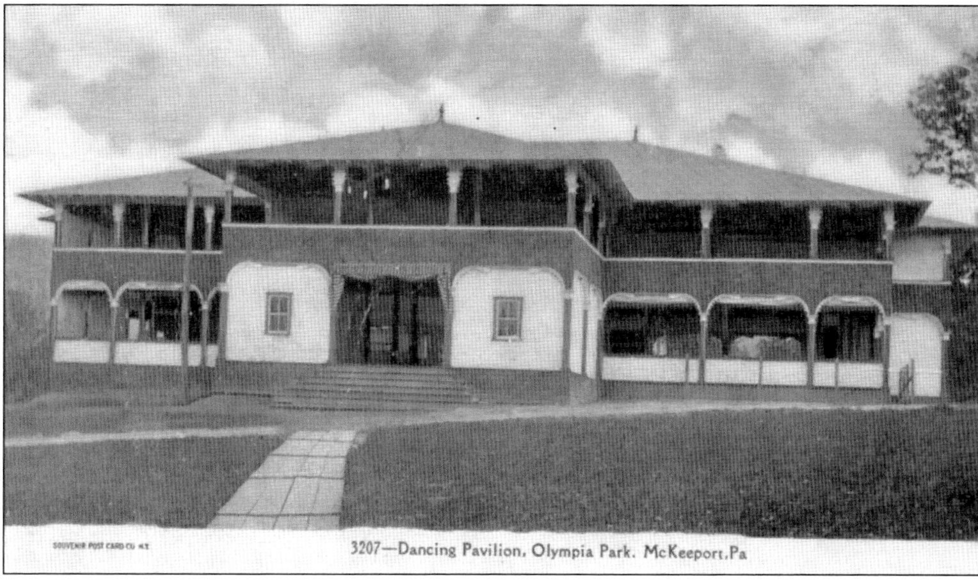

The dance pavilion was located at the southern end of Olympia Park. Local and touring bands and orchestras provided music for guests. The dance pavilion became a roller-skating rink around 1920, when a new dance hall was built.

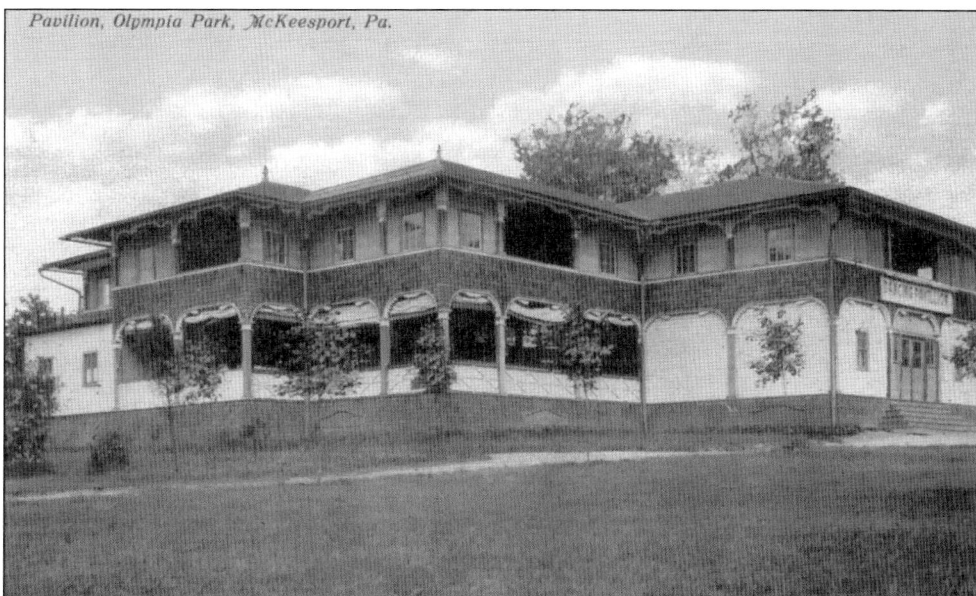

This is another view of the dance pavilion. In 1901, a contest was held by the trolley company to name the new park. Out of almost 15,000 responses, two people from McKeesport both suggested Olympia Park, and they split the $25 prize. (Courtesy of Chuck Jarrell.)

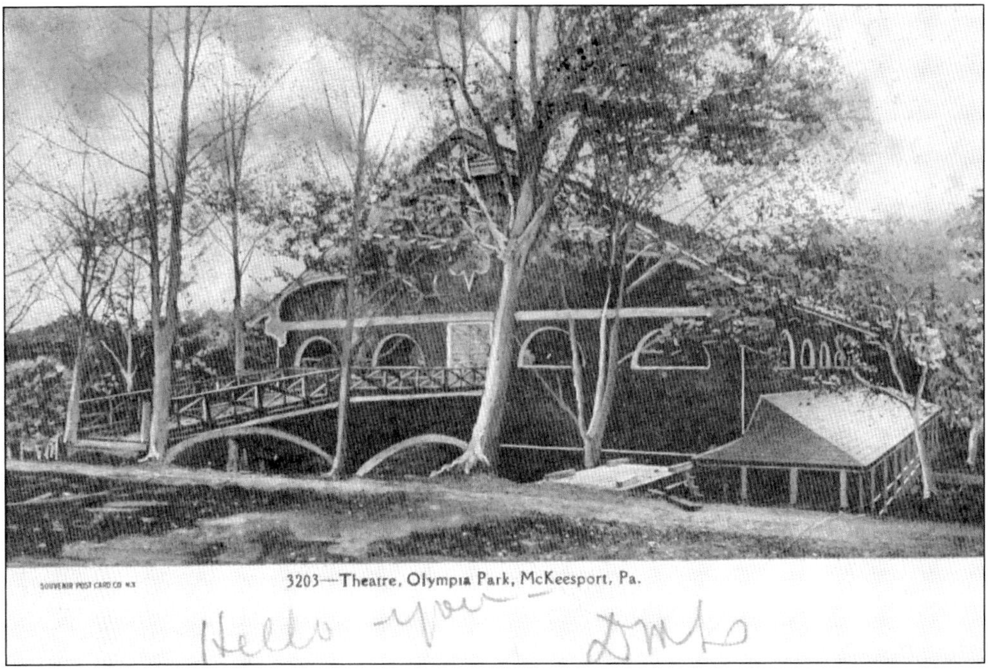

The theater at Olympia Park seated 2,500. John P. Harris was retained to provide the entertainment, including vaudeville and other theatrical performances, and by 1903, he was managing the entire park. The theater was replaced by a dance hall in the early 1920s.

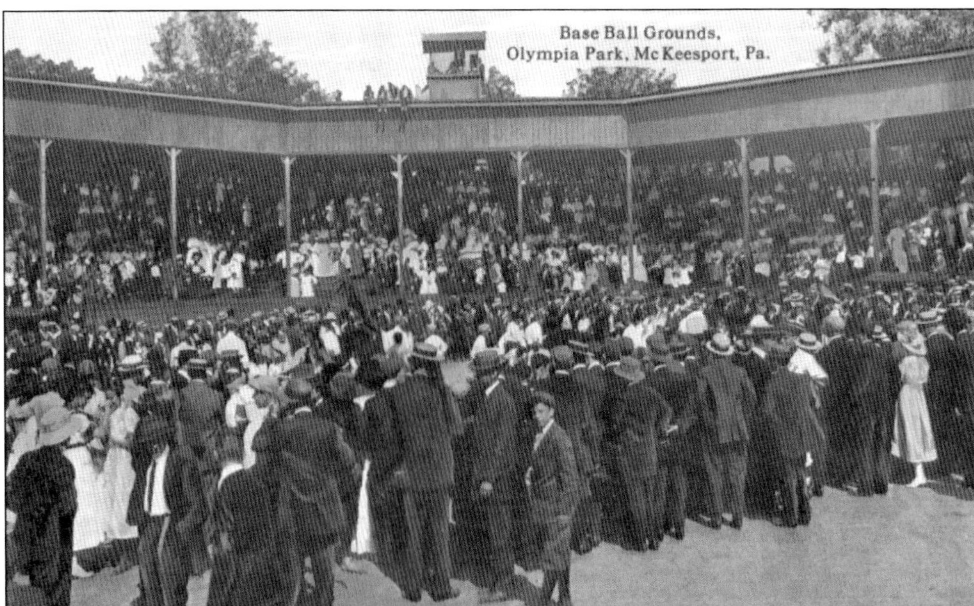

The baseball grounds seen here were to the north of the main entrance. The grandstand seated 1,000 people. In 1925, the field was relocated to the lakeside to make room for a parking lot. (Courtesy of Leonard Chemsak.)

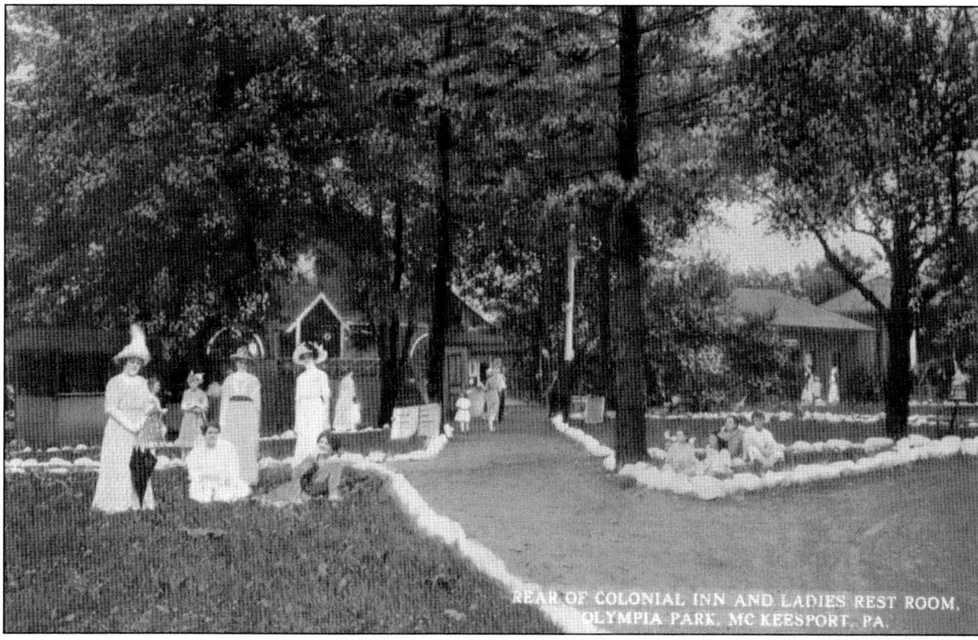

Many beautifully landscaped pathways led through the park, including the walkways pictured here, which were located behind the Colonial Inn near the ladies restroom. Olympia Park was billed as "Nature's Own Creation." (Courtesy of Leonard Chemsak.)

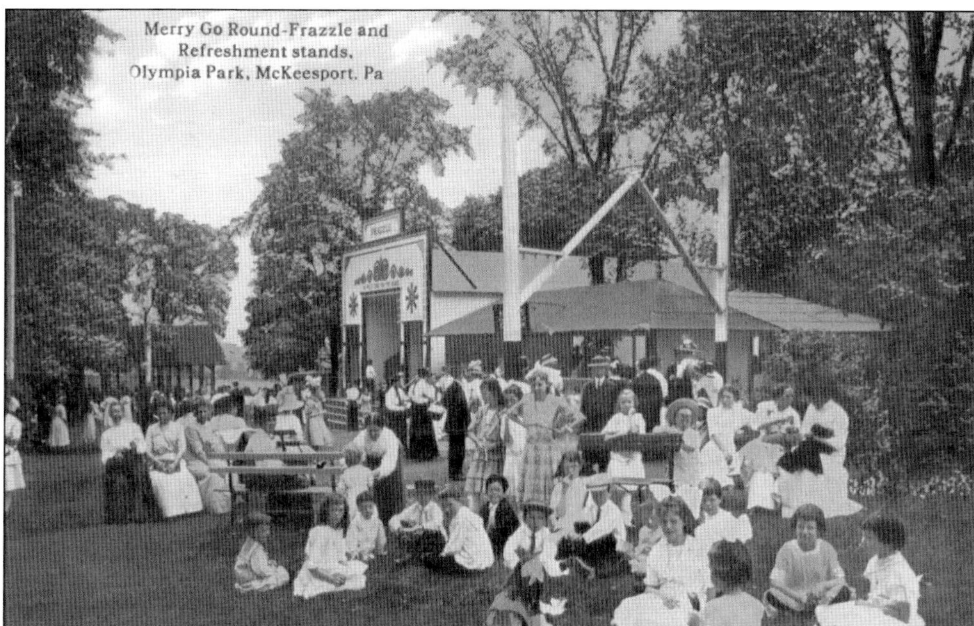

Only the edge of the merry-go-round can be seen in this image (left). This carousel was one of the original rides in the park. The Frazzle, in the building at the center, was replaced by the Whip.

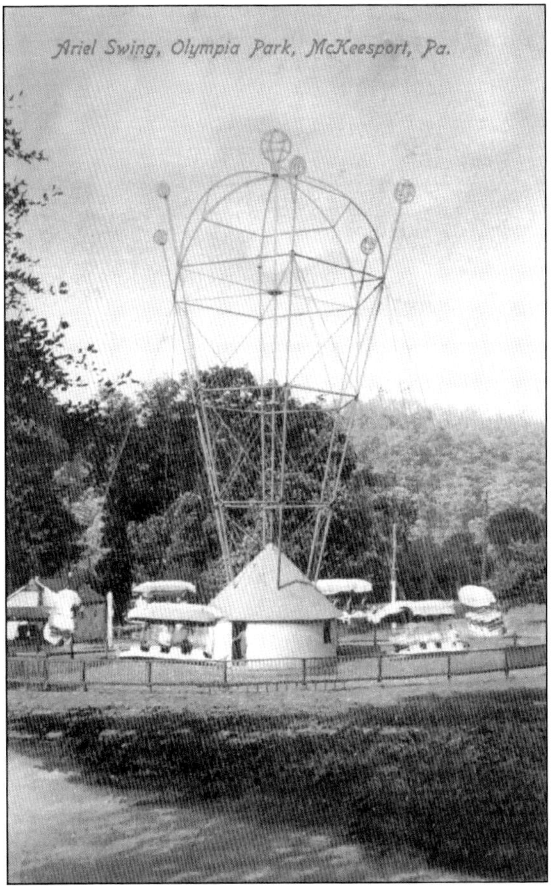

A staple ride at amusement parks, the Ariel Swing was another early attraction at Olympia Park. Six cars, each carrying six passengers, thrilled the riders with the sensation of flight, capitalizing on the exciting possibility of airborne travel that was brought on by the early flights of the Wright Brothers. (Courtesy of Chuck Jarrell.)

The miniature railway, another early attraction at the park, wound its way through the picnic grounds and past the rides in the park. The railway remained a popular ride up until the closing of the park in 1942. (Courtesy of Leonard Chemsak.)

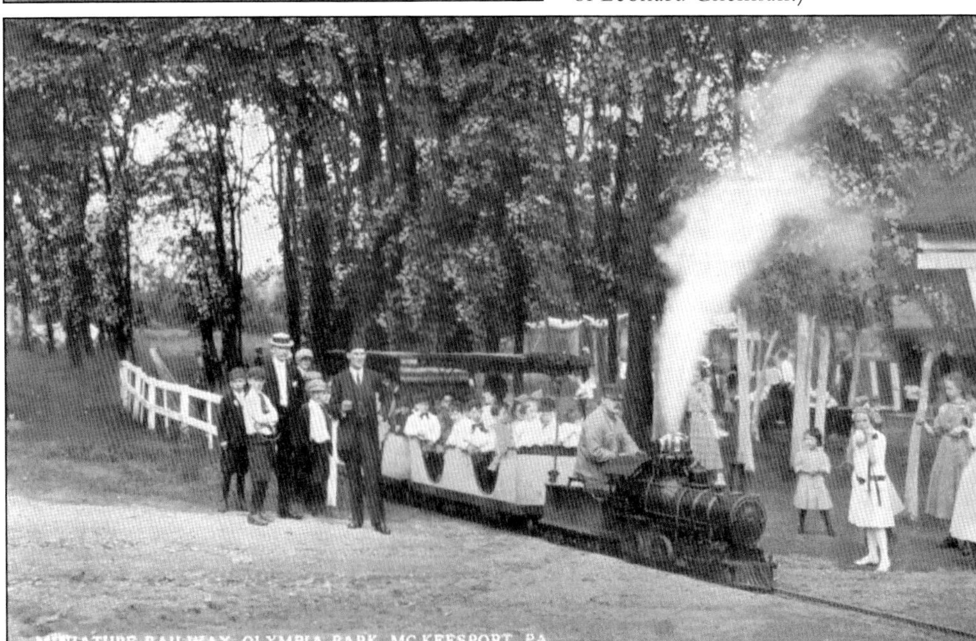

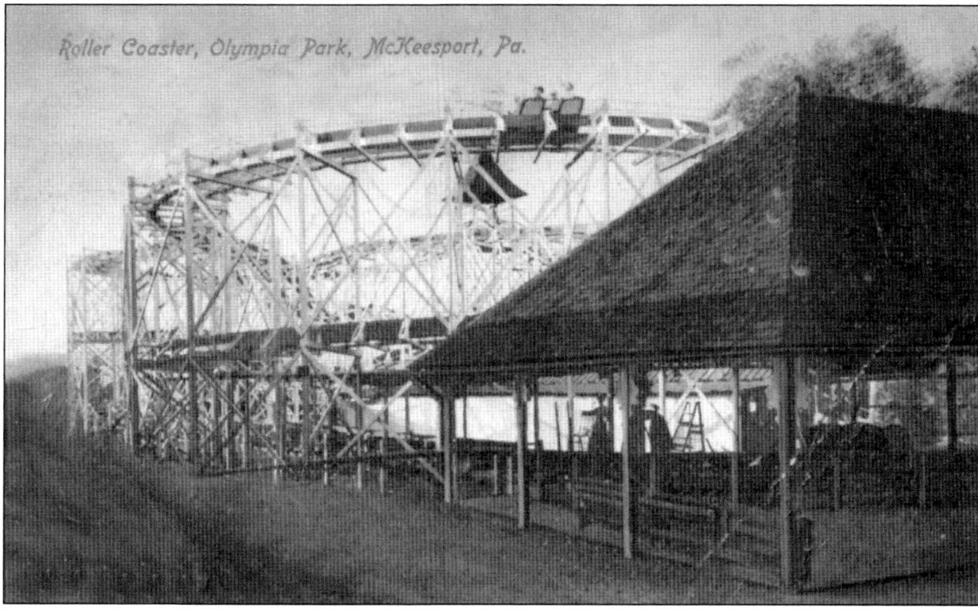

This figure eight–style roller coaster was one of the original rides in the park. It was located behind the first-base line of the ballpark. (Courtesy of Andrea [Luketic] Cartwright.)

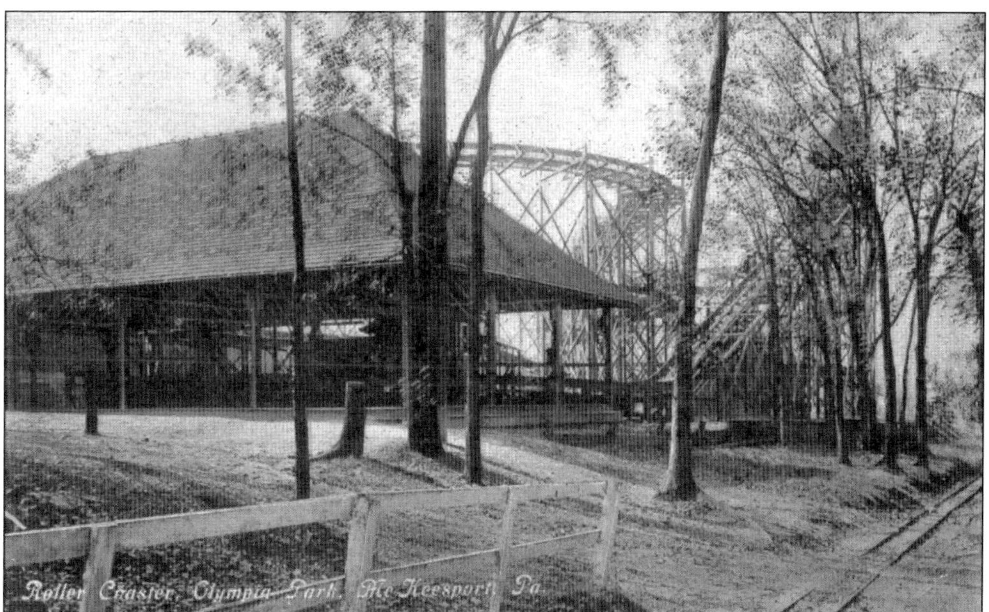

In 1921, this old roller coaster was replaced by a new one called the Leap Frog, which featured a "half-mile of dips." The track for the miniature railway can be seen in the bottom right corner.

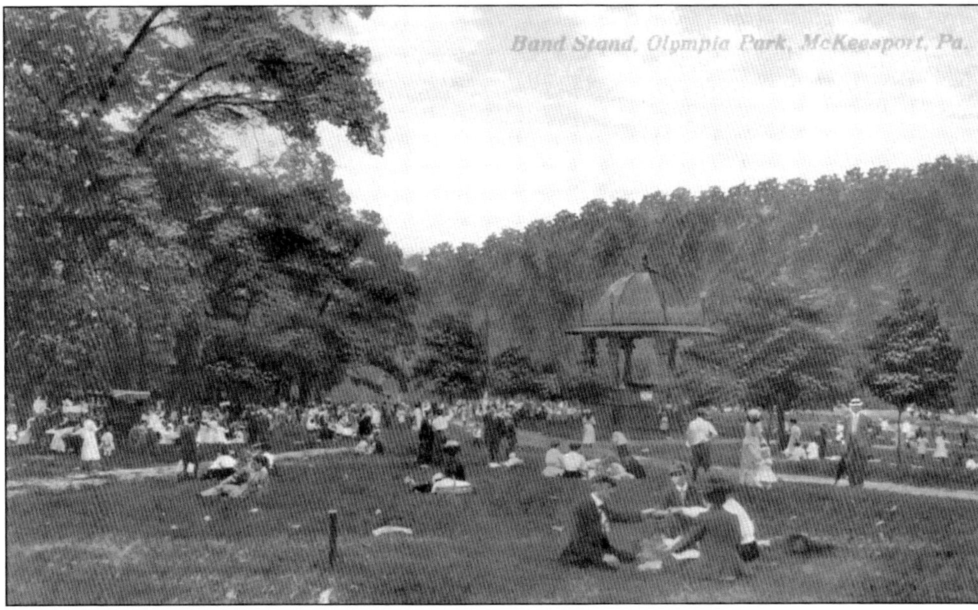

In 1901, the first concert given at Olympia Park was by the Electric Band of McKeesport, which was directed by Christian H. Wernke. The bandstand originally stood in front of the Colonial Inn, but in 1902, for the park's second season, is was moved to a large grove (pictured) at the rear of the theater in order to accommodate more people.

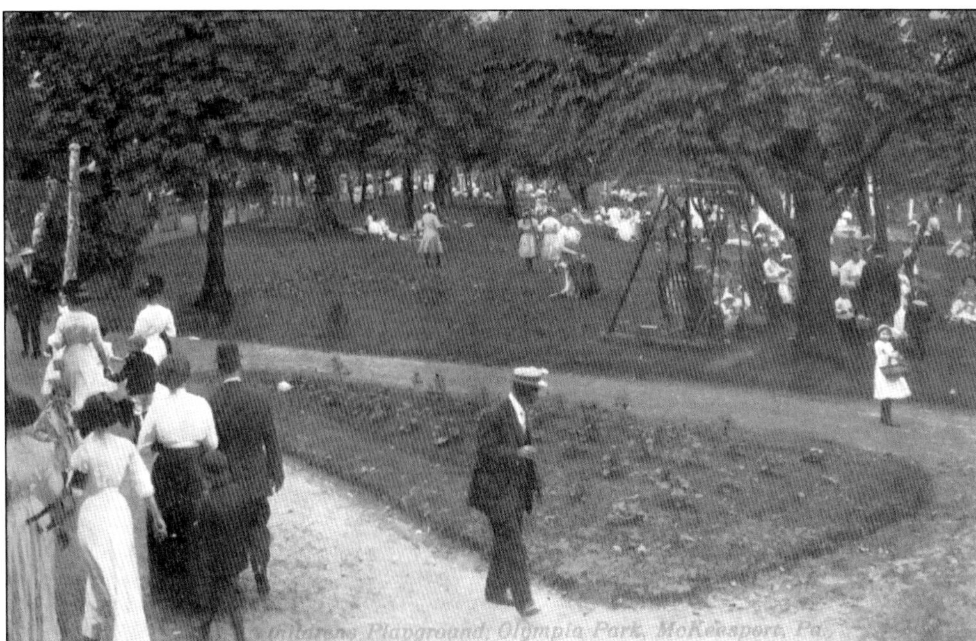

The children's playground was one of many picnic areas, scattered throughout the park, for families. This tree-shaded lawn provided space for the children to kick up their heels.

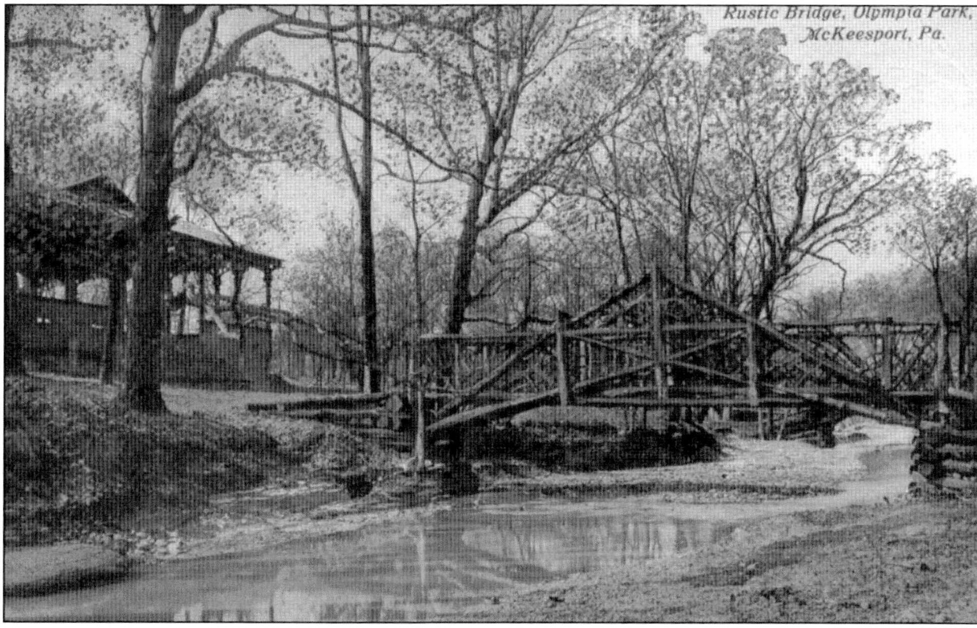

There were two rustic bridges in Olympia Park. This one was located at the southeast corner of the park, spanning Long Run, near one of the larger pavilions in the park.

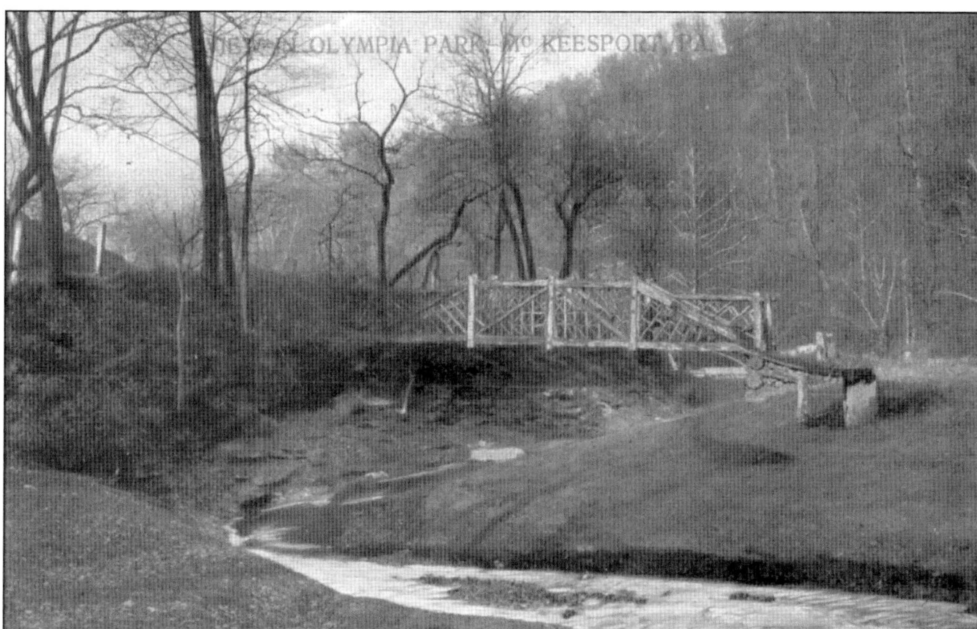

This second rustic bridge was located farther north along Long Run, connecting the island in the lake to the grove near the bandstand.

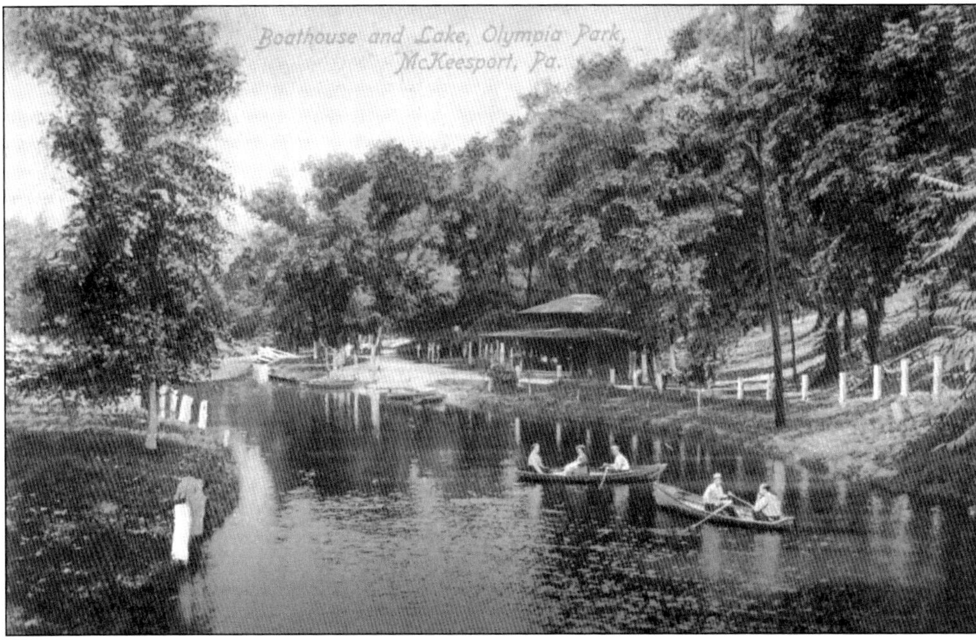

Lake Olympia was formed by the damming of Long Run, creating a picturesque location for boating. A boathouse was built for rowboat rentals. This photograph was taken from the footbridge in the previous postcard. (Courtesy of Leonard Chemsak.)

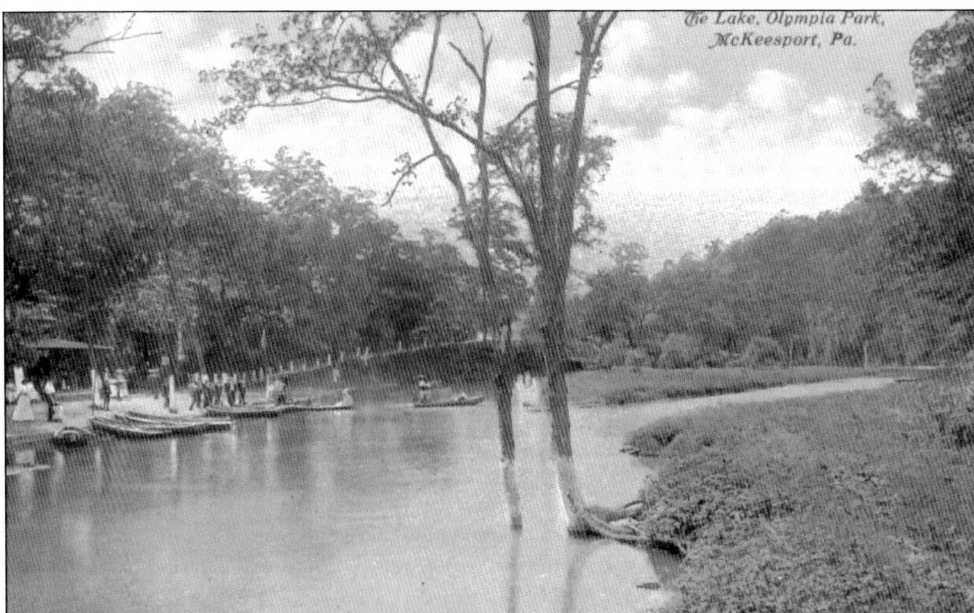

This view downstream includes the boathouse at the left and a line of boats awaiting rental. The tip of the island is also visible (center).

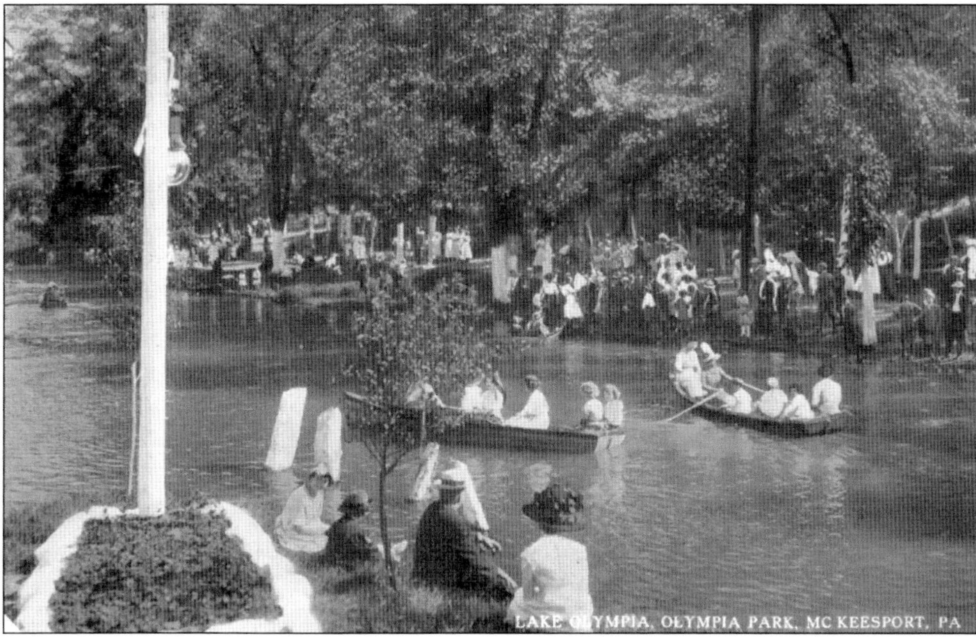

Above is a view of the lake taken from the tip of the island, and below is a view downstream. The annual school picnic day drew the largest attendance for the park. On June 6, 1905, school picnic day, a violent electrical storm occurred shortly before dusk and lasted through midnight. Power lines fell, and trolley service was interrupted. People took shelter in pavilions and standing streetcars. An additional show was put on at the theater to accommodate the stranded crowds. A special Baltimore & Ohio passenger train ran to the Versailles station to pick up some of the crowd, which caused a rush of thousands out of the park. Many people, including children, were stranded in the park overnight, as the streetcars did not resume operation until the next morning. (Both courtesy of Leonard Chemsak.)

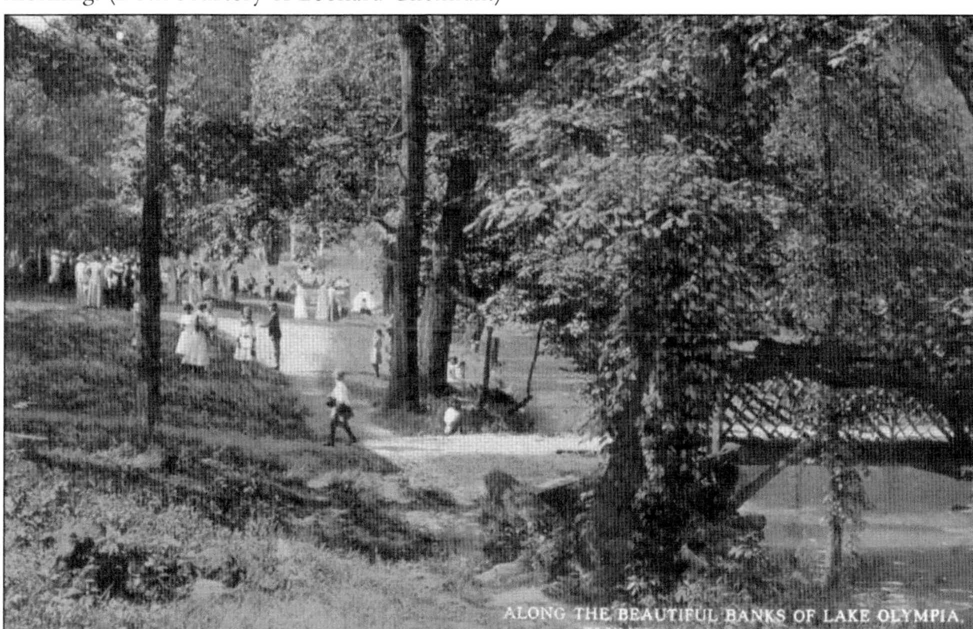

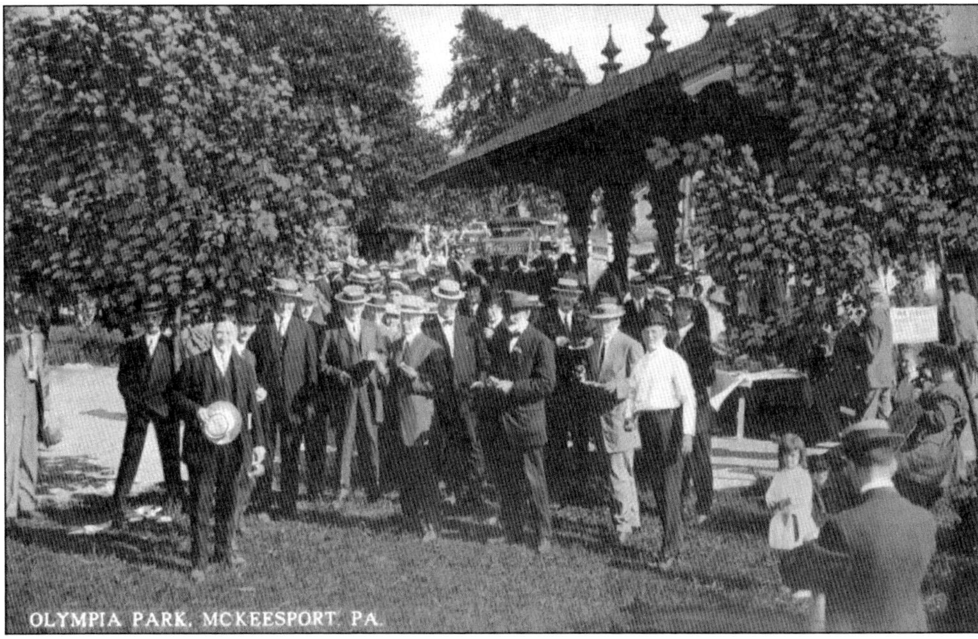

In this image is a group of men gathered at a pavilion for an ox roast. This photograph illustrates how fashion has changed. A day in the park consisted of more formal attire, and gentlemen were often seen wearing straw hats and three-piece suits, even in the heat of summer. (Courtesy of Leonard Chemsak.)

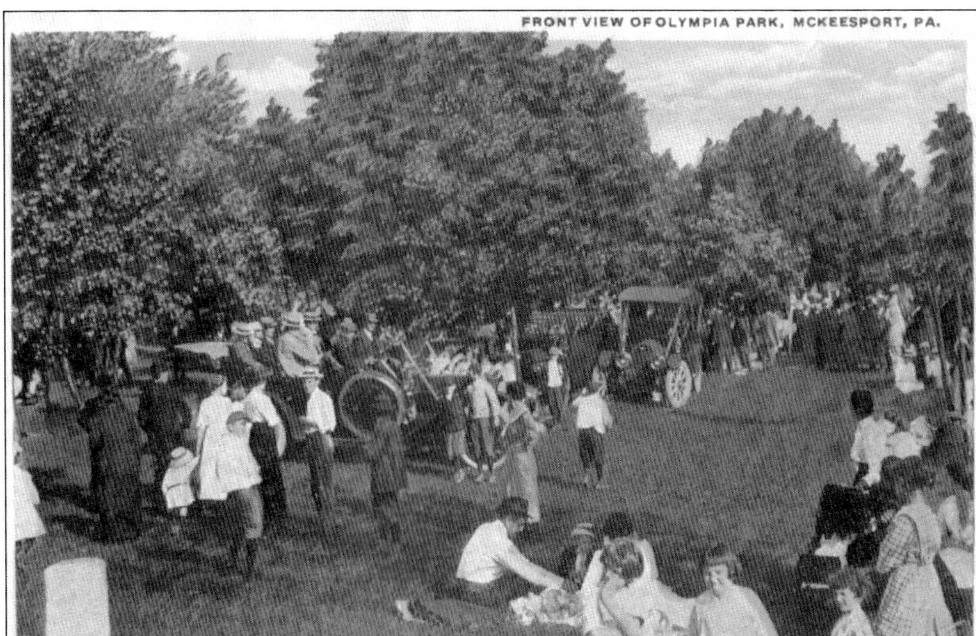

Though most park patrons arrived by trolley, Olympia Park also accommodated those who drove their own automobiles. These motorists parked in the grass until a parking lot was provided in the mid-1920s, located where the ball field originally stood. (Courtesy of Leonard Chemsak.)

Nine

EVENTS

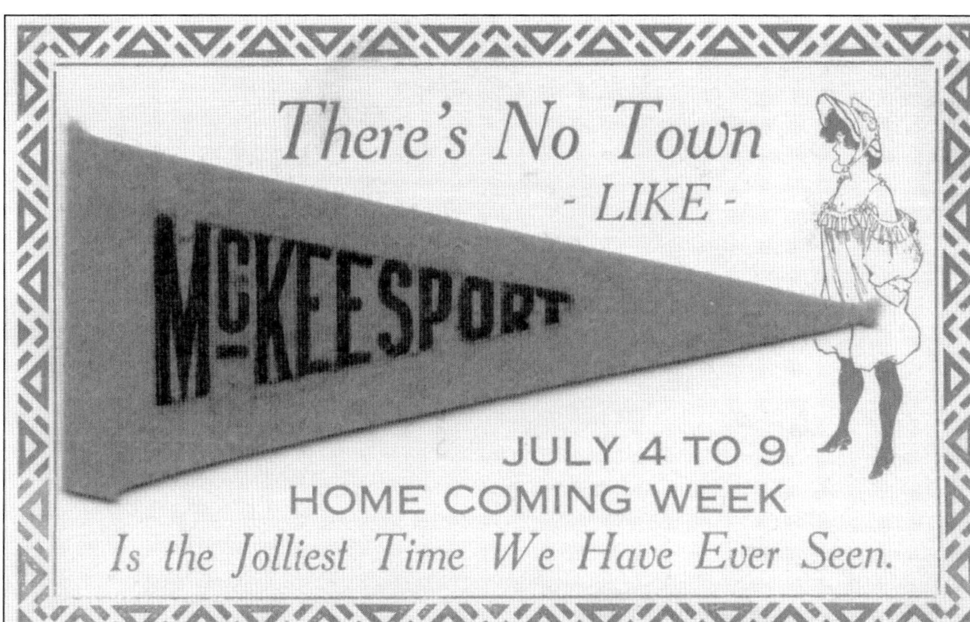

Four major events stood out during the golden era of the postcard: two major floods, one in 1907 and another in 1936; a natural gas boom from 1919 to 1925; and the Old Home Week celebration in 1910. The card seen here promoted the 1910 Old Home Week with "McKeesport" printed on a yellow felt pennant.

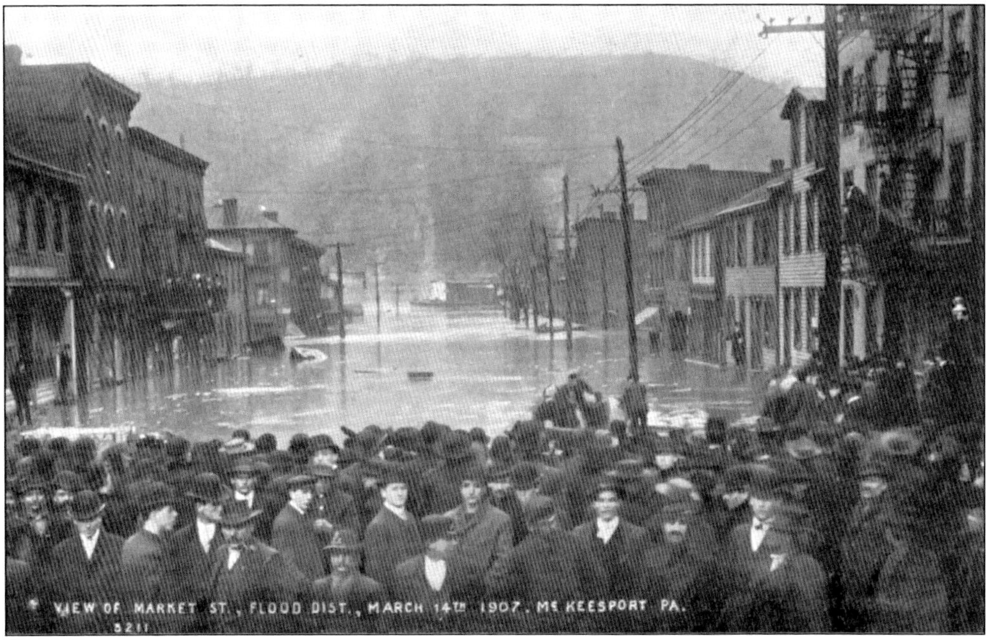

Looking north on Market Street, the effects of the March 14, 1907, flood can be seen. The water from the Monongahela River rose to over 34 feet, reaching as far as Third Street, where these spectators were gathered. The previous record was made in 1884, when the river crested at 33.7 feet.

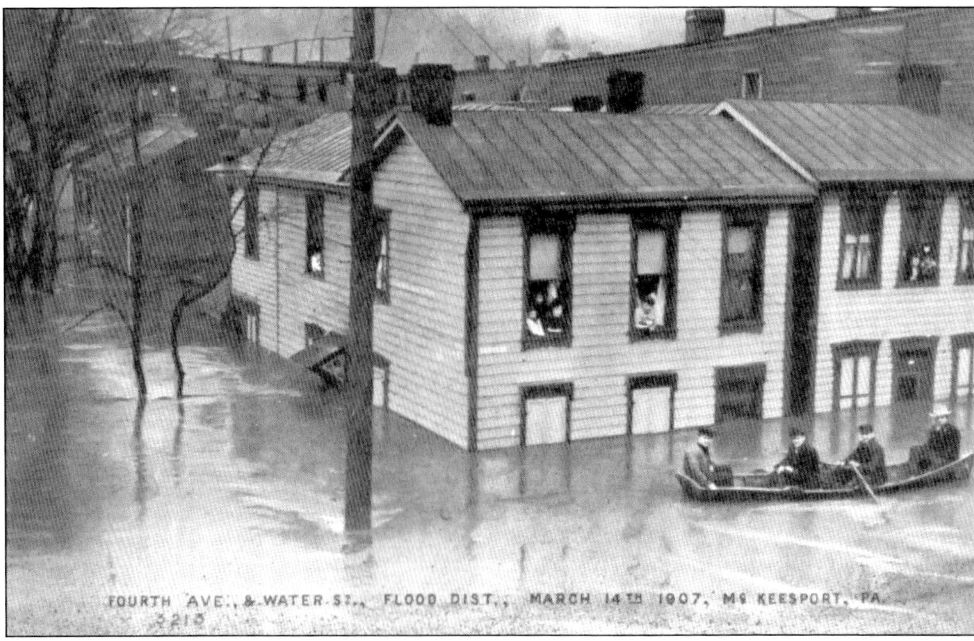

The houses at the northeast corner of Water Street and Fourth Avenue are pictured here. The water had completely flooded the first floors of this low-lying area. All major industries were shut down, and 19,000 men were temporarily out of work. The W. Dewees Woods Works was the first to be submerged. Some 800 houses were flooded, and more than 3,000 people were displaced. (Courtesy of Chuck Jarrell.)

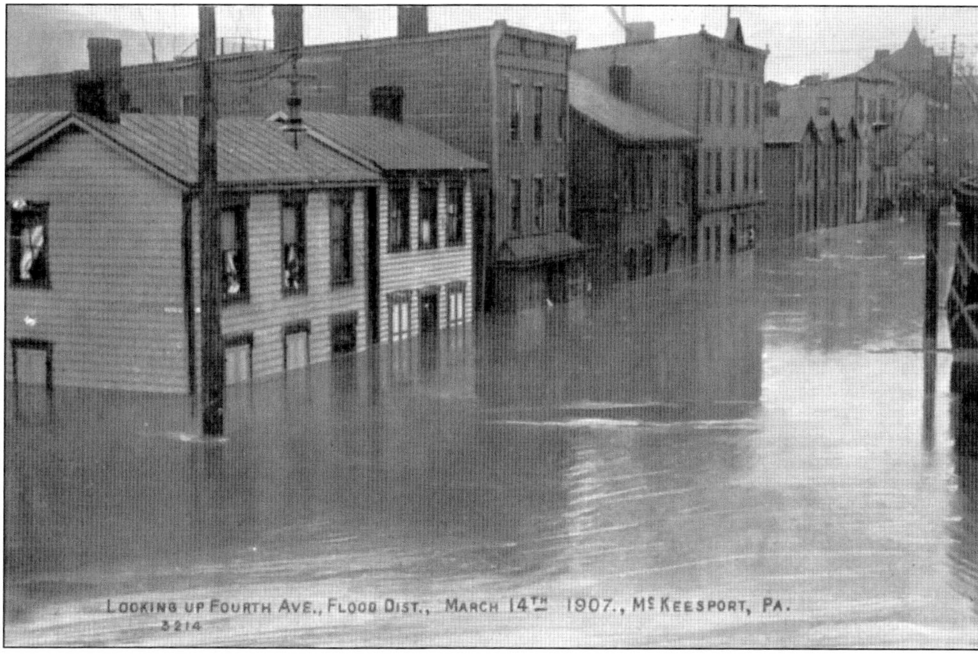

Looking east along Fourth Avenue from Water Street, the majority of the First Ward was inundated in the flood. In the Third Ward, a small fire broke out on Brick Alley, where fleeing residents neglected to turn off their gas lights. Two days later, a fire broke out in the Ruben Building, located at Fifth Avenue and Walnut Street. This blaze was caused by a gasoline explosion in the basement.

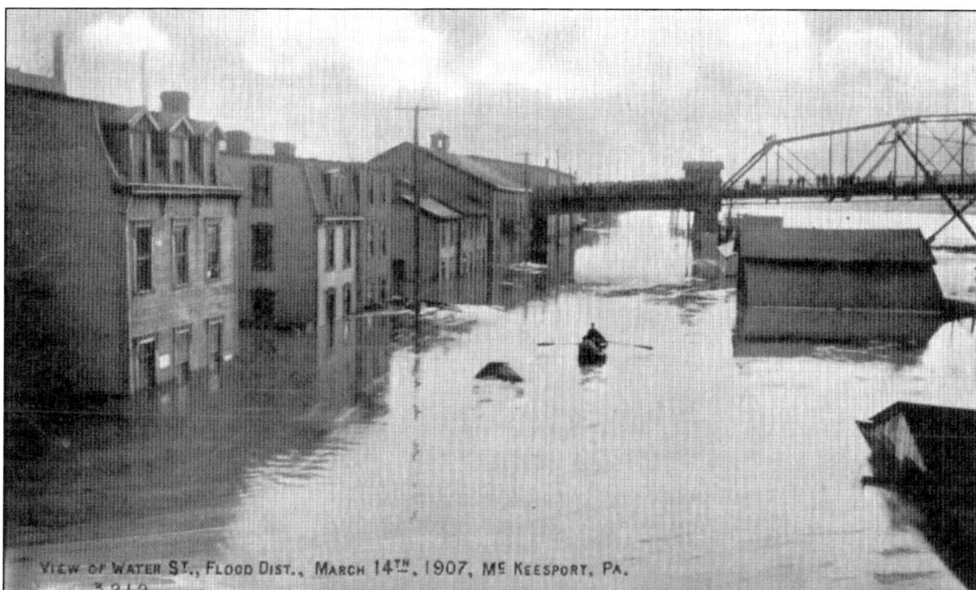

Looking south along Water Street from Fourth Avenue, the Fifth Avenue Bridge can be seen at the right. By March 16, services were returning to normal. The pumps were restarted at the water works, trolley service was partially restored, and the Monongahela River was once again below its banks.

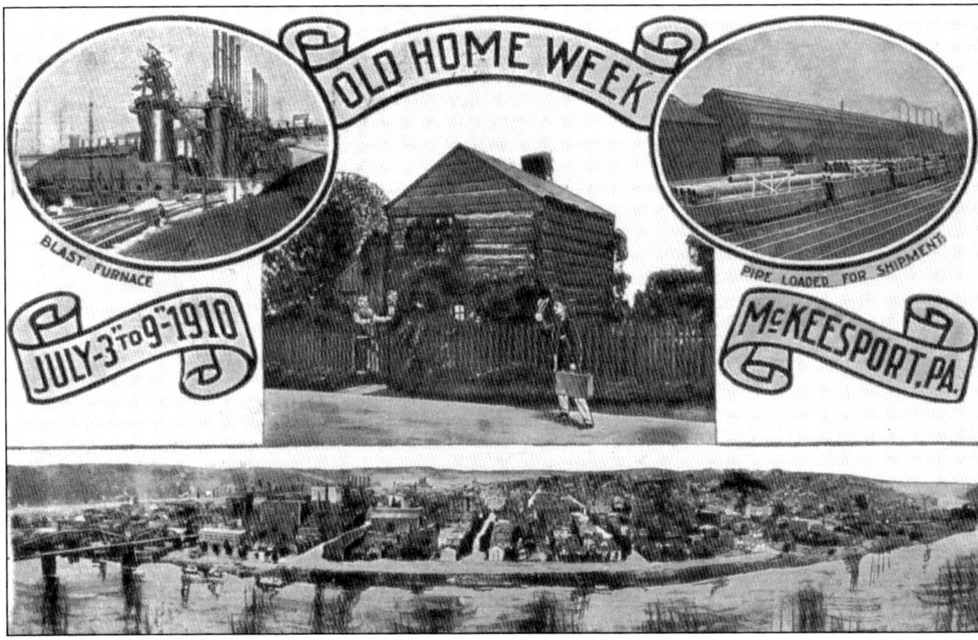

In 1910, McKeesport held a celebration of civic pride. Lasting from July 3 to July 9, Old Home Week included numerous events to both remember McKeesport's past and to celebrate modern progress, as seen in the above postcard where the images of modern factories are juxtaposed with the image of a log cabin.

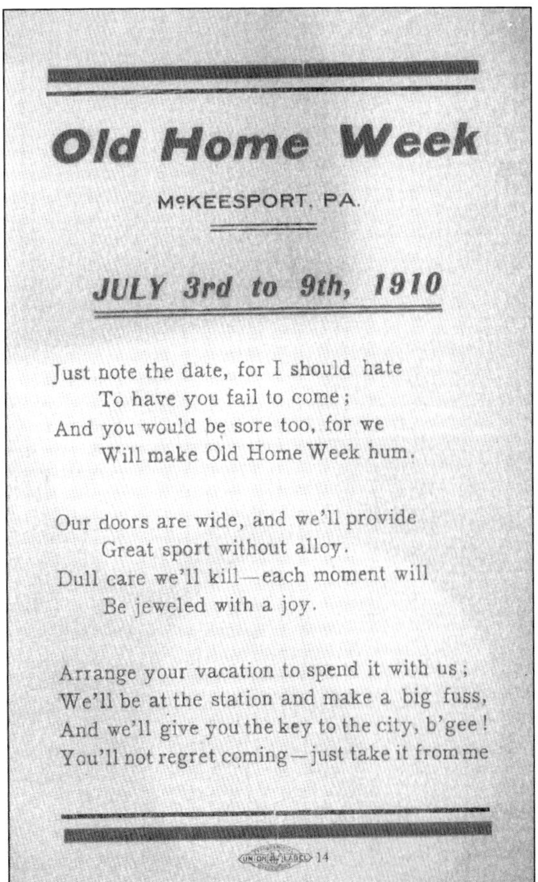

Old Home Week

McKEESPORT, PA.

JULY 3rd to 9th, 1910

Just note the date, for I should hate
To have you fail to come;
And you would be sore too, for we
Will make Old Home Week hum.

Our doors are wide, and we'll provide
Great sport without alloy.
Dull care we'll kill—each moment will
Be jeweled with a joy.

Arrange your vacation to spend it with us;
We'll be at the station and make a big fuss,
And we'll give you the key to the city, b'gee!
You'll not regret coming—just take it from me

14

Many postcards were sent out promoting this event. Even Edwin S. Stuart, governor of Pennsylvania, came to town for this celebration, praising the growth of the city in an address to the community. A fraternal parade marched along Fifth Avenue on July 6, and on July 8, an industrial parade was held.

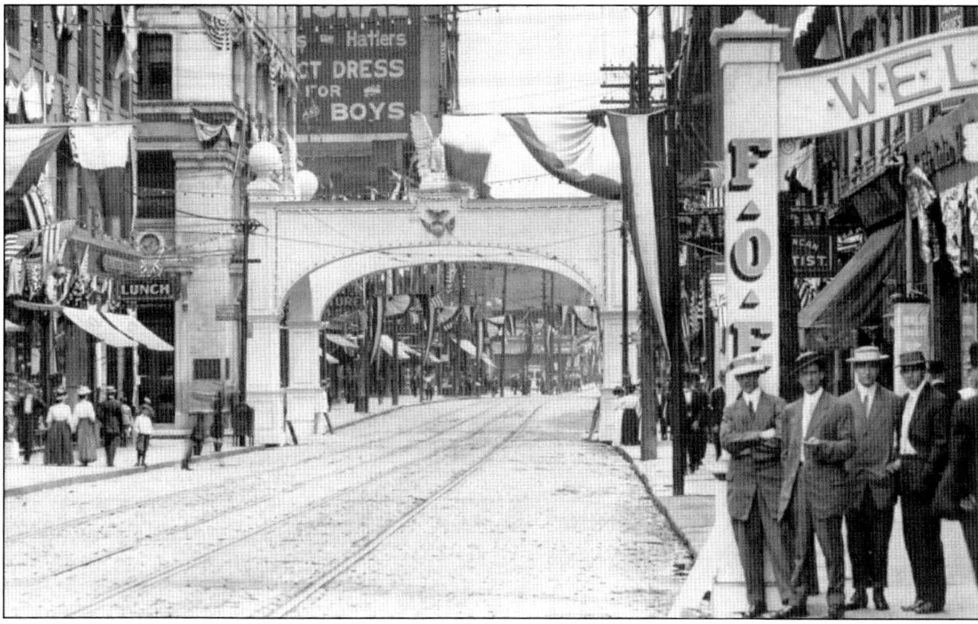

The triumphal arch built for this occasion spanned the intersection of Fifth Avenue and Walnut Street on the main parade route. The Fraternal Order of Eagles sponsored another arch. It went over the sidewalk in front of its lodge rooms on Fifth Avenue, and it can be seen to the right in this image. (Courtesy of John Barna.)

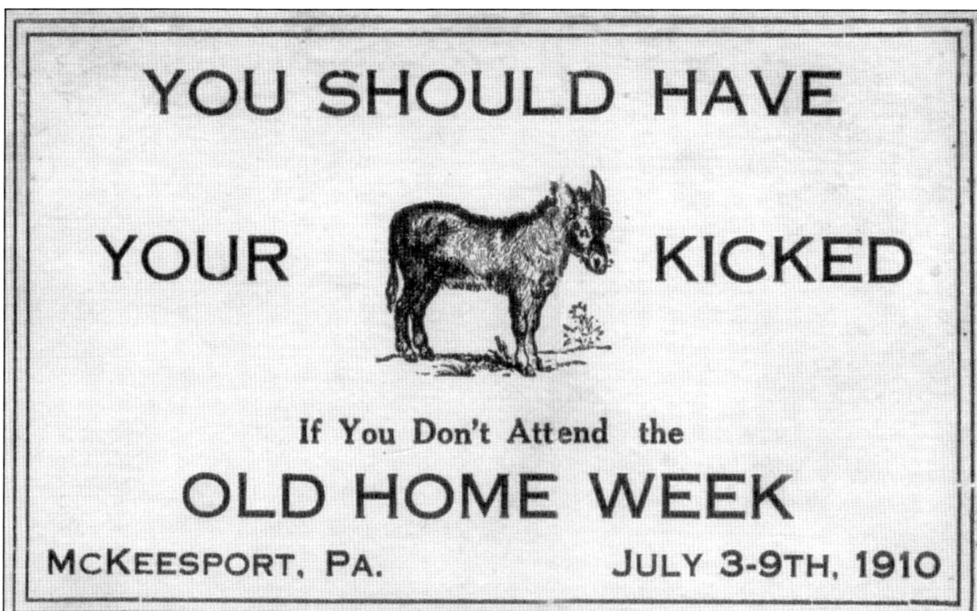

The numerous promotional postcards printed in advance of the event included this humorous card alluding to the dire consequences if one failed to attend. As soon as this celebration ended, the city began to consider hosting it as an annual event. This did not come to pass. The next Old Home Week celebration was not held until 1960.

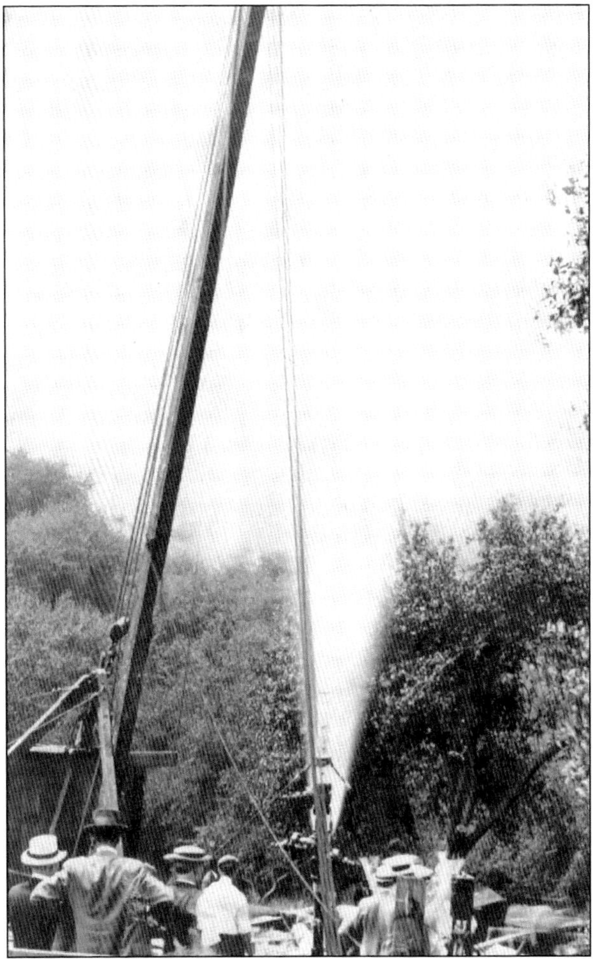

This shows the Spiegel Gas Well just outside of McKeesport in North Versailles Township. The well struck gas on July 7, 1915, and this was a harbinger of things to come. The boom in the McKeesport Gas Field began in 1919, centered in the Snake Hollow district of the Ninth and 11th Wards of the city, and extended into parts of adjacent Versailles Township and Versailles Borough.

This was a typical view in the McKeesport Gas Field, with the derricks crowding the landscape. The boom began with the Hamilton No. 3 gusher in September 1919. In December 1919, there were 116 companies drilling wells. By mid-January 1920, the number of companies had increased to 297. By late 1925, the gas boom had run its course.

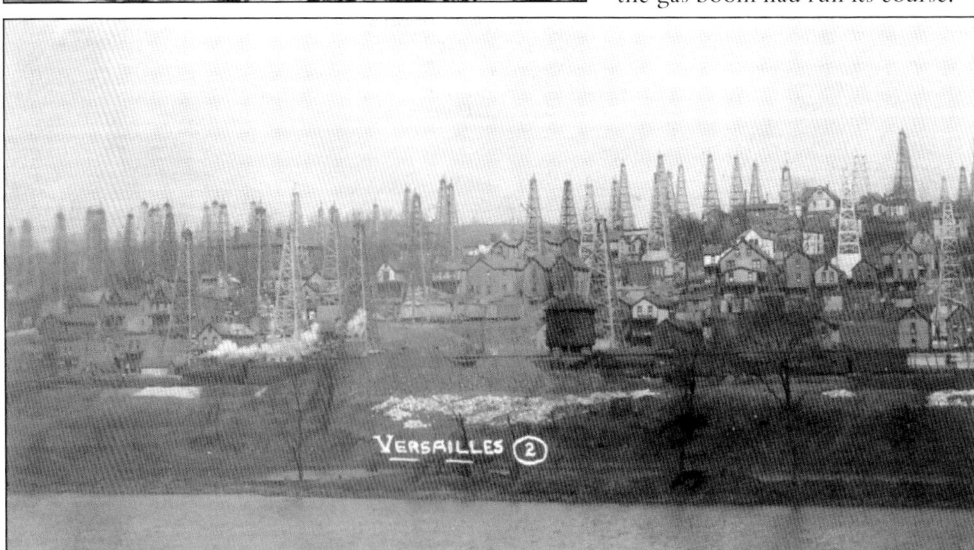

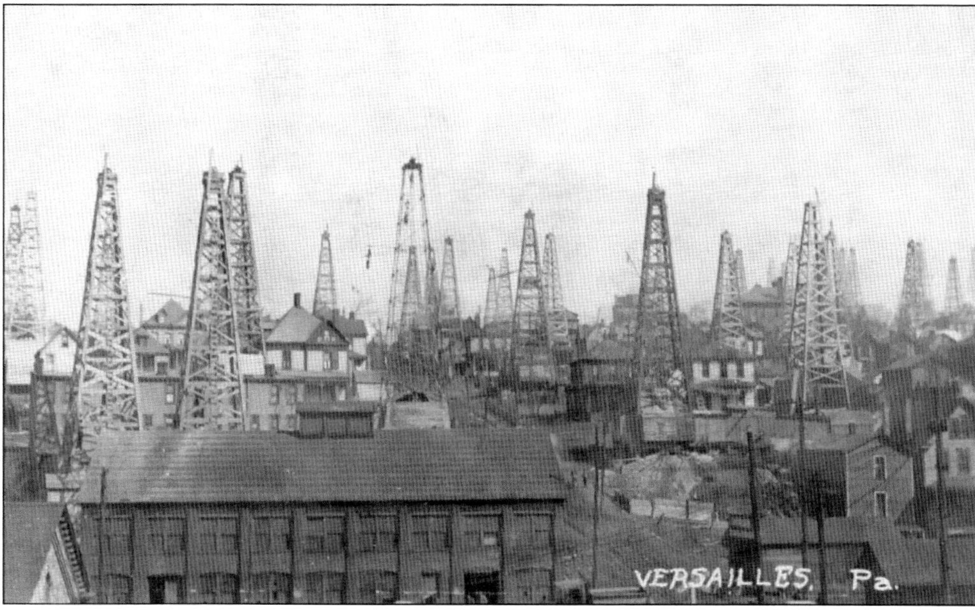

The total gas production over six years was 21 billion cubic feet. Nearly 650 wells were drilled in an area that could have been efficiently drained by 10. At least $13 million was spent drilling for gas that was worth only $3,150,000. This represented a loss of $9,850,000 and was a blatant indication of the over-drilling that had occurred.

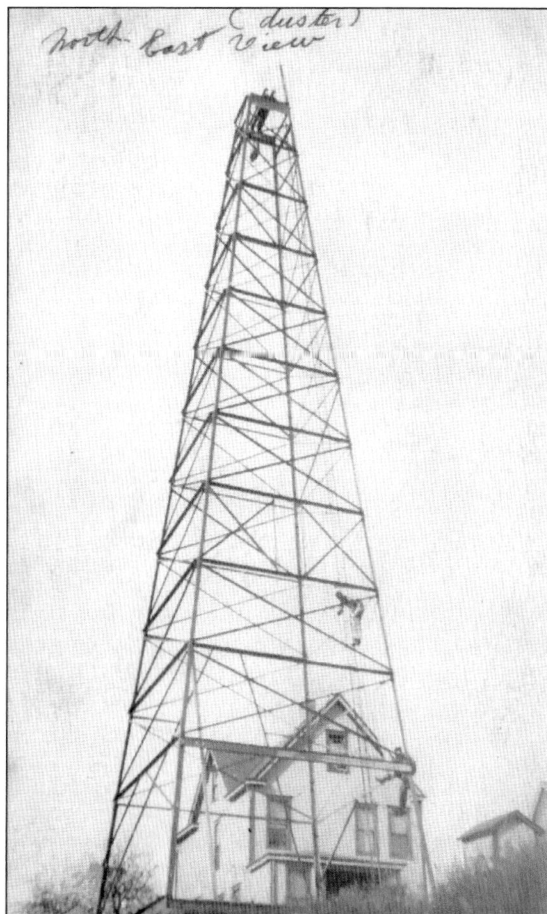

The Fischer No. 2 well was on the Reese property, which was located on Rockwood Street in Christy Park between Thirty-fifth and Thirty-sixth Avenues. This well typified the reality of the gas boom. After drilling 3,445 feet into the Bradford Sand, a gas-producing formation, the well proved to be a "duster," meaning it contained no gas. The well was capped on March 26, 1920. (Courtesy of the Edith Greaves Barrowcliff collection.)

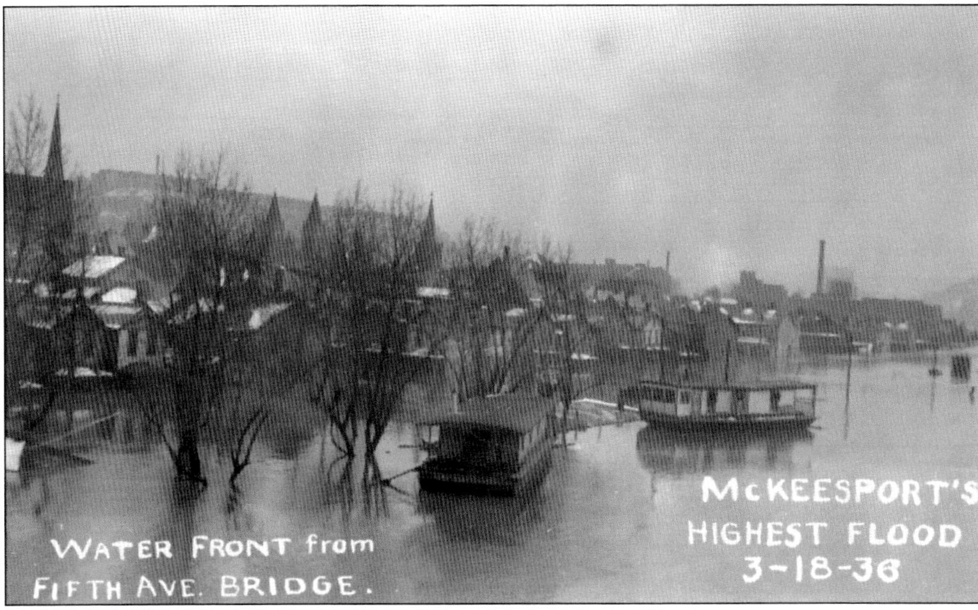

On March 17 and 18, 1936, McKeesport suffered another devastating flood. The rivers crested at more than 40 feet, surpassing the 1907 flood level. This view shows the scene along the Youghiogheny River between Sixth and Eighth Avenues. (Courtesy of Andrea [Luketic] Cartwright.)

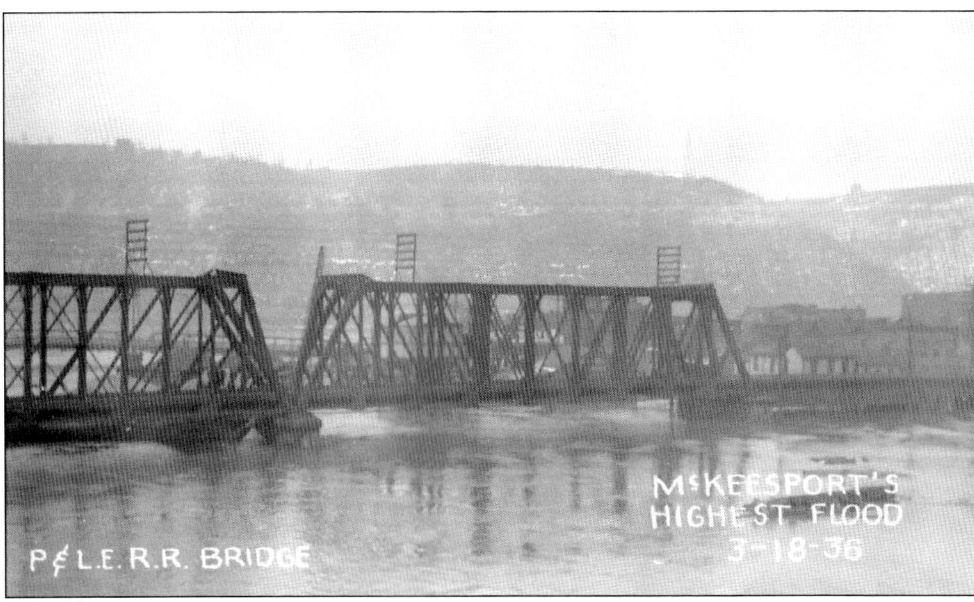

This image gives a better sense of the depth of the water. The piers of the Fourth Avenue railroad bridge are nearly submerged. Despite earlier warnings of the possible flood, residents were taken by surprise by the rapid rise of the rivers.

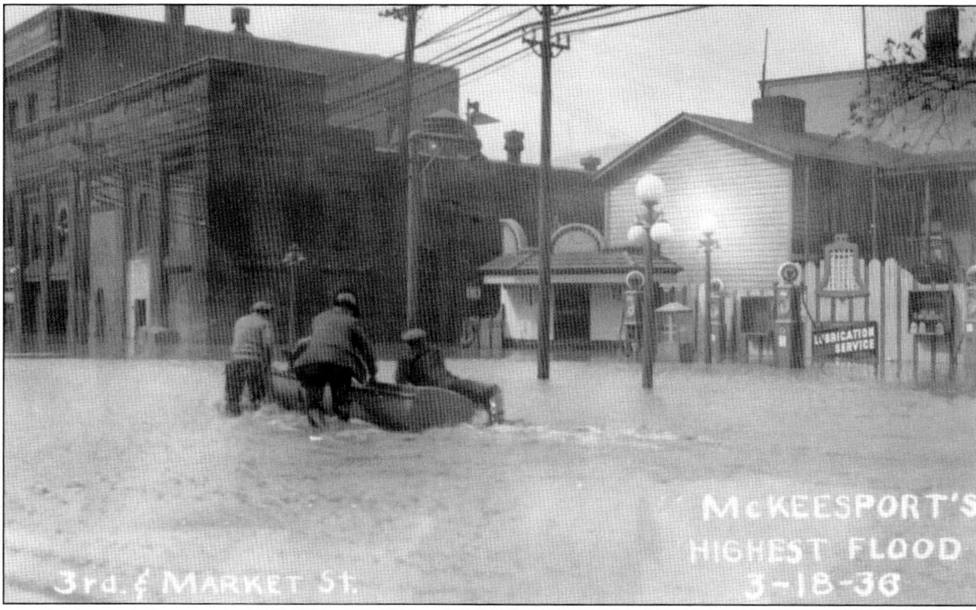

Men are pictured in a rowboat at the corner of Third Avenue and Strawberry Alley. The Third Avenue service station is on the right, and the Duquesne Light Company substation is on the left. The police department borrowed three skiffs from Olympia Park that it used, along with skiffs loaned by private owners, to evacuate people in the flood zone.

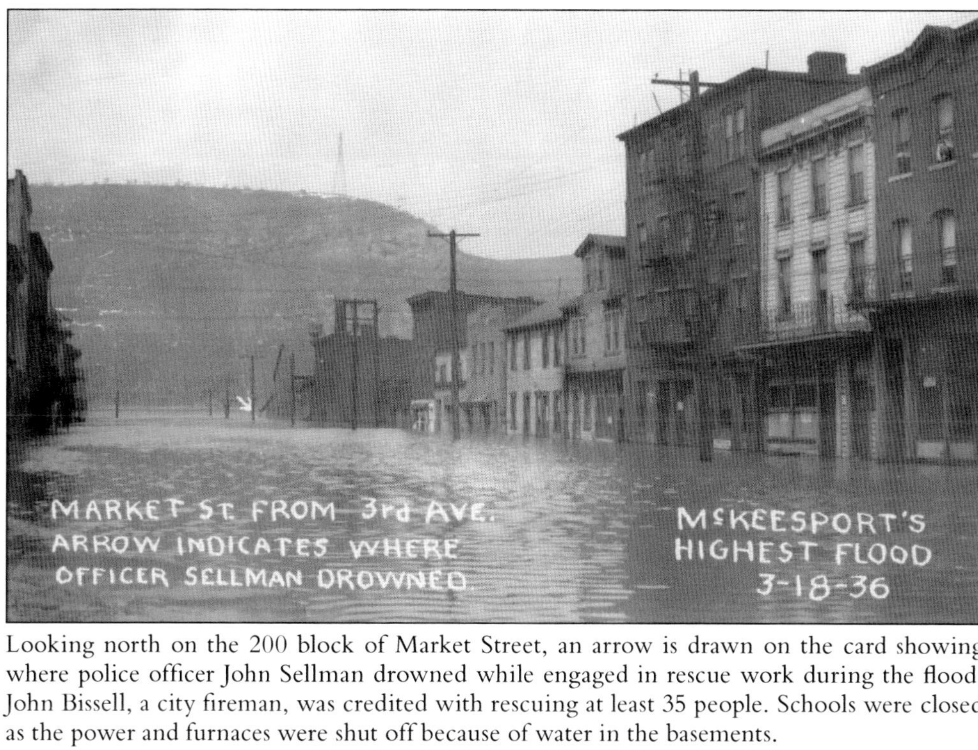

Looking north on the 200 block of Market Street, an arrow is drawn on the card showing where police officer John Sellman drowned while engaged in rescue work during the flood. John Bissell, a city fireman, was credited with rescuing at least 35 people. Schools were closed as the power and furnaces were shut off because of water in the basements.

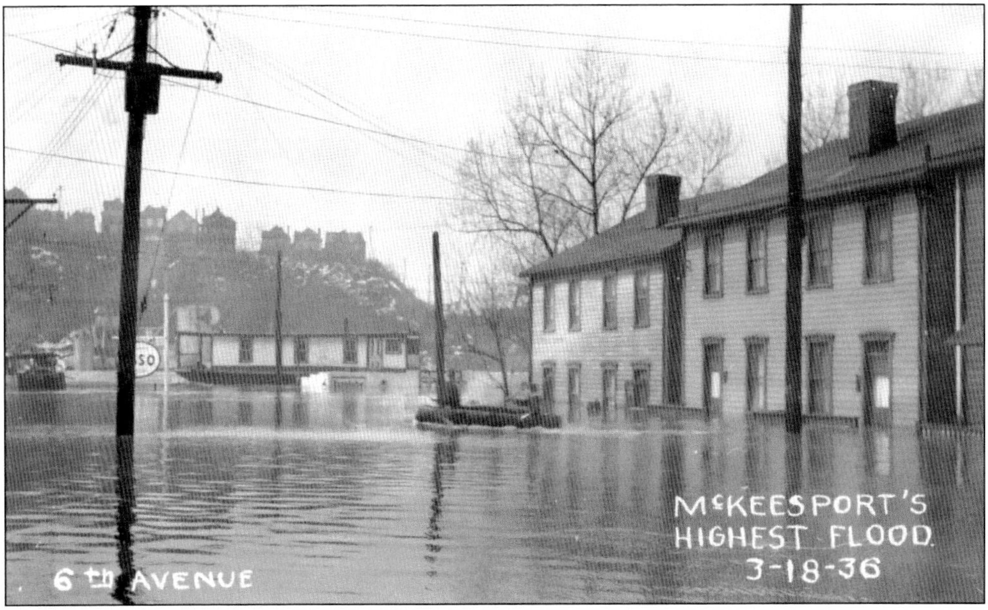

At the western end of Sixth Street, one can see two houses with their first floors under water and a houseboat just beyond them. The ESSO sign indicates the location of the submerged Riverside Filling Station. The National Tube Company, Christy Park Works, McKeesport Tin Plate Company, and other mills were shut down, leaving several thousand men temporarily out of work.

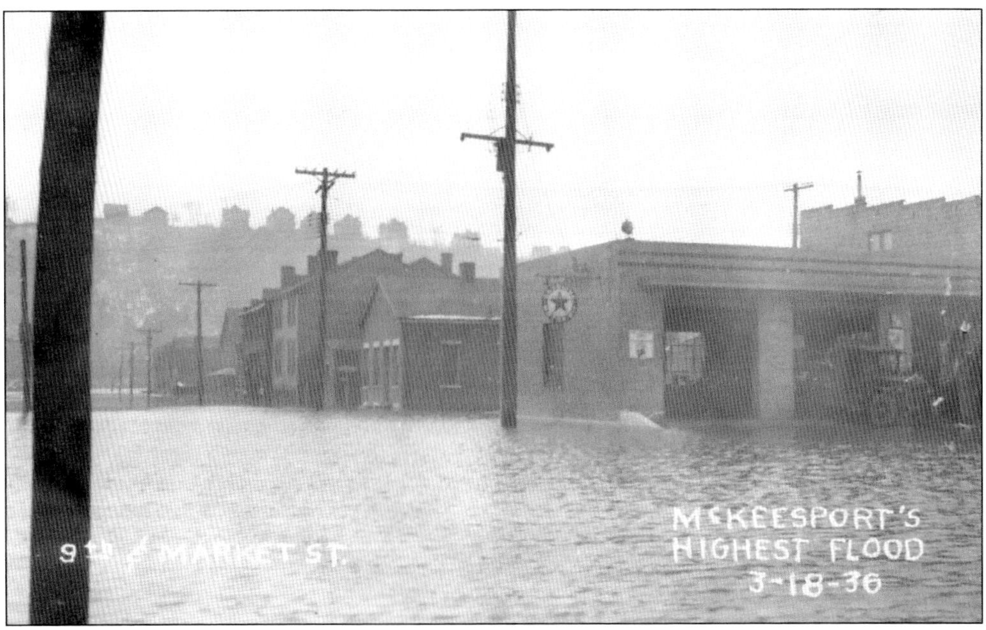

Seen in this image is the Guttman Service Station at the corner of Ninth Avenue and Market Street and the residences along Ninth Avenue. The cleanup after the flood began immediately. The American Red Cross moved into McKeesport to coordinate relief efforts. Several hundred Works Progress Administration workers with 25 trucks came to assist city workers in the cleanup effort.

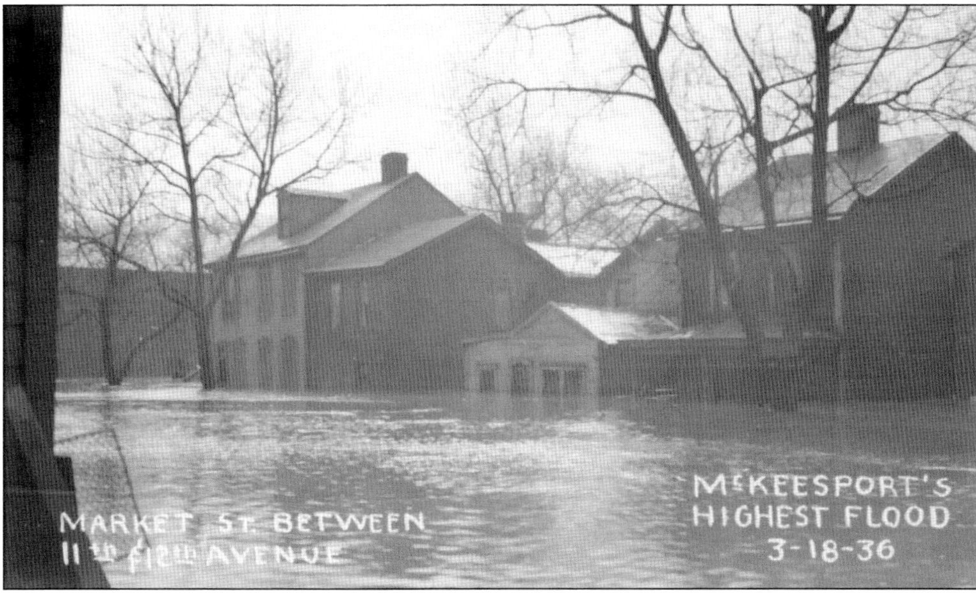

This image is of Eleventh Avenue photographed from the corner of Market Street. This was another hard-hit section of the city. By March 23, most electrical service had been restored and the water works were operating. Schools reopened, as did businesses and factories.

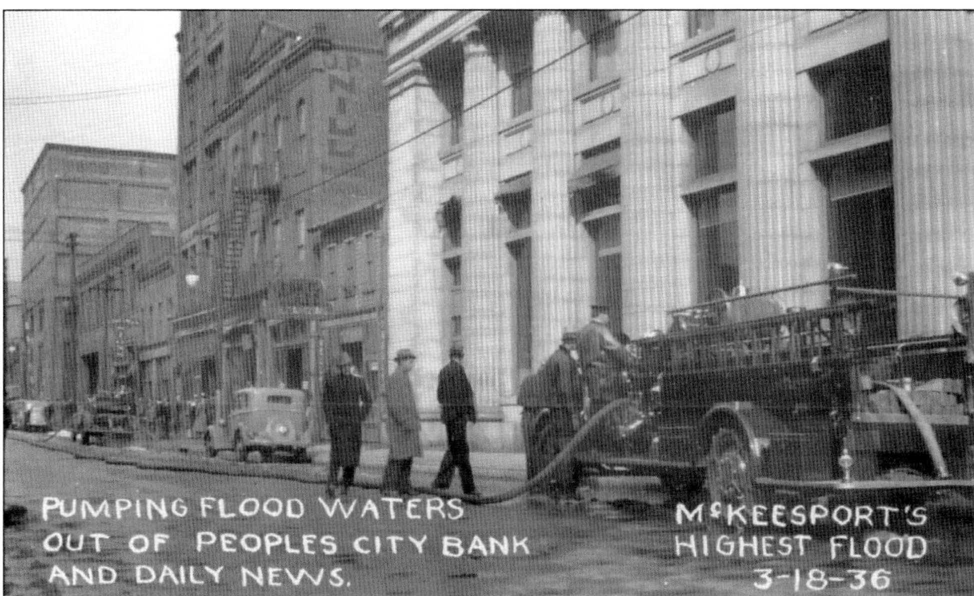

The area along Walnut Street, from Fourth to Fifth Avenues, is pictured here. From left to right, the basements of the Swift Packing Company, the *Daily News*, the Herrold Building, and the People's Bank building are being pumped out. The damages from the flood were estimated in excess of $1 million. In addition, millions of dollars in wages were lost, as was business for merchants.

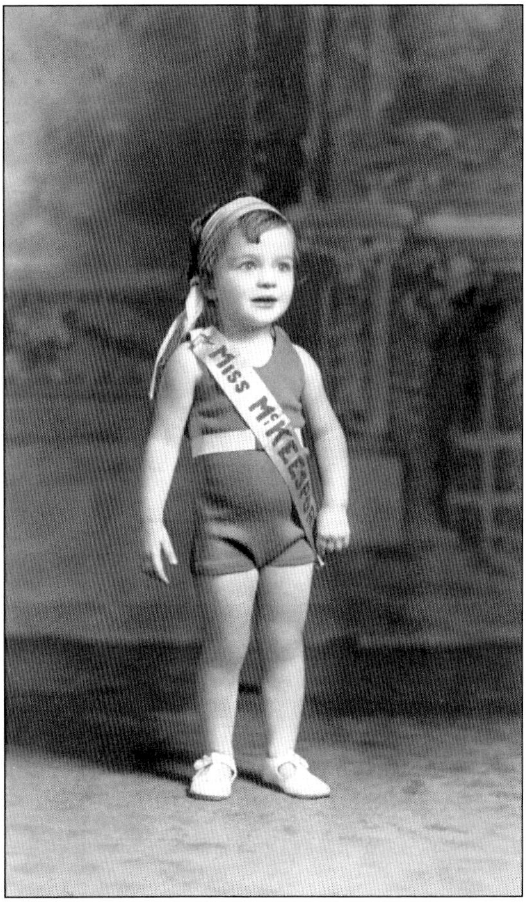

McKeesport held pageants for girls in various age groups, including a Little Miss McKeesport contest. In 1935, Henrietta Leaver won Miss McKeesport and went on to win Miss America, becoming the only McKeesporter to hold that title. The little darling pictured here is unidentified.

Pictured is one of the many generic postcards of the time, on which city names were filled in. Echoing this card, the authors offer a "Greeting from McKeesport." (Courtesy of Leonard Chemsak.

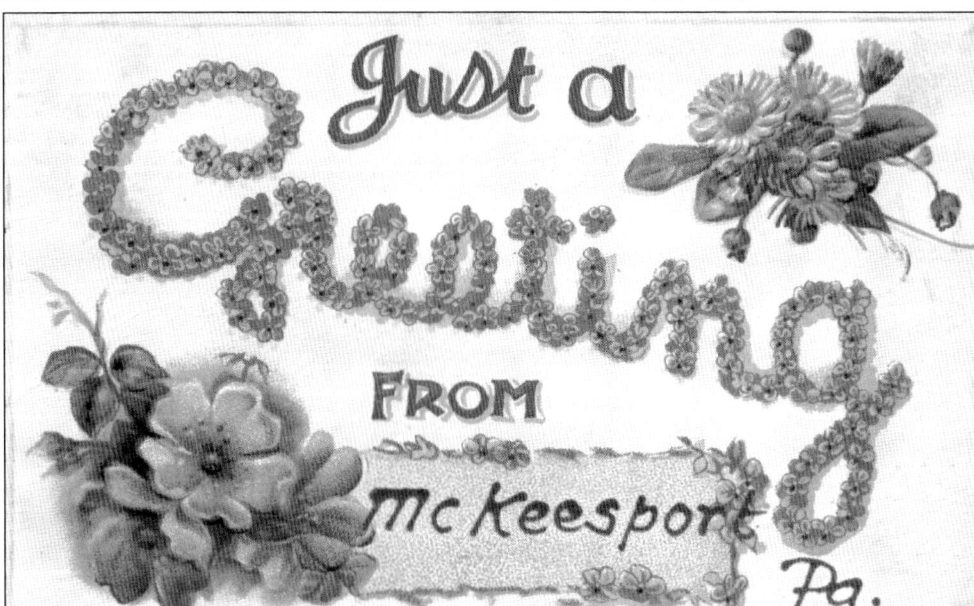

About the Organization

The McKeesport Heritage Center is a museum and research facility dedicated to preserving the history of McKeesport and the surrounding areas. Six museum rooms contain exhibits illustrating various aspects of McKeesport's past. Our research facility contains genealogy resources and local history archives, books, and historic photographs. Our research collection includes all of the past copies of the *Daily News*, McKeesport's newspaper since 1884, on microfilm. Highlights from our museum collection include prints by local artist Jeff Madden, McKeesport's first one-room schoolhouse, and a scale model of the National Tube Works. Our museum is free and open to the public. Our research materials are available to our members at no charge or for a daily fee for nonmembers. We are open Tuesdays, Wednesdays, and Thursdays from 9:00 a.m. to 5:00 p.m. and Saturdays from 9:00 a.m. to 3:00 p.m.

We are a private, nonprofit organization, and we appreciate all of your support. If interested in preserving McKeesport's past, please consider becoming a member. For more information, visit our website at www.mckeesportheritage.org, e-mail us at mckheritage@yahoo.com, call us at 412-678-1832, or visit us at 1832 Arboretum Drive, McKeesport, Pennsylvania, 15132.

Consistent with our mission to preserve history on a local level, this book was printed in South Carolina on American-made paper and manufactured entirely in the United States. Products carrying the accredited Forest Stewardship Council (FSC) label are printed on 100 percent FSC-certified paper.

MADE IN THE USA